Evolutionary Metaphysics

Evolutionary Metaphysics

The Development of
Peirce's Theory of Categories

by
Joseph L. Esposito

Ohio University Press
Athens, Ohio

Library of Congress Cataloging in Publication Data

Esposito, Joseph L   1941–
    Evolutionary metaphysics.

    Includes bibliographical references and index.
    1.   Peirce, Charles Santiago Sanders, 1839–1914—
Metaphysics.   2.   Metaphysics.   3.   Categories
(Philosophy)   4.   Pragmatism.   I.   Title.
B945.P44E86   110   80-15736
ISBN 0-8214-0551-9

For
My Father

Contents

Part Two (1870–1884)
The Metaphysics of Experience

Part Three (1885–1913)
Objective Idealism

Preface

Charles S. Peirce (1839–1914) has been popularly known as a logician and as the founder of pragmatism. While both of these descriptions are no doubt accurate, they sometimes help create the impression that he was a philosopher with varying and unrelated interests. In fact, just the contrary is true; Peirce was not a journeyman philosopher, and only recent fashions in philosophy have prompted or kept alive such a view. Rather, he was to a considerable degree a *systematic* philosopher, and today stands as the most recent, though hopefully not the last, of the great architectonic thinkers of the calibre of Aristotle, Leibniz, Kant, or Hegel. It is understandable that nineteenth-century scholars, particularly in America, were often unprepared to follow his arguments, which blend mathematics, logic, philosophy, and science; less understandable is that until very recently his work has continued to be misunderstood or seen out of context.

Peirce regarded metaphysics as an interdisciplinary study, requiring many kinds of knowledge and method. Accordingly, the present work does not treat of his writings on traditional metaphysical subjects (substance, cause, etc.), but rather attempts to portray his lifelong efforts to bring the advances of science, mathematics, and logic to the service of these subjects. Many of his philosophical arguments were motivated by goals not readily apparent in the arguments themselves; indeed, it is fair to say that nearly all of his many philosophical endeavors are linked in one way or another with a major metaphysical project first formulated during his student years at Harvard and carried forward over half a century. For this reason a significant portion of this work is devoted to an account of Peirce's philosophical writings before 1865 or so.

The need for such an account became apparent to me while working with a group of scholars on Peirce's unpublished papers in the Harvard University Archives, work preparatory to a new collected edition of his writings. His early metaphysical manuscripts, filling several massive folders, were uncharted territory at the time. Since then the Peirce Edition Project has been organized, promising upon its completion a new generation of Peirce studies, and the early writings have been greatly reorganized to facilitate examination and comprehension.

I am indebted to the Harvard Department of Philosophy for permission to use the Peirce manuscripts in the Houghton Archives, and to Harvard University Press for permission to quote from the *Collected Papers of Charles Sanders Peirce;* to Max H. Fisch, a wellspring on subjects Peircean and a model of scholarship at a time of increasing commercialization of philosophy; to Christian Kloesel for his work on dating and sequencing the unpublished papers; to Donald Buzzelli for helpful comments on the early metaphysics of Peirce; and to Kenneth Ketner as Director and moving force of the Institute for Studies in Pragmaticism at Texas Tech University—where research on Peirce can be conducted with unmatched economy—for the opportunity to use the resources of the Institute and for his gracious hospitality.

Introduction

Peirce has generally been regarded either as a philosopher with several systems of philosophy, or as one with two basic, though not entirely related, philosophic concerns—epistemology and metaphysics. Murray Murphey's pioneering work illustrates the first point of view;[1] the second is found in numerous works, but more recently in Israel Scheffler's *Four Pragmatists* (1974), where Scheffler remarks: "The direction of development in Peirce's thought is, roughly speaking, from the epistemological to the cosmological."[2] From such perspectives Peirce looks like a philosopher who often changed his mind, who was full of brilliant flashes of argument and insight but had no commanding form to his work. This impression has partly been justified by the fact that when Peirce did change his mind he conspicuously announced it to his readers. It is also significant that he never published a systematic book of metaphysical philosophy, that he often published in popular journals, and that his writings sometime appear to readers of the *Collected Papers* as episodic and fragmentary.

In his later years Peirce had ample opportunity to conclude that his lifetime efforts would not be long remembered. Had he known otherwise he might have been inspired to write a short book on his conception of the task of philosophy, a table of contents for future generations to follow. Instead he proposed giant works, works far beyond the scope of a single man to complete even in a lifetime. One rather obvious and simple reason accounts for the unsettled nature of his work: *the extreme complexity of the philosophic task as conceived by Peirce.* Early in his life he had assimilated the philosophies of Kant

1

and Hegel, and they had become second nature to him. In the process, however, he realized how much more would be required to bring architectonic philosophy into the second half of the nineteenth century. Thus Peirce saw the need for a vast reconstruction of the philosophic tradition in light of more recent developments in the natural and formal sciences.

Peirce conceived of philosophy as an ensemble of investigations centered around an enigma whose resolution would, in his words, "answer the riddle of the sphinx" and "unlock the door of philosophy." Near the end of his life, in 1907, he quoted from Emerson's poem "The Sphinx":

> The old Sphinx bit her thick lip—
> Said, "Who taught thee me to name?
> I am thy spirit, yoke-fellow,
> Of thine eye I am eyebeam . . . "

How do we fleshly mortals presume to name the sphinx? How can we see the very conditions necessary for seeing? In short, how can we who are part of the world come to be conscious of the world as a totality? This is very nearly a religious question, and for this reason Peirce remained reluctant throughout his life to dismiss as insignificant the founding insights of religious consciousness. Solving the enigma, then, would require the updating of religion as well as of philosophy.

From the start he could not disassociate epistemology and metaphysics; somehow each required the other, and this at once raised the problem of philosophic foundations, a problem with which he struggled in the late 1850's and early 1860's. In order to grant apodicticity to a potential knowing instrument, we must know something of the metaphysical nature of reality in order to be sure that even a potential fitness between knower and known is possible. But then knowledge itself cannot establish that guarantee, and all philosophy is without foundation. Following Kant, we may purify the domain of philosophy by keeping it within prescribed limits, i.e., in this case, within the limits of the world of appearances; following Hegel, we may be confident ahead of time of the influence of Reason's Concept upon the philosopher's groping insights. Peirce was dissatisfied with both procedures as he found them. Against

Kant he would argue that it was a bona fide cognitive stance to think the unthinkable transcendental object, and well within the province of philosophy to speculate upon it with the proper logical tools; against Hegel he would argue that a dialectic of Reason in nature could not be postulated without a basis of precise and detailed logical and scientific investigation. Although Kant would give him the greatest practical guidance in his early career, it would be with Hegel that he would ultimately reconcile himself in later life. From the very outset of his career the young Peirce acutely felt the difficulty of being able to *begin* his own philosophy free from uncritical dogmatism.

Metaphysics for Peirce begins in the mainstream of ordinary experience. It does not seek to establish a bulwark in one act of intuition or assertion, but gradually builds an edifice from the results of specific investigations into the structure of scientific knowledge. In his earliest speculations, between the years 1854 and 1863, Peirce sought the elementary categories of knowledge and nature. Yet such a quest required not only that the knowing mind be determined by a matrix of relations, but also that it could somehow come to know those relations. To explain this he constructed a hierarchical theory of categories containing a system of recursion between levels. This was an initial, exceedingly hypothetical formulation of abstractions, based upon a preliminary analysis of the conditions of knowing. These conditions involved in one way or another the manifest ability of one facet of reality to become reflected in another; in short, the ability of something to stand as a *sign* for something to something. Peirce had concluded that even before the question of adequacy could be raised, we had to confront the limiting condition of knowledge as a kind of sign-structure of some real structure or object. This in turn required that metaphysics be irreducibly *triadic* in nature, comprising three elements: a knowing subject, an object known, and a representing medium. No matter what ontology was accepted, all three dimensions were required for metaphysics. Foundationalism attempts to eliminate two of these in favor of a unified and privileged ontological condition, but in doing so it refutes itself by giving status in its very argumentation to one or both of the rejected dimensions. If it bases knowledge on objects-in-themselves, it does so only because it assumes that mind can representationally constitute the object 'as it is'; if it accepts only appearances as representations, it fails to notice that it does so only as a result of one or more inferences based upon arguments whose concepts and general form imply and require a dimension other than appearance; and if it begins only with a pure transcendental knower, it has nothing whatsoever to philosophize upon unless it adds a dimension to be known apart from the self. All of these were problems that Peirce sought to avoid.

Once Peirce had some tolerably clear idea of his philosophic method, he began, after 1862, with a study of the forms of scientific explanation and logical predication. There he discovered that the very triadic structure which governed the overall conduct of metaphysics was itself microscopically revealed within the forms of logic and explanation. In this manner the triadic system of categories began to receive indirect confirmation. It is, after all, conceivable that some significant feature of thought or experience might not come under a proposed ensemble of categories. If so, this affords evidence that the list in question is incomplete or misformed. To help clarify this issue Peirce carefully distinguished the *short* list from the *long* list of categories. In the former list were those categories which were necessarily to be found in all philosophical subjects, while in the latter list, ultimately based upon the short list, were those categories which had a more localized and contextual application. In his lifetime he made considerable headway in perfecting the analysis of short-list categories, but, as we shall see, only intermittently did he take up the onerous task of detailing the long-list ensemble. Only the short list approached a degree of confirmation satisfying him.

In the years after the publication of his paper on the 'new list' of categories (1867), during the 1870's and early 1880's—in the latter case during his tenure at Johns Hopkins—Peirce sought to apply the more theoretical speculations of the earlier years to specific areas of research, a number of these within the purview of psychology and physiology. By combining a unified theory of inference with a sign-theory of cognition, he was able to assemble a general theory of cognition and to place it within a general theory of scientific explanation. A full formulation of this task was never completed at the time; what we find instead are specific portions of the argument, or general introductions for more or less popular consumption.

Finally, while still in his forties, Peirce retired to the countryside of Pennsylvania, separating himself from the sophisticates of Cambridge, New York, and Baltimore, and for the rest of his life worked on a series of projects designed to unify the theoretical and practical dimensions of the work of his earlier years. At this time he attempted to formulate "the one intelligible theory of the universe" $(6.25)^3$—*objective idealism.* Since its inception in Schelling and Hegel, that philosophy alone, he felt, had been sensitive to the problem of the enigma of the sphinx and had sought a "two-sided" solution at once in *Naturphilosophie* and *Phänomenologie*. Peirce continued the same course, and as he progressed he began to realize that the early abstract theory of hierarchical categories required a *telos* to give it dynamism and vitality. Thus habit-breaking chance gave way to habit-taking order, Firstness to Thirdness, abstractions to living concepts, and belief fixing to pragmaticism.

From his earliest work Peirce's thought had tended toward the direction of a dialectical view of reality and experience. The elements of the dialectic changed from time to time, but the underlying form remained the same. Particularity, determination, systematization, and consciousness all resulted from a relational reciprocation of polar extremes, each the opposite of the other relative to their mediating synthesis, but each the same when looked upon as outer limits. For example, the limit of determination and particularity becomes once more indetermination and universality. Consciousness ceases both in the purest of mathematical intuitions and in sensuous intuition. In this light everything that comes to philosophic reflection is already mediated, and the very essence of reality is that it be manifested to something beyond itself. This is the general model of Peirce's scientific metaphysics, a model, I shall argue, that follows a developmental pattern both in terms of its internal constituents and in terms of the general interpretation given it. That pattern attains three discernable stages: *abstract unity, concrete plurality,* and *concrete unity*. These follow to some degree the Hegelian triad of Idea, Nature, and Spirit, though Peirce attempted a far more detailed elaboration.

Although Peirce was the first to conceive the task of creating a genuine *scientific* metaphysics in modern form, he was far from fully realizing it. Since his time modern science has become increasingly creative, philosophical, and speculative, while philosophy, on the other hand, has lost its sense of quest and participation in the activity of science. (The departmentalization of knowledge in academia may be at the root of this, particulary in a context in which the pursuit of knowledge becomes closely intertwined with competitive matters of finance.)

Peirce's vision of metaphysics is, however, far from dead. Recently its updated agenda has been outlined by R. M. Martin:

> Our task now is to formulate a metaphysics on the basis of the broad theory of logical form now available. . . . We can not do better than start, as Henrich Scholz did, with the truth-functions, quantifiers, and identity. We then add the calculus of individuals (Lésniewski's mereology) and an event-logic with event-descriptive predicates. And then a systematic semiotics on top of this.[4]

In a futuristic passage written as part of his "Minute Logic" (1902), Peirce himself suggested the outline his own thought and that of coming generations ought to follow:

> The new conception will not be content to be restricted to the particular phenomena it was devised to explain: it will insist upon applying itself to analogous phenomena, and to others analogous to these again, without stint. For that purpose it must be widened and probably simplified and rendered more agreeable to reason. It will not be content with explaining the history of thought, but will aim to explain history in general. It will not be content with accounting for man, but will wish to grasp all the forms in the universe, which is greater than man. It will not be content with an accidental universe, but will wish to assimilate every possible universe that the mathematician can suggest. It will not be content with allowing to the unreflective view a sort of subordinate legitimacy, but will insist upon elevating it to a truth in full harmony with its own.
>
> These tendencies are irrepressible: in the long run they will cause that which they need to come into being. (2.33–34)

To fill in more fully this program for scientific metaphysics, we may add to Martin's suggestions the need for comprehensive philosophies of quantum mechanics, of thermodynamics, and of cosmological relativity, as well as a general theory of organization incorporating these philosophies of science with information theory and semiotics. Such projects would considerably enliven philosophy's lagging sense of discovery, and in this respect the work by Peirce described below affords inspiration as well as insight.

Part One

(1855-1869)

Early Metaphysics
and
Theory of Categories

Chapter
I
Metaphysical Essays

Peirce began to study philosophy seriously during his years as a student at Harvard (1855–59). Among the more important works he read during this period were Jouffroy's *Introduction to Ethics,* Schiller's *Aesthetische Briefe,* Kant's *Critique* and *Prolegomena,* Hume's *Treatise of Human Nature,* James Mill's *Analysis of the Human Mind,* and the works on logic and metaphysics by Sir William Hamilton. A list of books (MS. 1555) he compiled in 1858 also reveals that he was familiar with some of the works of Aristotle, Locke, Mansel, Whewell, and Whately, among others.[1] Peirce tells us (MSS. 1606, 1608) that Whately's *Elements of Logic* had been a major formative influence upon him. By 1860, if not sooner, he was also reading the dialogues of Plato.

Peirce read widely in non-philosophical subjects as well, from the classics to chemistry to the works of Louis Agassiz and Lyell. But generally the most enduring influences at this time, those closest to his philosophic heart, derived from the writings of Kant and Schiller. From the very start of his career as a philosopher Peirce seemed most inspired in the company of German philosophers. Along with a fellow student, Horatio Paine, he first opened the *Aesthetische Briefe* around 1855 at the age of sixteen, and shortly thereafter commenced a three-year study of the *Critique of Pure Reason.* Years later he would recall the "indelible impression" Schiller's work made upon him, calling it "a good book for an infant philosopher," and noting:

> My good angel must have prompted me to take up first that branch of philosophy [esthetics] which ought immediately to follow the study of the categories, and to study it in a German book which though it was too old to be sensibly influenced by Hegel was nevertheless one of those books in which the three categories in an almost unrecognizable disguise played a great part. (MS. 310)

The three categories barely recognizable in the *Briefe* were those Peirce worked out in his first study of the work, and which he would call the *I*, *It*, and *Thou*. In the *Aesthetische Briefe*, as in the earlier *Philosophische Briefe*, Schiller was writing in response to the predicament of philosophy produced by Kant's *Critique*. And in spite of his claim that it was upon Kantian principles that his position in the letters was based, Schiller was in fact involved in an effort to undermine completely the subjective approach of the *Critique*.[2] By postulating two coexisting tendencies—the *sensuous drive* toward the finite, particular, and temporal, and the *formal drive* toward the infinite, universal, and eternal—and by introducing a historical/genetic analysis of the relation of philosophic thought to culture, he was undercutting the privileged position of the Sensibility and denying the very possibility of a truly transcendental philosophy. Critical philosophy, he argued, was one-sidedly analytic and incapable of accounting for the ultimate harmony of goodness, truth, and beauty, or for the irreducible reality of the human personality. Thus reason and analysis had to be tempered with esthetic sensibility as the only means of harmonizing the two conflicting drives of *feeling* and *law*, and this elevated, dynamic sensibility largely involved the ideal of beauty as the unity of contingency and law.

In a forensic from his sophomore year at Harvard, "The Sense of Beauty never furthered the Performance of a single Act of Duty" (1857), Peirce recasts Schiller's formal and sensuous drives into what he called the *I*-impulse and the *It*-impulse, with their unity producing a *Thou*-impulse. Following Schiller, he argues that the two impulses need not clash or remain within separate realms.

Rather, each contributes to the workings of the other; the formal impulse does not succeed in reducing the manifoldness of sensation to the barest unity of transcendental selfhood, nor does the sensuous impulse succeed in proliferating the self into a chaotic variety of unrelated sensory episodes. Instead, an underlying harmony is possible due to a third impulse that leads to the "perfect balance" of the other two. This harmony makes possible the true realization of the person according to a "purely *a priori* idea of humanity" (MS. 1633).

The role of beauty as a synthesizing force in nature and mind is revealed in some remarks contained in a notebook of philosophical aphorisms (MS. 891). There Peirce jotted down, around 1857:

Action   Life   BEAUTY   Character   Rest

In another passage from the same notebook, dated 12 August 1856, he describes the soul as an interplay of action and passion, and gives to beauty the task of activating the soul from a passive state; this it does, paradoxically, by its being a "patient notion" that distracts the soul from its usual attentions and allows a natural harmony to unfold. By 1857 Peirce was attempting to blend the polar inpulses of the soul with the three basic categories, and in the process to reestablish a harmony between the analytic and synthetic methods of Kant and Schiller. From MS. 891 we have the following outline:

I: Reason Faith	Goodness	Love of Order	Unity	Reality	Permanence
THOU: Affection Love	Beauty	Love of Man	Totality	Limitation	Causality
IT: Sensation Hope	Truth	Love of World	Plurality	Negation	Community

By this time Peirce's study of Kant had progressed to the point where he was ready to embark on the task of a more detailed recasting of Kant's own categories within this new framework. Years later he wrote of this period:

Kant, as you remember, calls attention to sundry relations between one category and another. I detected some additional relations between the categories, *all but* forming a regular system, yet not quite so. Those relations seemed to point to some larger list of conceptions in which they might form a regular system of relationships. After puzzling over these matters diligently for about two years, I rose at length from the problem certain that there was something wrong with Kant's formal logic. (MS. 441)

Actually, Peirce was simultaneously involved in two tasks at this time, attempting both to set out a short list of categories much like the *I, It,* and *Thou* and to establish a dialectic for generating a "regular system of relationships" among the categories. The years 1859–1862 were taken up, a far as his philosophical efforts were concerned, with these tasks. They are years of intense, if youthful, metaphysical speculation, which, along with the several years later leading to the 'new list' of categories, comprise some of Peirce's most provocative output.

1. Preliminary Essays

Peirce's first attempt to produce a systematic metaphysics resulted in a series of short essays which at one point he listed as follows:[3]

1. On the Definition of Metaphysics (July 1859)
2. Metaphysics as a Study (June 1859)
3. Proper Domain of Metaphysics (21 May 1859)
4. That the PERFECT is the Great Subject of Metaphysics (21 May 1859)
5. That There is No Need of Transcendentalism (21 May 1859)
6. The Logical and Psychological Treatment of Metaphysics (3 July 1860)
7. The Fundamental Distinction of Metaphysics (30 June 1860)
8. Proposition. All unthought is thought-of (25 July 1859)

9. Remarks*
10. Where shall we find the Perfect?*
11. Kant's Categories*
12. New Names and Symbols for Kant's Categories (21 May 1859)
13. Of the Stages of the Category of Modality or Chance (22 May 1859)
14. Explanations of the Categories (22 May 1859)
15. Table*
16. Remarks*
16½. The Infinite, the Type of the Perfect (3 July 1860)
16¾. Math. infin. . . [unclear]*
16'. The Orders of Mathematical Infinity (13 July 1860)
17. Sir William Hamilton's Theory of the Infinite (27 July 1859)
18. Comparison of our Knowledge of God and of other Substances (25 July 1859)
18'. Conflicting Attributes of God*
19. That Infinity is an Unconscious Idea (25 October 1859)
20. Of Pantheism (25 October 1859)
21. Of Objects (25 October 1859)
22. Of Realism and Nominalism (25 July 1859)
23. Two Kinds of Thinking (23 October 1859)[4]

The fact that he composed the list in something other than chronological order seems to indicate that he considered the essays to comprise a systematic development of ideas from general principles and distinctions to their elaboration and explication. There is even a "Summary" included in these papers, though not mentioned on the list, in which Peirce enumerates the accomplishments of the essays. I shall now summarize the contents of the more significant papers.

The idea of metaphysics. Peirce defined metaphysics as the study of the elements of consciousness. As part of philosophy, it is unlike natural science in that it does not base its claim upon observation. It is also to be distinguished from psychology, the science of thoughts, in that it only reflects upon the results of scientific observation. This reflection takes the form of an analysis of *a priori* conceptions and is the restricted "proper domain" of metaphysics.

Peirce justified the *a priori* nature of metaphysics in two ways, in both instances by a kind of presupposition argument. First, for any proposition to be understood we must understand its terms and conceptions; hence we cannot begin metaphysics with propositions, but with a primordial mental activity, called on various occasions *meditation* and *cultivation*, that is directly capable of comprehending elementary conceptions. Here Peirce is very close to Fichte in maintaining that first philosophy begins with an act of cognition. Second, the provable propositions eventually derive from propositions that are "original truths," and these latter must be either universal or negative. In either case the propositions must be *a priori* since experience "*unreasoned upon*" is particular and affirmative. In "Metaphysics as a Study" Peirce writes: "Nature is not in the habit of calling out 'Charles!', 'What?', 'Nothing'." Hence the conceptions of metaphysics must be part of the *a priori* configuration of the mind and its activity. But of whose mind? Peirce's answer is: everyone's! But only insofar as each person uses his mind 'naturally' and 'normally':

> Nothing can be more important therefore than that [metaphysical notions] be tested by normal minds; but lamentably most minds are upon most subjects, or upon most subjects about which there is any question, abnormal.

For such an argument to even begin to make sense, we must assume that the conceptions Peirce has in mind must be exceedingly general; they must be conceptions capable of being analyzed, as he puts it, "without any reference to their objective validity."

The phenomenology of consciousness. Metaphysics considers whatever can be an object of consciousness, and this object Peirce simply denotes as A. "This *gives* by addition of a negative (not A) that of which we can not be conscious" ("On the Definition of Metaphysics"). Now everything either exists or does not, he continues, and if the latter it is either possible or impossible. But anything possible can be conceived and so it is also an object of consciousness. Hence the not-A is either existent or impossible. Peirce continues: "Now that which is inconceivable and impossible is out of our *all*, hence *all* not-A is existent and A and not-A have existence in common." It appears that Peirce is begging the question here. After all, what is at issue is whether or not the not-*A*, that of which we are not conscious, may *exist*, and so by definition if we are conscious of it, it is not not-*A*. What he seems to have in mind, however, is that propositions like 'Not-*A* does exist' and 'Not-*A* is impossible' are still *about* not-*A*, and so not-*A* is being thought of, though only by means of some sort of definite description containing 'that of which we are not conscious'. In later essays the mind's ability to intend an object of which it could not be directly conscious, such as an infinite set, would play an important role in his argument.

Peirce noticed at this point that out of the above distinction comes an even more fundamental distinction between an act of consciousness and that of which consciousness is conscious. Here he anticipates Husserl's distinction within pure phenomenology between a noetic act and its noematic content. Peirce simply refers to the distinction as that between Subject and Object. Out of this he further distinguishes the Subject as self and the Object as phenomenon, calling the relation between them one of apperception. This trichotomy reveals three areas of research in pure metaphysics: (1) the self and its (passive) feelings, (2) the (active) volitions of the self, and (3) the representations apperceived by the self.

In the essay "Proposition. All unthought is thought-of" Peirce further elaborated upon the relation between Subject and Object. We either think of an Object positively as thought-of, or negatively as unthought. But with respect to the latter we *think* this object as unthought-of, and yet no unthought-of is thought. And so the unthought-of, strictly speaking, *is not*. This in turn raises the question of the particular nature of the relation between our thought of the unthought-of and the unthought-of itself. If the unthought-of does not exist, then though we think we are thinking of it we are not. Hence anything that we actually do think, even that which is putatively unthought, is thought-of, and, what is more, actually to think it we must in some manner also *apprehend* it. Normal minds are capable of this, though only the metaphysician understands why.

But then Kant's distinction between the conditioned phenomenon and the unconditioned noumenon began to raise a difficulty for Peirce. How is it possible to apprehend the unconditioned? In an "Elucidation" of the above essay, dated 30 June 1860, he considered this problem. In the *Critique* Kant had defined truth as the agreement of knowledge with its object.[5] To Peirce this definition naturally follows from the claim that our thoughts are caused by unapprehended noumena, and so in a trivial sense must always agree with their object. The more interesting question is: How can any representation possibly be false? We consider a judgment false, he argues, when our faculties act improperly, so that whenever we use them in the natural manner, truth must be the inevitable result:

> Now to whatever is thought-of there is a normal way of thinking-of; and that normal way gives a true thought of the thing; and that is an apprehension of the thing. And so even when the normal way of thinking of a thing gives an unintelligible result, it is either because it can't be thought of or because we have an unconscious idea of it.

The first alternative has already been eliminated, and that leaves only the second. "Whatever is normally unintelligible is true," Peirce concludes. An idea such as that of infinite space cannot be directly apprehended as an object and yet *is* apprehended, and so must be an "incomprehensible truth."

In a later essay, "The Fundamental Distinction of Metaphysics," the basic distinction between thought and thought-of is further refined. In such a distinction there is implied the view that apprehension is a process whereby a Subject brings itself into the act of apprehending an Object, and this embodies the traditional distinction between Reason and Sense. Thus the 'fundamental distinction' appears in all of philosophy, inasmuch as philosophy must make a distinction in its subject matter between the *a priori* and the *a posteriori*, or between what Peirce calls *Images of Reason* and *Images of Sense*. This same distinction appears in psychology as one between *Images of Inner Sense* and *Images of Outer Sense*, and metaphysics proper— as the study of all that we are conscious of *a priori*—generalizes this distinction as one between *Images as Images* and *Images as Representations*. At this point Peirce felt that he had improved upon and had gone beyond Kant's distinction between noumenon and phenomenon. In the essay "Of Objects" he discarded the noumenon as the thing "regarded simply" in favor of the object or thing "regarded as thought-of." Then the fundamental constituents of the field of consciousness become (1) the object thought-of, (2) the "influxual" dependency of the thought on the thought-of, (3) the result of that dependency in the form of an unconscious idea, (4) the actual representation, to whatever extent possible, of that idea, (5) the act of representing, (6) the acting soul, and (7) the self or mind's representation of itself as acting. Thus Peirce drops the transcendental object, but adds the transcendental ego, and in so doing moves away from Kant and closer to the post-Kantian idealists.

With such a shift it no longer becomes necessary to produce a transcendental deduction of the categories, for now the noumenal realm of actual transcendental objects is entirely beyond metaphysical consideration, even while the notion of the noumenal remains a part of metaphysics; and as a result there is no need to link our ideas deductively with their necessary conditions, as long as those necessary conditions are construed as lying beyond the thought-of. Peirce's next task is to show in a more detailed fashion why a transcendental deduction is not needed.

Transcendentalism. In the *Critique* Kant observed: "I entitle *transcendental* all knowledge which is occupied not so much with objects as with the mode of our knowledge of objects insofar as this mode of knowledge is to be possible *a priori*" (A11, B25). Peirce had concluded that such an approach was "worthless" and maintained that "we can assign a better test for the objective validity of conceptions than their necessary relation to cognition" ("Transcendentalism"). Kant had argued that the unity of experience could only be possible if the changing manifold of intuitions was itself subject to a representation of a manifold, one that was both formal and *a priori*. Such representations were the rules of synthesis, or categories. Thus the "objective unity" of empirical consciousness must result from these and only these rules (A123), and it was the task of the transcendental deduction to have established this. However, if Kant had been asked upon what he had based the *a priori* nature of the categories, he would most likely have replied, "upon the deduction itself." Peirce, on the other hand, considered the deduction worthless because he believed that the *a priori* conceptions necessarily had to be grounded in some manner other than transcendentally. And this could be shown if it could be established that while the categories and the whole synthesizing apparatus could be transcendentally deduced *a priori*, the premises upon which the deduction was based could only have themselves been dogmatically grounded. It is not difficult to locate such hypothetical premises in the deduction itself, and we can easily imagine the young Peirce putting his finger on one or more of them in his diligent reading of the *Critique*. For example, Kant assumes that "if the objects with which our knowledge has to deal were things-in-themselves, we could have no *a priori* concept of them" (A128). But in the context this claim clearly begs the question, and would require the entire perspective of the *Critique* for its elucidation and justification, a project to which the later idealists found themselves not committed in the slightest. So it was also with Peirce, who had evidently suspected a hidden circularity in the pure deduction of the *a priori* nature of the categories, and who set out these suspicions in two closely-related arguments written in 1859, found in "That There is No Need of Transcendentalism" and "Transcendentalism."

(*i*) Kant and Whately had argued in their logical studies that the principle of the syllogism had to be assumed, for any justification of it would require its employment.[6] If this were so, Peirce maintained, for error to be possible in judgment the very "observing power" of the mind and its *a priori* conceptions would have to contain falsity in the formation of the premises. Now the only recourse the transcendentalist has is to reveal this falsity by showing to the mind using the *a priori* conceptions that these conceptions somehow involve the mind in a contradiction. But, Peirce continues, the *a priori* conceptions "are merely phenomena." Thus it makes no sense to say that they are false relative to the premises and operations of the mind, and so the conclusions cannot be false either, if derived from sound operations. Therefore "there is no need of a deduction of conceptions."

(*ii*) Reasoning involves the comparison of propositions, and propositions may be either related inferentially, not related inferentially, or contradictory. Here the transcendentalist assumes that he need concern himself only with propositions of the first kind, so that any given proposition may be deduced from the others. However, deducibility produces justification only if the other deducing propositions are justified. Thus either there are some propositions that are their own evidence, or else in the transcendental system of propositions all propositions are equally plausible. But if they all have an equal *a priori* plausibility, then the plausibility a given proposition derives from some other proposition is less than that which that proposition has by itself. If each proposition has plausibility *n,* then the plausibility of its being true based on its deduction from *m* number of propositions is n^m, which is less than *n.* For it to attain greater plausibility it must be deduced from more highly plausible propositions, and even if these latter are deduced from other still more plausible propositions, eventually deduction ceases to generate plausibility and we must fall back on some other method of justification.

In his *Logic* Kant takes up the objection of the skeptic that the only way to compare knowledge with its object is to know the object already.[7] To him such circularity can be avoided by establishing the formal conditions without which knowledge would not be possible, and this was not difficult insamuch as formal truth is merely the agreement of an act of cognition with itself. Kant realized that only formal truth could be established in this way. A transcendental logic would be required for the deduction of objective truth, and this in turn would require a transcendental aesthetic (A55, B79). Clearly Peirce was of the opinion that the skeptic's objection was more pervasive than Kant had made out, applying to the very deduction of the categories.

The second argument (*ii*) may well have been suggested by a passage in Sir William Hamilton's *Logic.* In "Transcendentalism" Peirce wrote:

> In the appendix to Sir W. Hamilton's Logic it is shown that any two of the three propositions of Identity, Contradiction, and Excluded Middle prove the third. We cannot know that all *a priori* synthetical propositions are not thus connected, so as to support each other. But it seems to me that it would be most extravagant to say that we are entitled to use in speculation the principle of Identity *because* the doctrine of contradiction and excluded middle support it. For if the truth of these propositions are not certain upon their own evidence, either of them derived less support from the other two than it does from itself.

In Appendix V of the *Logic* ("Laws of Thought") Hamilton says of the three laws, "Begin with any one, the other two follow as corollaries."[8] Besides correcting him on this, Peirce denied that logical deducibility could logically justify any or all of the three separately or together.

Although Peirce rejected the transcendental result of Kant's Transcendental Analytic, he retained much of Kant's method of using logic as the source of the fundamental conceptions. Thus in "The Logical and the Psychological Treatment of Metaphysics" he speaks of two approaches to metaphysics: "One starts by drawing the conceptions from logical relations and thence reasoning to their place in the mind; the other starts by drawing the conceptions from the system of psychology and reasoning to their logical meaning." The former is less psychologically accurate, he tells us, but more metaphysically true, and so it is the method he adopts.

The idea of the perfect. In May of 1859 Peirce wrote a series of papers which indicate that for some time he had been thinking of reformulating Kant's categories in such a way as to reveal their underlying interrelationships. The result is an argument combining Kant's twelve categories with the three relations of *I, It,* and *Thou.* Everything in nature and mind has three stages, he argues, and so must Kant's four main categories—Quantity, Quality, Relation, and Modality. The first stage involves "bare unity," or self-consistency, and is called the *Null* or *Simple* stage; the second stage involves "more or less," that is, degree, and is called the *Positive* or *Human* stage; not surprisingly, the third stage is the result of the combination of the previous two and is the stage of *Perfection* (see Fig. 1).

Fig. 1

	SIMPLE	HUMAN	PERFECT
QUANTITY	Unity	Plurality	Totality
QUALITY	Negation	Reality	Infinity
RELATION	Community	Causality	Influx
MODALITY	Conceivability	Compatibility	Actuality

The first stage, perhaps best understood in Hegelian and dialectical terms, is the stage of absolute indifference that turns something into its opposite or 'null'. Simple quantity is unity, and "*Unity* is that number which makes Number conceivable without itself realizing that conception. It is the Negative of Number."[9] Simple quality is negation; it is unpredicated quality that stands in relation to nothing and so ceases to be what it is precisely as quality. Simple relation, or "dependence," as Peirce calls it, is community: "*Community* is that relation which makes dependence conceivable but has not that which is necessary to positive dependence, succeedence in time. It is the negative of dependence." Simple modality, called variously "occurrence" or "form of fact," is conceivability; it is that possibility "which has not that which makes possibility possible," and is a "merely formal possibility," a possibility with not even yet a logical hold on actuality.

The second stage involves differentiation not fully realized. Positive quantity is mere plurality, while positive quality is reality (or sometimes "affirmation"); it is quality possessed in degree. Positive relation is causality inasmuch as causality indicates a degree of relation "more or less intimate," but the relation is neither completely estranged, as with community, nor perfectly intimate, as is the case with the perfect stage of relation. Positive modality is compatibility; it is the degree of modality that already has some hold on the actual to the extent that it 'can be' with some finite degree of probability.

The third stage is formed from a combination of the previous two. Perfect quantity is totality; it is "that Number of a substance that has become so many as to be one again." Perfect quality is infinity; once again it is that quality "so real that [it] ceases to have degree of reality and becomes a negation of degree. It is negation combined with reality." Perfect relation is influx: "that dependence that has a Causality too intimate to have the distinctive mark of Causality, difference in time, and has become Community. It is Causal Community." Perfect modality is actuality, a probability so great that it ceases to have probability "and our belief in it rests again on its mere reception into the mind."

The fourth of Kant's categories, modality, Peirce found most troublesome. In the paper under discussion he suggests that its three stages are possibility as mere conceivability, compatibility (or probability), and actuality. Yet Kant had grouped them as possibility/impossibility, existence/non-existence, and necessity/contingency. Besides, in the paper entitled "That the PERFECT is the Great Subject of Metaphysics" Peirce had given the stages of modality as possibility, actuality, and necessity, considering necessity to be one of the four perfections, along with totality, infinity, and influx. Why, then, did he change his mind?

The answer is at least partially found in the paper entitled "Of the Stages of the Category of Modality or Chance," written the day after the essay on the Perfect mentioned above. As the categories are outlined by Kant, Peirce asks, are possibility and necessity to be understood logically or physically? If the former, a meaning must be given to logical existence as well. But there is no such meaning, and so the categories must pertain entirely to the physical. This means that there is no sense to the category of 'physical non-existence': "All the non-actual must be physically impossible, for it is non-actual because nothing made it exist and it is physically impossible that anything should be which nothing has caused to to [be]." This also means that physical possibility and necessity are "coextensive" with actuality. The only possibility that remains a mere possibility is conceivability or metaphysical possibility. Yet this distinction raises a further problem with respect to necessity. If the necessity of an affirmative is the same as the impossibility of the negative, then necessity cannot be a stage of conceivability, and this means that there is an error in Kant's list. If we accept the idea of actuality as something that "does not admit of more or less," the three stages of modality must be conceivability, compatibility, and actuality. It became evident to Peirce, then, that Kant's error lay in his taking modality from the logical functions of judgment and not from the metaphysical analysis of *a priori* conceptions.

It has already been suggested that Peirce had interpreted the relation between the categories in something approaching Hegelian fashion even though there is little, if any, evidence to indicate that he had read Hegel before 1860. We may then wonder where he got the idea that Kant's triads revealed a *developmental* pattern that culminated in a state of perfection. Schiller's synthetic method has already been acknowledged as an early influence, and was doubtless of some importance here. Another possibility, suggested by Murray Murphey,[10] emerges from the *Critique* itself, where Kant observes (B110) that the third category can be formed by a combination of the first two. He even illustrates this with the concept of number, as did Peirce, and several pages later (B113) notes that the Scholastic categories—*unum, verum, bonum*—are conditions not of things but of knowledge, and have their counterpart in unity, plurality, and totality. Here the unity of the concept combines with the variety of truthful consequences to produce a completeness of knowledge. Significantly, of the last—complete knowledge—Kant writes: "Thirdly, and lastly, there is *perfection,* which consists in this, that the plurality together leads back to the unity of the concept, and accords completely with this and with no other concept. This may be entitled the *qualitative completeness* (totality)" (B114). Similarly, in the introduction to his *Logic* Kant speaks of the logical and esthetic perfection of knowledge and specifically describes this in terms of quantity, quality, relation, and modality. There he observes, "In the perfections just mentioned, there are always two elements which, by their harmonious union, produce perfection in general, viz., Plurality and Unity."[11] It is likely, then, that with guidance from Schiller Peirce discovered evidence for the three stages in Kant's own work; he did not, however, adhere to Kant's warning that such notions be regarded only as stages of knowledge. Instead, for reasons not yet entirely clear to him, Peirce took them to be stages of reality as well.

The four perfections—totality, infinity, influx, and necessity (or actuality)—represented for Peirce the "four difficulties of Metaphysics," for human experience was subject only to the categories of the positive or human stage, and so could not adequately and directly comprehend total quantities, infinite qualities, influxual relations, and necessary modes. Yet it was still the task of metaphysics to consider these, if only on the grounds that they can be thought-of. And so in the essays of 1859–60 Peirce took up the analysis of the concept of infinity.

The idea of the infinite. In a brief essay called "The Infinite, the Type of the Perfect" Peirce suggested that a study of our human knowledge of the infinite could shed some light on the stage of perfection, adding that "whatever is true of [the infinite] will hold good for the Perfect stage of the other conceptions." The idea of the infinite, he argues, is something of a paradox in that the infinite is definitely something thought-of even if it is not comprehended; it is both thought-of and unthinkable; "Its thinkability gives it existence, while our impotence makes it unthinkable" ("The Nature of our Knowledge of the Infinite," MS. 921, 23 October 1859). We do 'think' or refer to the infinite when we speak of, say, half of an infinitely long line. Similarly, when we say that we may neglect infinitely small quantities, there is something we say we are neglecting. But what is the *something* we neglect?

It is not a thing, nor the attribute of a thing, Peirce argues in "Why we can Reason on the Infinite," (MS. 921, 25 October 1859). However, it is a something we predicate of something, for example, of a line. Now the predicating relation is based on the perfect stage of the category of relation, on influx, in other words, and so infinity must be a form of influxual dependency, specifically an unlimited form of such dependency. In a sense, then, it is an attribute, but not one that can be thought of independently of what it qualifies. As the perfect stage of quality it can be neither a partial or limited, nor a negative, attribute of something; it must be predicable, yet somehow must also be something that adds nothing specific to the predicated. The predicate 'black' adds something specific (color) to 'crow', but 'infinite' adds nothing specific to 'line'. An infinite line is still merely a line and nothing more. "Infinity," Peirce concludes, "is that influxual dependency of qualities which is further from negation than limitation is." It is an unlimited attribute, and so, properly speaking, not an attribute at all.

How does such an unlimited attribute come to be known? Peirce considered this question in "Sir William Hamilton's Theory of the Infinite" (MS. 921, 27 July 1859). In the *Lectures on Logic* Hamilton had argued that the infinite is conceived only by thinking away all attributes from the finite; as such it is "no object of thought."[12] For him even a thought of infinite space is inconceivable. Peirce rejects this *via negativa* and argues instead for the positive character of the infinite. If the infinite is an unlimited quality, and if "there are no qualities except those thought, since only by being thought does it become a quality," the infinite must be thought. However, "in my immediate consciousness I cannot realize any quality infinitely," and so, Peirce concludes, not everything is in consciousness in an immediate fashion. Something may exist in consciousness as an *idea*, and this is how the infinite, if it can be said to 'exist' at all, would exist. Somehow "the idea may be infinite and the thought finite." Peirce describes such an idea as "the impression made upon my mind by the object of thought." Thus he is not speaking here of a Kantian transcendental idea, but of an impression made by something actually infinite. It is not an idea imposed by the legislation of Reason, though it is like a Kantian idea in the sense that "no object adequate to the transcendental idea can ever be found within experience" (A327, B385). Now, however, the infinite is not just an unlimited quality, but a quality having some mode of real being. It is not only thought, but thought-of, and Peirce is left with the formidable task of justifying the reality of such an object.

What evidence is there that an infinite reality in whatever form exists, not merely as an idea, but as an object as well? In one attempt to answer this ("That Infinity is an Unconscious Idea," MS. 921, 25 October 1859), Peirce turned to faith as the justification of last resort: "Now Faith says, the infinite does influence the soul—as infinite. It follows that we have an unconscious idea of it." In speaking of faith in such a context he may have been influenced by the arguments of Henry Longueville Mansel's *The Limits of Religious Thought* (1859), a work Peirce is known to have studied carefully. Like Hamilton, Mansel considered the notion of the infinite a negative idea which indicated "a relation, if only of difference, to that of which we are positively conscious."[13] However, Mansel went further in attempting to account for our putative notion of the infinite. We cannot directly know the infinite, and yet it is not an idea we can dispense with easily: "While it is impossible to represent in thought any object, except as finite, it is equally impossible to represent any finite object, or any aggregate of finite objects, as exhausting the universe of being. Thus the hypothesis which would annihilate the Infinite is itself shattered to pieces against the rock of the Absolute."[14] Mansel concludes that we are "compelled, by the constitution of our minds, to believe in the existence of an Absolute and Infinite Being."[15] The reason thought can only represent the finite is that "to be conscious, we must be conscious of something; and that something can only be known as that which it is, by being distinguished from that which it is not."[16] This means that "to be always conscious of the same object, is, humanly speaking, not to be conscious at all" for "existence itself . . . is only conceivable in the form of existence modified in some particular manner." In other words, "consciousness is . . . only possible in the form of a *relation*."[17] But the infinite is all-encompassing; it is not something subject to modification in some particular manner.

Mansel rejects the attempts of idealistic philosophers like Schelling and Hegel to grasp an Infinite reality beyond consciousness through its finite development. Such attempts, he concludes, are self-refuting in that they enlist reason in service of the task of transcending reason:

> They thus assume, at the same moment, the truth and
> falsehood of the normal consciousness. . . . Such a theory is
> open to two fatal objections—it cannot be communicated,
> and it cannot be verified. It cannot be communicated; for
> the communication must be made in words; and the meaning
> of those words must be understood; and the understanding
> is a state of the normal consciousness. It cannot be verified;
> for to verify, we must compare the author's experience
> with our own, and such a comparison is again a state of
> consciousness.[18]

For very much these reasons Peirce too had come to conclude that
philosophy must be tested by normal minds, that transcendentalism
is useless, and that every man must be his own metaphysician. And,
like Mansel, Peirce remained unwilling to dismiss talk of the infinite
as sheer logomachy. We cannot apprehend the infinite, and yet, as
Mansel had put it, "the shadow of the Infinite still broods over the
consciousness of the finite."[19] This fact is a mystery of faith, and is
the clearest indication that "belief cannot be determined solely by
reason."[20] That metaphysics requires a turn to faith was Peirce's
conclusion at this point as well, though, unlike Mansel, he was
already engaged in an effort to ground this conclusion rationally in
a system of categories. In taking up Mansel's challenge to the idealists
Peirce was seeking to develop a new language of communication
about topics not thought-of in the usual manners.

In two of the final short essays of the series we have been considering, "Of Realism and Nominalism" and "Comparison of our
Knowledge of God and of other Substances" (both 25 July 1859),
Peirce maintained that our ideas must be given a realistic interpretation. In the first paper he writes: "It is not that Realism is false, but
only that the Realists did not advance in the Spirit of the scientific
age. Certainly our ideas are as real as our sensations. . . . An *idea* I
define to be the *neumenon* of a conception." And in the second he
asks: "But has space a corresponding neumenon? There are no innate
ideas. Is it then a thing out of us? It is an innate idea. It will be seen
that I take a realistic view of this subject." But what is this view?
Peirce does not tell us at this point; nor is it likely that he had any

clear comprehension of it himself. We know that the idea must be in the mind and that it cannot be thought or apprehended. As a noumenon of a conception it must stand to the conception in a manner similar to that relating phenomenon and noumenon. It must cause the conception in some sense, and the conception must in some way retain the marks of its origin. But these questions remained for further elaboration, and particularly for a fuller development of the system of categories.

2. THE TREATISE ON METAPHYSICS

The topics considered in the previous section are given fuller expression in a proposed treatise on metaphysics Peirce worked on from 1860 to 1862. There is little evidence to indicate that he changed his opinion radically during this time. The topics he takes up once more are (1) the definition of metaphysics and (2) the refutation of the dialectical and transcendental methods; in addition, he considers (3) the principles of metaphysics.

The definition of metaphysics. Because Peirce accepted "the arbitrary impossibility of an apodictic deduction of metaphysics" (MS. 920), it followed that metaphysics could not rest on one simple foundation. As the analysis of fundamental conceptions, it could be looked upon subjectively, objectively, or "in a way which is as nearly expressed by—practically—as any other word" (MS. 920). Observation plays no part in metaphysics because "any science got from observation may be subsequent to some other" (MS. 920). As an *a priori* science metaphysics concerns itself with the primary conditions of all science, and so could only result from the natural unfolding of the mind. For this reason it is ultimately tied up with the distinction between knowledge and wisdom. Knowledge is acquired empirically, while wisdom results from reflection on the conceptions employed in acquiring knowledge. This reflection is something each person must carry out, for otherwise metaphysics could be the kind of knowledge acquired from reading metaphysical texts. As Peirce says, "Why is metaphysics so hard to read? Because it cannot be put into books. You may put suggestions towards it into books but each mind must evolve it for himself."[21] In making this point it is possible that Peirce may have been influenced once more by Kant, specifically by his distinction between *cognitio ex datis* and *cognitio ex principiis,* wherein

Kant distinguishes historical knowing (learning) from knowledge that results from the active production of Reason (A836–37, B865–66).

To the extent that metaphysics deals with the conceptions of the mind it can be looked upon as a branch of psychology. Yet, Peirce notes, psychology in the form of *rational psychology* itself rests on metaphysics, so that we are presented with two possible methods of studying metaphysics: "One starts by drawing the conceptions from the system of psychology and reasoning to their logical relations and meaning; the other draws the conceptions from no system but from the thoughts as they present themselves in their Logical form. . . . The latter seems to me to be the truly metaphysical course."[22] This latter approach, based on "no system" and beginning with thoughts "as they present themselves" to reflection, may be considered a phenomeno-logical one. In choosing it Peirce was already assuming a great deal of accomplished metaphysics, in that he was assuming that our thoughts do in fact possess a logical form and that upon inspection this form can become apparent to us. It was undoubtedly reading Kant and Hegel that convinced Peirce that there was such a form in thought. In his book of aphorisms (MS. 891) he wrote on 13 July 1860: "Metaphysics is the study of form. In the study of matter we have at least some idea of our subject and therefore are never wholly in the wrong, but a modified form is in no degree the same as the unmodified form, therefore in metaphysics we are never partly right." Fortunately, this passage, while sufficiently dramatic for a book of aphorisms, did not reflect Peirce's working attitude toward metaphysics, for he also stated as part of his approach: "I believe in mooring our words by certain applications and letting them change their meaning as our conceptions of the things to which we have applied them progress" (MS. 920). This is more the method followed in actual practice. In the previously considered essays he had divided the thoughts "as they present themselves" into a set of three dichotomies. Using the phenomenologically neutral notion of an "image" he distinguished *a priori* and *a posteriori* images (as in philosophy), inner and outer images (as in psychology), and images proper and images as representations (as in metaphysics). In the Treatise he goes on to suggest that reciprocal relations may also be possible among the dichotomies. For if metaphysics may be looked upon either objectively or subjectively, as logical analysis or psychology, it may turn out that *a priori* images are merely *a posteriori* images looked at simply as images, or that *a posteriori* images are really *a priori* images looked upon as representations, or that to regard an image as an image is to regard it as inner in that it can only be apprehended in immediate consciousness. In some fashion the three dichotomies are not mutually exclusive, and so neither are the sciences based upon them.

Although "pure" metaphysics remained for him the study of images as images proper, Peirce continued to insist that the metaphysical grounding of elemental truths was not possible. Why then did he continue to hold that there are both primal truths and *a priori* conceptions? The answer to this seeming dilemma lies, at least in part, in his view that for a conception to be *a priori* is not the same thing as for it to be elemental. The logical method consists in the study of "the logical relations of conceptions since definition is itself a statement of relation," and this is possible because "conceptions cannot have a logical relation (that is, one that is contained in the very thought itself) unless they are complex" (MS. 920). Peirce's meaning becomes clearer in a remarkably modern, almost Quinean, passage (from MS. 891) written 25 November 1860: "I have come to the conclusion that our primary conceptions are not simple but complex; that our elementary conceptions are not independent but linked complexedly together; that nevertheless properly speaking we have no *a priori* synthetical propositions, and that axioms are only definitions." Accepting this view has implications for how metaphysics shall proceed. It is to this question that Peirce next turns.

The dialectical and transcendental method. The threefold conception of metaphysics and the "impossibility of achieving a synthesis of it" has historically led to the formation of three schools of metaphysics, which Peirce calls the *dogmatical*, the *psychological*, and the *logical* schools. It is possible that he intended these "schools" to derive from the three approaches to metaphysics—the objective, subjective, and practical—though this is not clearly indicated. Indeed, Peirce would never make explicit whether he identified the 'practical' with the 'logical' treatment of metaphysics, noting only that "the logical examination of truths is the same as the practice of Logic" (MS. 920, p. 15). When members of each of the three schools conclude that their own method is the exclusive approach to metaphysics, three erroneous methods result—dialectics, transcendentalism, and

rationalism. The former two Peirce would consider and subsequently reject, while noting that inasmuch as he himself belongs
to the logical school, rationalism would be a "constant topic . . .
and need not be specially considered" (MS. 920, p. 18).

(i) *Arguments against dialectics.* Though dialectics may at times be
used by the psychological and logical metaphysician, it is a character-
istic outgrowth of dogmatism in that it assumes the existence of
first principles. Its 'ground' is that "the light of necessary truths is
a participation of the infinite reason" (MS. 920, p. 19). Peirce argues
this rather surprising position in the following way: the dogmatist
holds that the truths of experience must ultimately be deduced
from certain major premises, yet no knowledge could be deduced
from premises whose truth is not given. Thus if knowledge is
derived from the deduction from first principles, the truth of these
premises must be given in the very statement of the principles.
But there are only two ways a proposition may contain its own
necessity: either it is analytic, "or else it must as a fact have an
existence which is self-dependent." The former is ruled out if
science is to generate genuine knowledge, and so the latter must
obtain. But this means that first principles are statements concerning
the only self-dependent entity we know—God: hence a dogmatic
dialectician must maintain that in knowing, we participate in the
divine nature.

Psychological dialectics involves a similar assumption, except
that it substitutes consciousness for God and maintains that consciousness "contains not mere images of the object thought of but
is an immediate seizing of the object itself" (MS. 920, p. 20). Peirce
calls this the Theory of Immediate Perception, and in a short essay
written around this period, "Immediate Perception" (MS. 1103),
he declares "the Doctrine of Common Sense to be well fitted to
Reid's philosophical calibre and about as effective against any of the
honored systems of philosophy as a potato-popgun's contents
might be against Gibraltar." Common sense can not serve as a
starting point because it does not indicate any way we can establish
such a starting point beyond a redundant appeal to common sense;
it restricts us, Peirce concludes, to one line of inquiry, that of finding
out which claims are held with greatest conviction. But "there is no
criterion by which it may be determined whether a given conviction
is normal or not." By this he means that no such criterion is

immediately known. While Peirce maintained that it was intelligible to appeal to normalcy in referring to the process of concept formation, it was not appropriate when referring to analysis and justification of metaphysical concepts. The data of metaphysics, the *a priori* conceptions, must in some sense be construed as being 'given', but how such data are to be analyzed is not given immediately or apodictically. Only as a result of an analysis of fundamental conceptions could such a claim to immediacy be justified, and then surely not on grounds of common sense. And so because an immediate data of consciousness does not reveal its own constituting conditions we should use instead what he calls "indirect reasoning *a priori*" as a means of establishing its credentials. From such reasoning it would be apparent that "perception is in fact a mere residuum of analysis, and what belongs to it is not a question of common sense but of analytic simplicity." Peirce does not deny that at times some form of intuitionism can be useful; however, all three methods of inquiry—the intuitive, the deductive, and the analytic—should be available to the metaphysician:

> To make [intuitionism] our one principle of investigation, [and so] never to dogmatize [so as] to proceed from acknowledged axioms as all natural sciences do, never to analyze so as to find what is simple in thought and not merely what is primitive, is not only to throw away two thirds of our means of investigation, but is to sow the seeds of the overthrow of that principle of faith with which we set out. (MS. 1103)

Immediate perception is not acceptable, then, because there is still room for analysis; it confuses the primitive with the simple, and must be tempered by metaphysics, considered as the analysis of conceptions into their simplest configurations.

Finally, logical dialectics is based on the assumption that there must be some abstractions that are literally real, for it claims that in studying the structure of logical forms we can attain genuine knowledge. The ontological argument for the existence of God is one such form of logical dialectics, Peirce suggests, in that it views our thought of a necessary being as evidence for the reality of a necessary being.

Peirce now presents a three-part refutation of the three forms of dialectics: dialectics is refuted as a *system*, a *tendency*, and an *intention*, with the first of these containing three objections, a philosophical, psychological, and logical objection. By dogmatism as a 'system' he meant the idea of a completed philosophical system based on certain first principles, while by dogmatism as a 'tendency' or 'intention' he meant the endeavor or intent to construct such a system.

Considering first the philosophical objection to systematic dogmatism in metaphysics, Peirce notes that metaphysics must be prior to all the sciences. Yet the dogmatic dialectician holds that knowledge of external reality can result from the study of metaphysics, and that such knowledge must be based on a founding principle. However, metaphysics cannot supply a principle that would be the foundation of knowledge of fact, without itself being based on some knowledge of fact. In short, metaphysics would have to cease being metaphysics and become physics or some such science instead. If it were a science it would be capable of producing synthetical propositions; yet because "every previous principle of synthetical truth is synthetical, for it goes beyond the subject—the representation of the fact—to state its correspondence with something beyond itself, the fact" (MS. 920, p. 22), this would imply that metaphysics is based on prior principles which is simply contrary to our notion of it. In short, the dogmatist cannot be a systematic dialectician and a metaphysician as well.

Peirce turns next to the psychological objection that all knowledge involves a modification of consciousness, and so metaphysical knowledge is antecedent to all other modifications of consciousness. Yet the antecedence the dogmatist requires is one of a grounding principle prior to all modification of consciousness, and so if metaphysical principles are *known*, as it trivially seems they would have to be for metaphysics to be possible, they would have to involve a modification of consciousness. However, one modification of consciousness cannot stand as a principle to another modification of consciousness. Psychological priority does not justify metaphysical priority.

The logical objection is even more straightforward: if metaphysics were the logical antecedent of all sciences, it would logically contain those sciences, for the premises can be said to contain the conclusion, and so all science would be prior to itself, which is absurd.

Peirce then briefly considers the following responses of the dogmatist to each of the previous arguments: (1) there *is* a science prior to all science, the science of the reality and nature of the Divinity; (2) while we are not conscious of possessing divine knowledge, the knowledge we do possess manifests the truth of its Creator; and (3) even the mere consciousness of a certain conception (that of a necessary being) affords genuine knowledge of that being. But Peirce felt that these claims should be summarily dismissed because they are clearly based on a number of ramified metaphysical assumptions, and therefore actually belong to applied rather than to pure metaphysics.

If dialectics fails internally by producing only truisms based on common sense, can it at least be justified as a provisional method of investigation? Peirce next considers this question. What we must ask, he argues, is how probable the principles of dialectical investigation are likely to be. If they are metaphysically interesting then they are going to be considerably abstract in nature, and then it becomes necessary to make a judgment as to whether, and, if so, to what degree, a given abstract proposition applies to given specific circumstances. Recalling the previous remark about metaphysics as the study of form, Peirce once more concludes that "in thinking of the concrete, if we err, it is by a reasonable distance from the truth. In the world of abstraction, on the contrary, there is no extension and consequently the slightest error is as absolute as the greatest" (MS. 920, p. 25). Because one abstract proposition differs fundamentally from any other, unless the correct propositions are the premises settled upon by dialectical investigation, there is a very strong likelihood that the conclusion will be erroneous. In the search for truth, Peirce reminds us, the deductive method is at a great disadvantage to the inductive method; in the latter, deviations from the truth may cancel each other out, but in the former, an initial error is a total error and compounds itself greatly. Consequently dialectics as a method of investigation is considerably less reliable than even the Baconian method.

Finally, dialectics is rejected even as an intention, that is, even as an idea of a proposed method of investigation eventually culminating in a system. By now this should be obvious, for the difficulties with dogmatic metaphysics are internal to it, and so are inescapable. Even as an intention it only ends up either espousing what we already know through common sense, and so does no better than common-sense philosophy, or else it lapses into speculations that can in no way be justified.

Peirce's refutation of dogmatism raises a number of difficult questions, one of which I shall consider at this point: Does he mean to deny by such arguments that there are any axiomatic metaphysical propositions? The evidence would seem to indicate that he does not. Rather, what he appears to deny is that we may exclusively use the mind to uncover in a rationally integrated way all of the fundamental tenets of our knowledge and all of the basic operations of the mind. In short, his rejection of dogmatism amounts to a rejection of episte-mological foundationalism. In contrast, he conceives of metaphysics as a ship already afloat, which nevertheless must be built and rebuilt, plank by plank, while underway. The boat departs christened 'common sense' and arrives at its destination as 'metaphysical truth'. But then this raises the question of whether the blueprint for the reconstruction was already aboard before the journey began. Here Peirce denies that such a blueprint can be produced by the mind. For if dialectics cannot be shown to stand on a rationally cognizable foundation, while at the same time abstract metaphysical propositions are intelligible, as they seem to be, then such propositions must derive from some non-mental source which Peirce simply labels "divine Reason" (MS. 920, p. 28); and such metaphysical prop-ositions, he suggests, must somehow be the results of inspiration.

This is a rather paradoxical turn in Peirce's account of dialectics, for it would seem that he had already rejected philosophical dialectics as the view that necessarily presupposes such an infinite reason. Now he seems to claim that because dogmatism fails, it somehow succeeds! Metaphysical propositions cannot be given a foundation in dialectical argument, and so they must have a foundation external to the activity of mind. (The other possibility is that they are utterly foundationless, but this leads to skepticism, which Peirce rejects outright.) Is this an inconsistency, and if so why didn't Peirce notice it? It may be that he thought that by appealing to introspection he was not giving metaphysics a foun-dation at all, but instead was grounding it, so to speak, on a groundless faith. A dogmatist, he may have thought, is one who is simply dogmatic about the truth of his fundamental metaphysical conceptions, and overlooks the fact that they cannot be rationally justified. What he might then have meant by the expression "true dogmatism" in the brief section of the Treatise entitled "Inferences Regarding True Dogmatism" (MS. 920, p. 28) is simply the view that the fundamental conceptions have not been justified, and this may have been the extent of his own commitment to dogmatism. Dogmatism is clearly false to the extent that it thinks it can fully certify unconditioned truth through consciousness; of this he was sure. For "pure consciousness . . . thinks nothing before experience." However, dogmatism is true to the extent that it sees metaphysics as the unfolding of implications: "Yet if we arrange what we already know, it will be more easy to arrive at new experience. . . . Abstractions are revealed in consciousness and in the world, and our studies of them in one place hold good in another. There is that much truth in dialectics." This is a considerable amount of truth indeed. In fact, echoing Peirce's reply to him, the dogmatist might say that this fact cannot be a concern of pure metaphysics, but must result from the application of pure metaphysics. In order to avoid the necessity of rationally justifying metaphysics, and so of running into the logical difficulties he had already analyzed so well, Peirce must fall back upon a 'revelation theory' which, if it is to have any justification at all, must derive its justification from an entire metaphysical perspective. Once more metaphysics would have to be ahead of itself.

This problem, by no means solved or even clearly formulated in these early essays, would grow in importance through the years in Peirce's mind. He realized that direct, immediate, and intuitive justification would not do for metaphysics—he was at least that much in sympathy with the prevailing Anglo-Saxon attitudes of the time—yet he also realized that piecemeal, inductive justification was insufficient by itself. And so he sought a third, "indirect" justification, which at one point he must have thought that he had found in the transcendental method, for he wrote: "I have thus shown that we can have no dialectics until we have had a Transcendental Philosophy" (MS. 921). However, as we have already indicated, Peirce had become suspicious at the outset of the effectiveness of such a method, even while considering it closer to his own 'logical' or 'practical' approach than was dialectical dogmatism.

(ii) *Arguments against transcendentalism.* The abuse of the psychological school is transcendentalism, that is, the view that the nature of external reality can only be determined by investigating the operations of the mind. As such it takes three forms: a strictly psycho-logical form that seeks the answer in the activity and intuitions of consciousness (Kant); a dogmatic form that seeks it in the justification of the major premises of knowledge (Hume); and a logical form that seeks it by bringing our conceptions to the logical test of contradiction (Hamilton).

Psychological transcendentalism seeks a justification for meta-physics in the authority of consciousness, Peirce argues, "but the authority of consciousness must be valid within the consciousness, or else no science, not even psychological transcendentalism, is valid; for every science supposes that and depends upon it for validity" (MS. 920, p. 31). Or else, like Hume, it seeks it in our elementary impressions, and again no internal or logical authority can be brought to bear as a measure for assessing these perceptions. Or else, finally, it seeks it in the logical nature of our conceptions; but once more our "conceptions are determinations of abstractions and so far are the same nature" (MS. 920, p. 33).

Dogmatic transcendentalism does not realize that our major premises "merely state how our consciousness is modified." If such premises are unwarranted, so must be transcendentalism and meta-physics in general insofar as it must rely upon consciousness. It is better to assume, Peirce concludes, that metaphysics has no premises and is instead "pure analytics" (MS. 920, p. 33).

Finally, logical transcendentalism, which seeks a conformity of our principles and conceptions to the principle of logical consistency, overlooks the fact that the notion of contradiction is only applicable to "certain supposable predicates which are unrealizable and therefore necessarily false" (MS. 920, p. 33). If a concept is cognizable it cannot be self-contradictory, and if a principle is reasoned upon it too cannot be contradictory "if the procedure has been normal" (MS. 920, p. 32).

Metaphysical fideism. The failure of both dogmatic and transcen-dental metaphysics critically to establish their founding premises suggests the need for an entirely different perspective for metaphysics, one that embraces this failure itself as a critically established fact. This new perspective is fideism, the view that the founding premises must be based on faith. In Peirce's view this is what both the Kantian and Humean positions must ultimately come to. In Kant there must be faith in the relevance of the Ideas of Reason and in the apodicticity of the non-inferential element of cognition, while in Hume there must be faith that our ideas are indeed copies of our impressions and that our judgments of causal relation have objective validity. And, as noted previously, Peirce rejected total skepticism as a self-stultifying impossibility, and partial skepticism because he believed that each faculty was limited to a specific role and so could not be used to detect and correct the errors of another faculty.[23] "By showing that faith is inherent in the very idea of the attainment of truth," he writes, "makes its acceptance *axiomatic*" (MS. 920, p. 39). This is no simple faith, but something capable of discrimination: "Some things we should not believe though the angel Gabriel told us, while true religion is instinctively accepted by the ingenuous mind"; and "wherever there is Knowledge there is Faith. Wherever there is Faith (properly speaking) there is Knowledge" (MS.920, pp. 39–40). As early as 1854, when Peirce was but fourteen or fifteen, we find indications of a complex fideism: "Let us start then with a reasoning which is above Logic, state Truths that have only to be conceived to be believed; and do not say, if you do not understand, 'It is foolishness'" (MS. 891). Clearly, this is no mere credulity, but a sophisticated theoretical position (fideism), which emerges out of a critique of dogmatism, transcendentalism, and skepticism. We might call this view *methodological fideism*. It is not faith in certain privileged premises, and does not build the entire edifice of metaphysics upon these premises.

Peirce only gradually began to understand and articulate what he required for metaphysical faith. After numerous revisions he concluded that faith was involved in simple logical assertion as "the recognition by consciousness of itself. It is the strength of that faculty by which abstractions are conceived . . . . It is the vigour of that part of the mind which is in communication with the eternal verities" (MS. 920, p. 40). In this sense there can be no truth without judgment, and no judgment without the conscious act of judging and assenting. By itself the mere procedure of reasoning cannot generate truth. Premises must be supplied to be reasoned upon, and in the very process of investigation commitment must be made to the working criteria of intelligibility. In this respect Peirce's views anticipate in a general fashion Polanyi's notion of a *fiduciary framework*.

Although Peirce described this notion of faith in theological language, remarks such as those cited above may indicate that such language had an esoteric meaning for him. Around 1854 he wrote once more in MS. 891: "It is almost impossible to conceive how truth can be other than absolute; yet man's truth is never absolute because the basis of fact is hypothesis." We may surmise that human faith is precisely this act of hypothesizing, and, if so, it is clear that faith becomes necessary for the attainment of "man's truth." It would take a lifetime for Peirce to elaborate on the complex relations between hypothesis, assertion, methodology, and faith. In later writings he observed: "One must acknowledge that there is something healthy in the philosophy of faith, with its resentment at logic as an impertinence. Only it is very infantile. Our final view of logic will exhibit it (on one side of it) as faith come to years of discretion" (2.118). On the non-formal side logic will become part of a wider picture involving goodness and beauty as well. This picture is briefly sketched out in the 1903 Lectures on Pragmatism, where we find Peirce claiming that,

> our logically controlled thoughts compose a small part of the mind, the mere blossom of a vast complexus, which we may call the instinctive mind, in which this man will not say that he has *faith*, because that implies the conceivability of distrust, but upon which he builds as the very fact to which it is the whole business of his logic to be true. (5.212)

In the early papers, however, Peirce is more concerned with metaphysics proper, and does not yet fully realize to what these claims about faith and logic must commit him. Having cleared away the erroneous conceptions of metaphysics, he is now prepared to commence building his own edifice.

The principles of metaphysics. Peirce claimed to have refuted dogmatism, but only to have shown that transcendentalism was "useless." After it is realized that the transcendental method is not entirely presuppositionless, it remains possible to utilize it, only now without pretension. And so one of the effects of embracing metaphysical fideism as a methodology is that transcendentalism "as a study of the out-reaching of the human mind retains its full value" (MS. 920, p. 40). This value lies in the descriptive dimension of transcendentalism, which analyzes the various structures of knowing and the known. Metaphysics cannot dispense with this task even when it requires no argument linking cognition with transcendental objects. These structures, which Peirce regarded as the "three leading conceptions" of metaphysics, are truth, innateness of ideas, and externality. One can hardly fail to notice the three fundamental conceptions at work here. The *I* emerges as innateness, the *It* as externality, and the *Thou* as the combination of these in the dyadic relation of truth.

(*i*) *Truth.* An account of the truth of concepts depends on a theory of truth. Here Peirce suggests that 'true' is a quality of representations, so that it becomes of utmost importance to delineate the various possible dimensions of representability. A representation may be a *copy* and its truth *verisimilitude.* However, verisimilitude is not identity and so is only partial truth. Thus if we regard our conceptions as unqualifiedly true, as we must in metaphysics, then this truth cannot be that of verisimilitude. Next, there is that which is conventionally represented by a *sign*, and here truth is *veracity.* Obviously, fundamental concepts are not true in this sense; something must *become* a sign, and so metaphysics would not be fundamental if it regarded its concepts as signs. In metaphysics "conceptions claim as much truth the first time they are presented as they ever do" (MS. 920, p. 43). Finally, there is a form of resemblance that is non-conventional, yet not mere verisimilitude. In this case truth is *verity* (or *perfect veracity*) and the representation is a *type.* Now if verity is not to become identity, and thereby dissolve the representing relation, it must be based upon the very nature of the represented and not be a mere copy. But the nature of something, Peirce suggests, is found in its constituting origins. If these origins are temporally far removed from the entity to be represented, then the connection between them would be entirely loose and conventional. What we require for perfect veracity is invariable and immediate connection, and this is found, according to Peirce, only in the relation between substance and its accidents, which he had called in the earlier essays *influxual dependency.* In the First Analogy of the *Critique* Kant had argued that it was only due to the "logical employment" (A187, B230) of the Understanding that we were able to distinguish substance and accident. Substance and its accidents really constitute a unity; yet that 'unity' is not one of identity. Relation between them exists, though that relation is one of *inherence.*

This was the tight formal relation Peirce was seeking for the verity of type. He then extended the argument to include the way conceptions represented their subject: a conception represents its object, the conceived of, the way an accident represents its substance. If this is granted, then conceptions must "perfectly correspond" to their objects in some manner crucially analogous to that in which the qualities of a given substance can represent that substance (MS. 920, p. 44); the qualities are not identical to the substance, for if they were, there would be no distinction between them and the substance, and yet without precisely those qualities the substance would be something different.

Our concepts, then, literally 'participate' in the reality of what is conceived. Of course, as a sign the word *being* does not literally represent its extension (a certain condition), but, Peirce claims, our conception or thought of being somehow does. As with our conception of infinity, the connection is not one of verisimilitude, for the 'infinite' and 'being' are not the sorts of objects the mind is capable of knowing directly. If we recall that influxual dependency is a category of the perfect stage, and that such a category corresponds to a relational *Thou*, it follows that a conception must be a perfect copy of the nature of something insofar as it displays that thing's logical form. To have a conception, then, is always to have a true conception, falsity only entering in the application and relating of conceptions, and our conceptions for this reason must have "a connection therewith in the nature of things" (MS. 920, p. 44). Herein is the guarantee of the apodicticity of normal minds.

(ii) Innateness of ideas. The structures of inner experience have traditionally been described in terms of the doctrine of innate ideas. However, Peirce finds a confusion behind such a doctrine. Innateness implies that our ideas originate within us. Yet it is of the very nature of an idea to be a *representation* of something beyond our direct awareness of it, and so if our ideas represent something beyond that awareness they must be similar in some degree to the objects represented. If so, then there is a real connection between idea and object, and thinking of the idea as innate fails to emphasize this, even aside from the question of the origin of such ideas. In place of the usual doctrine Peirce proposes the following analysis: rather than speaking of an "innate idea" it is preferable to speak of an "innate element" of the mind. Unlike an idea that enters into an of-relation with its

object, and thereby concerns truth or falsity, an innate element is not predicated of anything beyond awareness. And so it either has no truth or falsity, or else is universally predicated of represented objects, and thus can only be possible if it does so "without altering the fact" of the object (MS. 920, p. 46). If its predication modified one object in one way and another in another way, then that predication would be specific, and with respect to such objects we would be able to say that it is a true or false predication. Thus genuine innateness must be either not predicable or universally predicable in that special sense just given.

Peirce now asks what element of the mind has this character, a character both wholly inner and incapable of specific predication, and suggests that receptivity is the element that satisfies these conditions. Receptivity is an essential character of the mind. It is also capable of being predicated universally of any of the objects thought-of without altering their specific character. Peirce then concludes: "Receptivity enters into of-thoughts as mere sensation. Sensation has neither truth nor falsehood for whether it be predicated or not doesn't alter the fact. It is not even thought of as external. Sensation then is the first category of Innateness" (MS. 920). From the point of view of phenomenology there is no difference between blue-sensed and a blue color sensed; nor do we consider that the sensation is external to us. To say 'the mind sensed blue' is to add nothing to the notion of 'blue'. What is innate then is not an idea but an "element of motion of the mind" (MS. 920).

In an earlier draft of the above argument Peirce remarks that "we ought now to find the Sensous Objective Logoi and find which of these implies Innateness. Then this with Sensation would be the metaphysical categories of Innateness" (MS. 922). But at this point he finds the idea of such 'Logoi' to be "hazy." Sensation, he notes, invariably involves a manifold of sense, and a manifold is something more complex than a simple object sensed; this "something else" Peirce calls a *world*, by which he seems to mean a totality, complete in itself, but capable as well of differentiation. It is sensible because the manifold of sense is itself always intuitively sensed, and it is objective because it involves an immediate revelation. A *subjective logos* is purely conventional—Peirce gives as an example a spoken language—but an *objective logos* is one that involves "a pure thinking of a fact" (MS. 922). Somehow, then, a sensible objective *logos* is both particular and *a priori;* it is not constructed through reasoning and it is not a simple "this." We suspect that our intuitions of space and time are what Peirce may have had in mind here. For Kant, space and time both contained "a manifold of pure *a priori* intuition" and were the "conditions of the receptivity of our mind" (A77, B102). Peirce appears to be attempting to synthesize these active and passive features within a single notion. However, to understand more fully his notion of the innate, its domain and influences, we must move beyond the theoretical foundations of metaphysics, our concern here, to the theory of categories and the metaphysics of nature to be discussed in the next chapter.

(*iii*) *Externality.* In this final section of the Treatise, Peirce argues the now familiar thesis that there can be nothing that cannot be thought-of either as thought or as unthought. One of the implications of this view is that all falsehood is partial truth, for falsity involves judgment, judgment involves conceptualization, and whatever is conceptualized must be taken into the mind in a true or accurate (normal) fashion. It was at least partly for this reason that Peirce thought transcendentalism unnecessary. Hence 'snow is warm' or even 'snow is strong' is partially false, but also partially true in that it is true that snow is something of which we can predicate something else. Any proposition or conception capable of being reasoned upon is at least partially true, and if it is logically reasoned upon it is entirely true even if, like the Infinite, or Absolute, or God, it is unintelligible in its own nature. "Thus if it is false that John is in the garden" Peirce writes, "that picture is at least truthful as to the man though the background be erroneous" (MS. 922). However, to say 'snow zr gork' is not to say something reasonable, and so it is not to say anything capable of being comprehended by our minds.

What do these arguments show regarding the question of the relation between thought and reality? First, that there are two realms, the thought and thought-of, and second, that while they are two distinct realms there still remains a relation of representability between them. Whatever the thought-of may be, it is always capable of being represented as thought. It is not surprising, Peirce concludes, that traditional metaphysics has split into *idealism* and *materialism,* and into the combination of both as *realistic pantheism,* leading to the postulation of three distinct worlds (which look very much like concrete realization of the *I, It,* and *Thou*), namely, Mind, Matter, and God. These three worlds are characterized by Peirce as being

> completely unrelated except in identity of substance.
> Everything which springs up freely in one of these, the
> Mind, does so from the very nature and substance thereof.
> Verity is unity of substance. It is clear that these data
> answer the question How Innate Notions can be True to
> External Fact. The connection between mind and matter
> is thus a preëstablished Harmony. (MS. 920, p. 48)

Verity implies a unity of Mind and Matter, and these two unsimilar realms become linked through a representation of the one in the other by virtue of their sharing similar logical structures, or *logoi*. In an earlier draft of the above passage Peirce writes, "There is an un-sameness between the mental and the material worlds. I do not say a difference of substance, for each is the universe. The difference is in their predicates. The predicates of worlds are qualities. There is then a difference between the qualities which reign in the two worlds" (MS. 922). Did Peirce intend the harmony of the two realms to be occasionalist in nature? This is suggested from his remark that our conceptions spring up freely from the nature of mind itself. Yet he refused to call the mental and material worlds *different*, choosing instead the apparently weaker term "un-same." And when he spoke of the three worlds as completely unrelated "except in identity of substance," he may have intended to convey the notion that they were in fact fundamentally related and distinct from one or more perspectives. Peirce realized that such metaphysical subtleties would require argument. "Here then we have three worlds," he wrote, "Matter, Mind, God, mutually excluding and including each other; as I showed was possible in one of my letters" (MS. 920, p. 48).[24] Unfortunately this letter has not turned up, and so we are left with the task of reconstructing his argument from his fragmentary writings on the categories.

Chapter II
The Theory of Categories

1. THE THREE WORLDS

At least as early as 1860 Peirce had become familiar with the central arguments of Plato's philosophy; at the time his library already contained several volumes of Plato. In one notebook (MS. 988), dated 30 May 1860 and entitled "Metaphysical Axioms and Syllogisms," he set down a series of 'axioms' derived from the Platonic dialogues, primarily on the subjects of morality and epistemology. The latter are of particular interest to us here.

From the *Phaedo* (lines 65–66) we get "Axiom 6": "The Ideas of Pure Reason are Real Objects." This curious blending of Kant and Plato is said to be justified by Socrates' argument that justice, goodness, and beauty can be objects of knowledge. The following are also derived from the *Phaedo*:

Ax. 8. Every event arises from its contrary. [lines 70–71]
Ax. 9. Our abstract ideas are suggested by outward objects, by empirical ideas. [line 74]
Ax.10. Qualities of empirical objects are not possessed infinitely. [line 74]

Ax.12. We have ideas of abstract qualities. [said to follow from the above axioms]

Ax.15. All things possessing qualities, possess them by virtue of a partial manifestation of the abstract quality. [line 100]

From the *Gorgias* (line 476) Peirce obtains Axiom 16: "According as the agent does, so the patient suffers," while from the major argument of the *Theatetus* he gets "Proposition 4": "The Conceptions which each faculty gives us are peculiar to itself."

This notebook may have been more than a mere study guide to Plato. From his selection of the axioms, Peirce appeared to be looking to Plato for support of some of his own metaphysical opinions. He willingly read out of Plato the view that the abstract is the real, that the actual is a partial realization of the abstract, and that the actualization of the abstract involved a clash of opposites—agent and patient, form and matter. This perspective fit nicely, we can imagine, with the previously developed categories as stages of perfection. Peirce's task, then, became that of explicating how the real and the actual were related and how the one merged into the other. This effort would involve, in part, delineating the general relations between the real and actual as well as the more precise relations among the categories deriving from each of the three previously established fundamental conceptions. Of the three basic categories, Peirce wrote in MS. 917: "Though they cannot be expressed in terms of each other, yet they have a relation to each other, for THOU is an IT in which there is another I. I looks in, IT looks out, THOU looks *through,* out and in again. I outwells, IT inflows, THOU co-mingles." In other words, while these three elemental 'persons' could have nothing *more fundamental* in common, each may become one of the others if looked at from a certain point of view. Thus the *I* may become *It* in memory, or generally whenever we think of ourselves as an object; the *It* may become *Thou* in apostrophic exclamation, the *Thou* may become *It* in cruelty; the *It* may become *I* in pantheism, and the *I* become *Thou* in love. It is clear, however, and was clear to Peirce, that the *I* does not literally become *It* in memory, for memory requires an *I* that is remembering, and so "the IT of the I contains nothing which . . . the I of the I contains" (MS. 917). When I remember a part of my past it is "my" past I remember because I myself remember it; even if I recall vividly what my state of mind was at the time, what I recall are certain emotions, desires, and so forth, that *I* had. The only *I* in memory, then, is the *I* of the present. Similarly, if the *Thou* becomes *It* in cruelty, it is not because it can become *It* literally. The *Thou*, after all, is an *I–It* combination and so has part of the *I* already within it. For it to become literally *It* is for it to eliminate the *I* from it. To extrapolate upon Peirce's argument here, in death it may be possible for the *Thou* to become *It*, but this is a transition we have difficulty comprehending—"What becomes of the I? What was it originally?" we ask—and it is more likely that the *Thou* who dies remains a *Thou* now dead. If the three 'persons' are totally different, and inhabit three different worlds, then once a person in one world, always a person in that world.

Does Peirce overlook the rather obvious fact that a *Thou* to me as *I* is an *I* to the *Thou* 'itself'? If so, he does not notice that the three worlds are actually three-worlds-for-me-as-I, thereby giving priority to the *I* over the other two categories. Hegel took this direction in the *Logic* when he sought to begin with simple internality of Being and derive from its negation and synthesis Nothing and Becoming. Here Peirce appears closer to Sartre, who considered the reality of the Other to be "pre-ontological" and so not derivable from the self.[1] Both the self and the non-self are equally necessary, one to the other, and so "the *cogito* itself can not be a point of departure for philosophy; in fact it can be born only in consequence of my appearance for myself as an individual, and this appearance is conditioned by the recognition of the Other."[2] In rejecting a foundationalist and psychological view of metaphysics Peirce had come to much the same conclusion. In the 'logico-practical' approach we begin with the fundamental logical notions and then rebuild all of the facets of reality out of them. If the *Thou* is really an *I* for-itself this does not eliminate its being a *Thou* for me; but this also means that the *I* contained within it is not simply my *I*. A *Thou* is not created when I put my *I* into an *It* (as in pantheism); rather, the *Thou* is 'already there', so to speak, in the way indicated by Sartre, and this is what Peirce means when he says that the three persons are in different worlds. Sartre's evidence is phenomenological in nature, and so, for the most part, is Peirce's; however, Peirce also appeals to the logical claim that the three persons are also the three most elemental forms of spatial relatability, as point, line, and angle, indicating that he seeks for his categories a far wider range of application than Sartre had intended for his. And in this respect, as will become clearer, Peirce is much closer to Hegel in overall intent.

In a series of remarks entitled "On Classification" (MSS. 919, 922) Peirce set out to describe instantiations of the three elementary conceptions. The triad can be manifested in thought in the following manner: we distinguish the content of a thought from the act of thinking it and notice that in some instances the content of certain thoughts remains invariant, and so our thinking it retains an element of impersonality. In this respect our thought that '1 + 1 = 2', even if thought at various times, is actually just one and the same thought when looked upon from the point of view of its content—just as a pen used now and again is really the same pen. This constant feature in thought Peirce calls *abstraction*. There is also another element of thought, which, Peirce writes, "in itself has not the form of number" (MS. 922); by its very nature it is particular and is called simply *things-or-thing*. Out of these two opposing elements a third is formed by combination, producing this triad:

Things-or-Thing
Modification of Consciousness
Abstraction

Of these Peirce holds that "the middle one only has a real existence among finite beings" (MS. 922). Here consciousness is a relational *Thou* that combines the *It* of thing with the *I* of pure abstraction.

He next considers a closely related triad involving language. For abstraction to come into consciousness the latter must contain a capacity to receive the pure form, and it must also be possible to predicate that form *of* consciousness. Consciousness, then, can be looked upon as a kind of 'substance' with a capacity to receive predicates, suggesting this triad:

Substance
Predicable making Predicate
Predicate

The mediating predicate must bring together substance and predicate, and this can only be possible if there is an underlying similarity between them; they must share something in common. But this must mean that within abstraction itself there is an *It*-like character that ties the abstraction down to this or that abstraction, and this Peirce calls its *meaning*. Along with this "peculiar form" there is the "common form," which is an abstraction within abstraction, and this underlying structure of the abstraction is designated the *language*. These combine to produce yet another triad:

> Language
> Expression
> Meaning

Again, only expression exists in the world of finite beings. For abstraction to come into consciousness, the meaning, or *It*-referring dimension, must be suited to the abstract *I*-referring dimension of language; only then will expression in the form of a conscious thought take place.

Peirce has now analyzed the application of the three basic categories to thought, distinguishing further particular triads of *kind* and *process*. He then seeks to elaborate on the structures of the latter. Just as there is no modification of consciousness unless abstraction combines with a specific dimension, which Peirce would soon call *sensation* rather than *thing*, so there is no expression unless meaning can combine with language. This ability of language to be suited to the expression of meaning he calls its *plasticity*, raising the question as to the categories of plasticity. Abstract language must be modified by meaning, and this modification is always a modification of a particular form. "If we speak of words," he writes, "this is the general construction of the sentence; I will accordingly call it *construction*" (MS. 922). For example, the meaning of the sentence 'snow is cold' is stated in the particular form '*S* is *P*' and to change the construction by rearranging the letters or words is to change the meaning, even if only insignificantly for conversational purposes. Peirce continues:

> Meaning puts expression into language first by the con-
> struction that is determined, second by the construction

that is indetermined. If the construction did not amount to construction, if it were *inconstruction,* there would be either silence or topsy turvy; if the construction were so fully determined as to produce a general inconstruction—a system too much a system to be systematic—it would make what we may call a *maze.* (MS. 922)

The three categories of expressibility or plasticity, then, are as follows:

Inconstruction
Construction
Maze

And once again Peirce concludes that only the middle category has existence among finite beings. Complete chaos or complete order does not exist in a realm where thoughts can be formed and expressed.

An interesting parallel to these categories can be found in recent information theory. Let us consider expressibility as a transmission process from sender to receiver, as something expressed through something to someone. Then if inconstruction predominates in the vehicle of expression no information (expression) is conveyed. For example, if the written code, as the vehicle of the expression of meaning, undergoes a random variation, resulting in inconstruction, then no message is transmitted. On the other hand, if the sender and receiver are 'fully determined' so that they form a 'maze', then again no information would be transmitted, for the receiver as part of a unified system with the sender would already contain the information being sent, that is, would 'contain' it in the sense that the unified system operated perfectly and each part required nothing beyond itself to maintain its role. In this case the system would be frozen and monotonous, and would lack the interesting variability that results from something's being systematic but not "too much a system."

As with his early study of Kant's categories, Peirce is once more thinking in terms of categories of process; he seeks to trace the transition of an idea or object from one state to another, and assumes that such a transition is incremental in nature. In the previous chapter we took note of his remark that during this period he sought to expand Kant's list of categories into a longer list revealing a regular system of relationships. The basic categories of *I, It,* and *Thou* represented the shortest list possible; now that list needed to be expanded by applying its basic logical forms to the various dimensions of experience. In this very task Peirce once more may have gotten some insight from a remark of Kant in the *Critique.* After introducing the twelve basic categories, Kant writes: "If we have the original and primitive concepts, it is easy to add the derivative and subsidiary, and so to give a complete picture of the family tree of the [concepts of] pure understanding" (A82, B108). Then such a combination of categories would yield "a large number of derivative *a priori* concepts."

The clue to what the regular system of relations might be is found both in Kant's perhaps inadvertent remark about tree-relations and in the basic structure of the three elementary categories. The latter embody monadic, dyadic, and triadic relations, but the same applies to even the most simple of branching structures as essential units of tree relations. Peirce clearly hoped to establish his system of relations upon these categories. It was his original intent that the unfinished treatise on metaphysics should serve as a preamble to such an undertaking, but only fragments of this effort remain. In the second chapter of the second book of the treatise there is a section entitled "Composition of Abstractions" (MS. 919). There he sought to discover the simplest possible relations among abstractions. This involved a proof of the proposition: "Every conception is of boundless complication in its own nature." There are, he notes, three ways any two abstractions or conceptions could be combined:

1. by being both thought at the same time
2. by one's being a thought of the other
3. by both being thought through a third

While Peirce does not supply us with an illustration here, the following is easily plausible: two conceptions may be thought at the same time in a hypen-relation, such as in 'hyphen-relation' itself, or more commonly in the simple predication 'round ball', with the notion of predication in the background; secondly, something may be thought *of* another when there is conscious predication of one to another, so that 'the ball is round' contains a different relation from 'the round ball'; finally, both previous relations can be combined by synthesis to produce 'the round ball is heavy'. The first relation, while combining more than one element, is essentially monadic in nature, the second, dyadic, and the third, triadic. If we formalize the first as AB and the second as A/B (A of B), the third would be C/AB ('heavy of round ball'). At this point Peirce concludes that "in the last case the third thought thinks of the others in the second mode," that is, C/AB is essentially of the form X/Y; in any string of predicates there is only one predicating 'of' relation and the rest are hyphenated. Thus only the first two relations are essential, and in the case of compounding conceptions, only the second is relevant.

In the particular of-relation of thought-of, the object thought of and the thought itself are the same, at least as long as we confine our view to abstractions. As Peirce puts it, both the thought and its object "belong to the same abstraction." What about the more usual predication of one 'thing' of another (not a thought), as for example 'round' of 'ball'? In this case he concludes: "When one thing has a relation to another, that wherein it has the relation must be complex, and the related members must have something in common." In an obvious sense the thing capable of taking on an of-relation must contain other of-relations. If something is to be predicated of something else, the thing subject to predication must be thinkable without its predicate. Unfortunately, this does not prove that prior to predication the subject is complex. Although we do not consider 'round' predicable of 'red', nothing said here so far precludes this possibility. Clearly, then, it must be Peirce's intent to argue that "two simple thoughts cannot have any relation in their own natures." Clarification of this ambiguity may be found in his observation that the "related members must have something in common." With this condition the subject, besides being something other than the predicate prior to predication, must contain *in its nature* something akin to the predicate. Thus 'red' contains nothing of 'round', but 'ball' contains something of 'round', namely, the predicate 'dimensionality'. From this Peirce concludes (1) that all thought compoundable involves a relation of simple to complex, and (2) that because a thought *of* a simple abstraction *is* that very abstraction, "there can be no plurality of elementary thoughts." In the former case he establishes the condition for the possibility of genuine complexity and in the latter he rules out a spurious complexity.

Next Peirce seeks to prove the proposition: "The field of thought is extensive." By an extensive field he means a homogenous network of relations among *similar* elements. Space and time, he suggests, comprise such a network.[3] But how might thought, with its seemingly intrinsic variety, comprise one? His answer is: by simply being comprised of acts of cognition. Whatever is thought "at once," he notes, can only be a simple conception, and if thought is a series of thinkings at once, with the links between simple conceptions being predications 'of', it must follow that our thought is part of a larger matrix of thinkable thoughts, and each of our conceptions must be linked to all others in some manner independent of thinking acts. Such a picture strongly suggests an underlying world of abstract Pythagorean interrelations. What Mendeleev would accomplish in 1869 with respect to the material elements (the Periodic Law) Peirce was now seeking to do in 1860 with the elements of thought, and in this light we are not surprised when he concludes that "the world [is] composed of numbers." In this vein he writes:

> The final elements of abstraction, since they contain in themselves the relations to one another, can contain nothing else (being simple) and hence are nothing but relations.
>
> The final elements being relations contain the idea of numbers and hence can contain nothing else. Hence for every number there can be but one simple relation.

In short, the list of positive integers is actually a list of simple relations, and not, as is commonly thought, a list of the names of the constituents of relations. If the constitutents are ultimately simple, mere place-holders, then, as Peirce notes, they are nothing but their relations. However, as there are many triangles, and therefore many ways three points may be related, there should also be many particular relations under the class of *three*. But here Peirce may be speaking of something even more abstract than, say, the general class denoted by 'two-dimensional configuration', for the "final elements" contain merely the "idea of numbers" and not specific numbered elements themselves. In this case 'three' is simply the idea of three-elements-in-relation regardless of the specific configuration of the relation.

At this point Peirce was less concerned with an analytically clear statement of this matrix theory of cognition than he was with the task of giving such ideas concrete instantiation. He rushed foward to develop specific instances of the simple number relations, and suggested the following as important examples:

> For 1. Ego
> Twofold. Primary and Secondary
> The Fourfold. Metaphysical, Mathematical, Dynam., Phys.

In the first instance oneness is akin to the category of the *I* as simple monadicity, and so it is plausible that he use the term 'ego' to illustrate it. 'Primary' and 'secondary', involving twoness, must then comprise the binary relation of *I* and *It*, with the latter depending on the former for its definition. In this case, however, there is contained in addition to the notion of twoness that of ordinality, perhaps indicating that Peirce was of the opinion that any binary relation required a priority or directionality to keep it from becoming monadic. The fourfold categories have no clear connection with number-like relations, and if they suggest other categories we suspect here a Kantian inspiration.

In the *Critique* Kant divided the twelve categories into two groups, the *mathematical* (quantity and quality) and the *dynamical* (relation and modality), but perhaps the four category headings suggested to Peirce that there were also four general categories, one for each triad of categories. If he was in fact familiar with Kant's *Metaphysical Foundations of Natural Science*, he may have noticed that Kant divides the *a priori* study of natural science—the metaphysics of nature—into four categories: *phoronomy*, the study of motion as a pure quantum; *dynamics*, the study of the basic interactions of motion; *mechanics*, the study of the more complex interactions of motion; and *phenomenology*, the study of motion as an object of experience. This scheme may have suggested to Peirce, in the order just given, the names of the fourfold categories—mathematical, dynamical, physical, and metaphysical. Also likely is the possibility that Peirce noticed Kant's remarks in the second edition of the *Critique* (B202) on the general modes of all combination (*conjunctio*), where the latter were divided into arbitrary and necessary combinations (*compositio* and *nexus*), with the first being mathematically treated and the second dynamical in nature. *Compositio* itself was divided into aggregation and coalition, while *nexus* was divided into physical and metaphysical relations.

Peirce no doubt pondered these remarks and may have modified this scheme to his liking, putting the metaphysical and physical categories of combination on the same level as the mathematical and dynamical.

As for the categories of threeness, missing from the above list, we may suspect that Peirce failed to list them not because of their unimportance, but because of their preeminent importance in his overall project. Any of the triads noted above exemplified to one degree or another the notion of triadicity, but none better than the *I, It,* and *Thou,* which themselves could function as transcendental categories pertaining both to relations and things, in both cases without loss of generality.

2. The Long List of Categories

From such preliminary work on the general structure of cognition, work that would be more fully realized in his later sign-theory of thought, Peirce was eager to propound a detailed system of categories with which to characterize not only the activity of mind, but also that of nature and of the world at large. Following Kant—who had claimed in the *Critique* that all *a priori* division of concepts is by dichotomy (B110), thereby taking one concept, analyzing it into two, and so ending with three—Peirce pictured reality as an unfolding by dichotomy of the abstract dimension of each of the three "persons" or "worlds" into their concrete manifestations. This unfolding of the basic relations he illustrated in two sketches found without commentary among the early fragments (Fig. 2). In both illustrations we see the ultimate reconciliation of opposites. *I* and *It* grow out of a common center, and reality, or abstraction, flows into sensation and the latter back to abstraction once more. In three brief but important essays, "The Course of Expression" (MS. 741), "Analysis of Creation" (MS. 1105), and "The Modus of the IT" (MS. 916), Peirce considers the question of how the abstract world becomes particularized. In the first two papers the key notion is the unification of form and matter to produce expression, that is: *abstraction + sensation → expression.* The "first condition" (MS. 1105) of creation must then be expression. In this case expression is consciousness-of in the form of a conception or feeling. Sensation and abstraction are "impersonal" and "intensive," but the combination of them produces something "personal" and "extensive." Peirce denies that we can dispense with expression and think the sensation or abstraction directly, because anything thought must be thought at a particular time, and neither pure sense nor pure abstraction requires a tensed dimension. Two examples of the necessity of expression given in MS. 1105 are (1) the necessity of a medium in the conversation of

Fig. 2

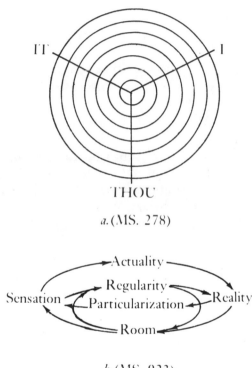

a.(MS. 278)

b.(MS. 923)

people and (2) the necessity of ritual and imagery in order for religion "to find the least realization."

As noted previously, expression is also understood as the unity of meaning (the "peculiar form") with language (the "common form"); this process of the determination of language by meaning Peirce calls *regulation*, giving: *meaning + language → regulation*. An illustration of this process is found in our thought of a line, where space or time as a 'language' combines with the abstract notion of length to produce a consciously thought-of line. Similarly, the thought of mere plurality, Peirce claims, is a plurality of mere points, though not arranged in any particular fashion. Other more ramified examples include the following:

> A prayer is not a prayer so long as the prayerfulness is wanting; neither is it one before prayerfulness regulates some rite, or at least some inward movement.

> The animal Kingdom is a Language. The four types are the regulations of that Language by the Meaning.

> The human life is a language. The character is the regulation by the meaning, which is the principles of action.

In another draft of MS. 1105 Peirce writes:

> Language is an abstraction not capable of realization alone, but combined (in a way of which we shall think directly) with other abstractions gives them realizability. Geometrical figures, letters, conversation, music are such languages. We seem to see their analogues in Vegetables, Animals, Chemical Compounds, Nebular systems, etc.

What, then, is the condition of regulation? Regulation is akin to a curve that changes systematically and is continuous throughout. Thus it involves a formal element that controls the meaning in a systematic way. In the case of a plurality of dots it is the condition that the dots not share the same space; in the case of language it is the control of grammar and the physical medium. And so regulation involves an element resistent to change, or *normality,* and an element producing systematic change, or *formality;* their combination then produces the variations Peirce calls *diflection,* so that: *normality + formality → diflection.* Formality contributes the particular rule and normality the condition that that rule be applied to a stable medium. Indeed, that something is a system, and not "too much a system," means that it orders particularity in some general fashion, but in such a way as to avoid monotony. Some examples of the necessity of diflection given by Peirce are as follows:

To speak we must have syllables. To make signs a body which remains the same in all gesticulation. In music we must have the scale, etc.

That a curve should express increasing increase it must have a dimension perpendicular to that increase.

The Types of the Animal Kingdom must be carried out in classes.

Greatness of soul emerges from frailty of flesh.

Love exists through difference of natures.

Diflection, however, if "carried to perfection" ceases to effectuate regulation, and so expression ceases once more. The language becomes as incapable of expressing the meaning by being over-systematized as it would be by being under-systematized. Thus Peirce writes:

If the body is absolutely under physical and physiological control there is no more gesture than if there were no fixity of body at all.

If human frailty were absolute we should be mere machines, so we should if human principles were absolute.
Lovers would be as indifferent if they had nothing in common as they would if they had everything in common.

And so diflection is a harmony of yet another hierarchy of reciprocal tendencies, now in the form: *coordination* + *inordination* → *ordination*. *Ordination* amounts to a constraint upon expression. A plurality of dots depends upon their remaining separate, yet they cannot become too separated lest they cease being a group. Similarly, physiology limits gesture, musical scales and rhythms the formation of melodies, language our prayers. Peirce also gives the following examples:

An algebraic curve must have a certain order or degree.

A limit to love is the incompatibility of natures.

The Types of the Animal Kingdom are limited by the classes to certain orders.

That expression involves ordination implies to Peirce that negation must be included in the expression of some meaning. We cannot imagine a plurality unless we simultaneously imagine a group; we cannot imagine a force without motion of a mass, although a mass is the antithesis of force and motion; and we cannot express the change of a curve without reference to its stationary focus. Ordination introduces an element of further particularity—or what Peirce calls "eccentricity"—as a balance to uniformity, thereby giving: *uniformity + eccentricity → particularization.* It is at this point that the manuscript in question, "Analysis of Creation," breaks off. In one draft of it Peirce calls the overall process whereby abstraction is particularized through expression a "fading process," and defines creation as "a faded abstraction regulating a language" (MS. 1105). From other quite fragmentary notes we suspect that he had intended to extend this 'fading process' according to the taxonomical scheme found in biology. For example, in a fragment from MS. 273 Peirce listed the following:

	Thought
(Kingdom)	Expression
(Type)	Regulation
(Class)	Diflection
(Order)	Ordination
(Family)	Conformity
(Genus)	Particularization
(Species)	Materialization
	Individuation

In this effort Peirce may have been inspired by the classification schemes in Agassiz's *Essay on Classification* and Whewell's *Novum Organon Renovatum.* Also in Peirce's library was Auguste Laurent's *Chemical Method, Notation, Classification and Nomenclature* (1855), a work which attempted to present a systematic theory of chemical classification and combination according to first principles:

"Combinations are formed according to very simple relations; and metamorphoses are also produced in virtue of very simple equations."[4] Whether and, if so, to what extent these works influenced Peirce it is difficult to say. He had accepted, from whatever source, the view that science could be carried on only in the light of rationally grounded methodological principles, which in turn, as Kant had argued, could only be formulated by an *a priori* analysis of the categories.

Peirce, however, was a long way from his goal of giving a detailed account of the process whereby abstraction becomes particularized. The illustrations in Fig. 2 indicate that the process involves both hierarchy and continuity. The seven concentric circles may have represented in his mind the seven taxonomical levels, and the center itself the absolute point out of which abstraction emerges. While it is difficult to be sure of his intent in these early fragmentary essays, it remains clear that although Peirce tried many schemes of categories—and although he left us nothing even approaching a final version—yet in all of what we have from this period, there is the persistent and clear assumption that actuality could be deduced from simple substantial categories in combination with basic relational categories. The most systematic early account of this deduction is found in "The Modus of the It" (MS. 916). This paper begins: "There are three Celestial Worlds. 1. that whose heaven is a speck, or the manifold of sense, 2. that whose heaven is of extensive manifestation, or the world of consciousness, 3. that whose heaven is of immense manifestation, or the world of abstraction." How are the three worlds related? We recall from the illustration in Fig. 2b that one such process involved a cycle leading from Reality to Particularization to Sensation, then to Actuality, and finally returning to Reality once more. If we construe actuality as belonging to the second world, then the problem becomes one of describing how reality combines with sensation to produce actuality as consciously experienced. If sensation is a "speck" and consciousness is "extensive," how can they accommodate each other? Peirce says in reply: "It will be clear that that which is in the sensible world can only enter the mental world by having in it a *revelation* which is in the abstract world." In short, sensation contains abstraction in some particularized form in order for it to come into consciousness. Peirce then describes the three possible forms of abstract revelation:

1. in the world of time: *arbitrariness*
2. in the world of space: *dependence*
3. in the celestial world: *absoluteness*

Sensation must contain the second form of abstract revelation, he concludes, because within our experience it takes the form of dependence and spatiality. Following Kant once more, Peirce considers space the subjective condition of sensibility. It is not an absolute revelation of the celestial world because it is an *It;* nor is it an arbitrary revelation of temporal sequence. It is a combination of both, for dependence is the result of the interplay of arbitrariness and absoluteness. It implies both that something is *related* and that *something* is related. Sensation, in short, has the character not only of being a *this-here,* but also of being a *what.*

Absoluteness, or absolute existence, can itself be revealed in three ways:

1. through the senses: *possibility, feasibility*
2. through the mind: *actuality*
3. in itself, abstractly: *necessity*

Consciousness, or conception, is the synthesis of abstraction and sensation, and the latter two share a form-taking capacity so that absolute existence can enter consciousness only through actuality. Peirce asks: "Why did the absoluteness reach mental and not mere sensual revelation?" He had previously argued that sensation itself must contain an 'abstract revelation', and so we could interpret this next question as asking why absoluteness entered the mental realm as well as the sensuous realm. However, it might also be interpreted as implying that abstraction does not enter sensation *for us* until it does so through the mind in its grasp of actuality. In this case sensation is a dimension of reflective consciousness and its 'given' aspect is only a myth of philosophers. This view would be more in line with Peirce's views on immediate perception. Unfortunately, his answer to this question does not resolve the problem: "Because conjoined with the feasibility was necessary form-of-fact, or mode. Form of fact is the way in which a fact is. . . . A necessary mode is one whose non-actuality is the same as [its being] not feasible. Clearly therefore for mere feasibility to become actuality it must have in it a necessary mode." In short, whatever is actual is abstract to the extent to which it contains a necessary form of fact. Now forms of fact can be necessary in one of three ways:

1. logically necessary: arbitrary existence as *community*
2. physically necessary: dependent existence as *causality*
3. absolutely necessary: self-dependent existence as *influx*

And once more he asks: Through which form of necessity can the necessary form of fact contained in actuality enter consciousness? For us, it can only enter through causality. We know of no communities bound by an internal logic, while at the other extreme the influxual dependency of substance and quality is too perfect for us to comprehend fully. Causality, on the other hand, combines both tightness and looseness, the former because one object determines another in some respect, the latter because it does not determine it in every respect. Influxual dependency (or "derivation") combines with arbitrariness in this case to produce causality. By itself such dependency can operate in three manners:

1. in a possible mode: as *negation*
2. in an actual mode: as *reality*
3. in a necessary mode: as *infinity*

(Here, as opposed to previous work, Peirce seems to equate actuality and reality, but this is a mere terminological digression.) Under the heading of influxual dependency we are considering the derivation of accident or *quality;* respectively, negative qualities, real qualities, and infinite qualities. In Kant's table of categories the categories of quality were *reality, negation,* and *limitation,* and from the Anticipations of Perception it is clear that he took reality to involve an intensive degree of sensation, with a continuity of possible realities existing between reality and negation. Yet if limitation is merely reality combined with negation (B110), how could reality be limited, even if intensively? Kant spoke of diminishing degrees between reality and negation, but never of degrees 'larger' than perceptual reality, that is, degrees that were extensive and not instantaneous. Peirce may have seen a terminological problem: either 'reality' should be used to mean something like the 'highest qualitative degree', so as to retain the notion of limitation, or else it should have been used to mean a given qualitative degree, in which case it would take the place of limitation and the latter would be changed to the highest qualitative degree (infinity). It seems that he settled on the latter option. Reality is here considered a matter of degree and involves empirical consciousness; in other words, reality is what he has been calling *actuality* all along, and this latter is the more appropriate term here as well. For us, as conscious beings, causality reveals the dependency of quality only as an actual mode; it is more than something with mere possibility, but there is no necessity in it. However, in itself causality implies an element of necessity, for, Peirce argues, in order for negation to become actual it must be joined with the infinite quality of the necessary mode.

What is the nature of this infinite quality? We already assume that it involves 'celestial' abstraction that is absolute and self-dependent, and Peirce now tells us that it must "relate to quantity since it is that which everything must have in order to be." For Kant, quantities took three forms: *unity, plurality,* and *totality.* Peirce accepts these and now gives their meaning within the unfolding modus of the *It:*

1. infinity necessarily derived from community: *unity*
2. infinity actually derived from causality: *plurality*
3. infinity necessarily derived from self-dependent existence: *totality*

In the first instance quality is derived necessarily, but from an arbitrary community. Since it is arbitrary, a plurality is, in Peirce's words, "denied" it, and so it remains unity. If we keep in mind that 'community' implies here the greatest possible degree of separateness, then nothing in it as yet can determine plurality. Thus all that we can speak of at an instant is a single element. When dependent existence takes the place of arbitrary existence, plurality results. For Kant, extensive magnitude was possible by a successive synthesis of the productive imagination (A163, B204). And so to Peirce even a unity is a plurality by virtue of continued existence; what is necessary is that the quality be "derived from the steps of the counting process, hence from causality." However, a successive synthesis still does not achieve a state of genuine totality, but only one of unified plurality. Such a totality must be implied as a condition for even the possibility of plurality, raising the question of what in totality produces, when combined with unity, plurality. Peirce's answer is: *total shape:* "A total shape is one the diversity of which is so great that it ceases to have any diversity but every thing which has shape has it in all its diversity." An undifferentiated plenitude comes to mind. Here differentiation increases to the point of elementary particles, wherein each is itself an undifferentiated plenitude. We would expect, then, that such a plenitude would have properties similar to the infinite qualities it influences, that is, that it would be isomorphically akin to unity, plurality, and totality, making the three total shapes:

1. negative qualitative totality: a mere point, *elementariness*
2. real qualitative totality: *extension*
3. infinite qualitative totality: *immensity*

Then for qualitative expression to become possible for consciousness, immensity, or "immense manifestation," must join with elementariness or punctiformity to produce extension. How does the immense manifestation take shape? Again, by taking on one of the three quantitative forms:

1. as unitary shape: *time*
2. as plural shape: *space*
3. as total shape: *heaven*

With the last element of this triad we have returned once more to the celestial world, coming full circle, and so Peirce concludes: "Time becomes space by conjunction with a heavenly world. That of consciousness. And this turns the IT to THOU."

Let us glance back over this arduous philosophical journey. We began by seeking the process whereby sensation combines with abstraction to produce consciousness, and we discovered seven stages to the process:

abstract revelation
absolute existence
necessary forms of fact
influxual derivation
infinite quality
total shape
immense manifestation

Each stage reveals a progressive particularization of abstraction culminating in consciousness. This can be illustrated in Fig. 3, a diagrammatic reconstruction of the 'modus of the *It*'. Diagrammed in this fashion it reveals some additional points not directly taken up by Peirce, but very likely assumed by him:

Fig. 3

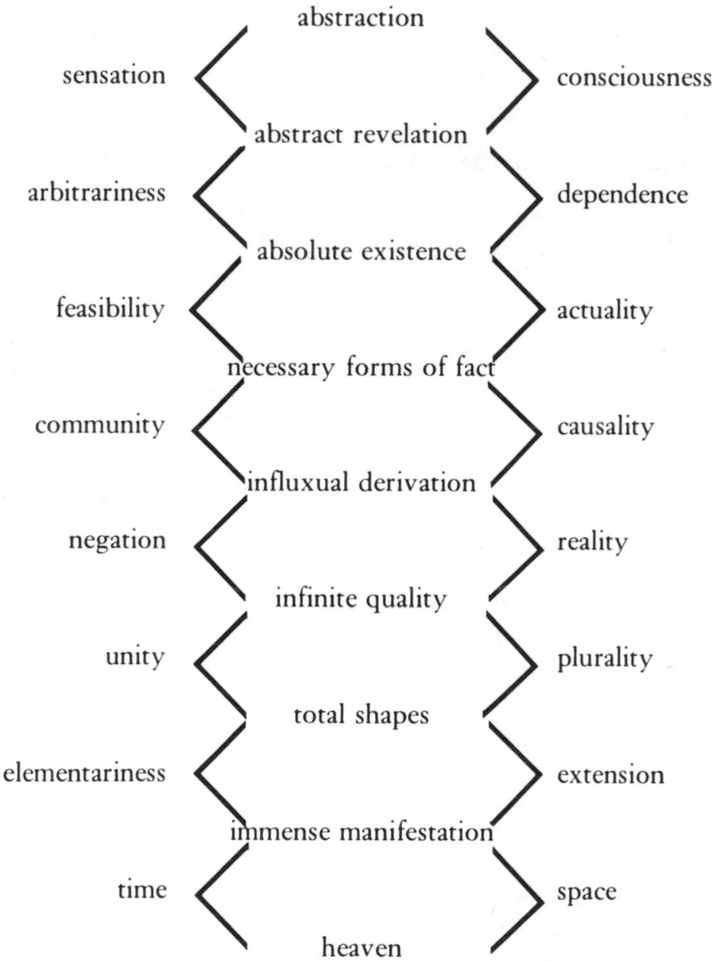

From Fig. 2b we suspect that the unfolding of concepts is circular in nature, and if so, the top of Fig. 3 should be connected to the bottom, thereby identifying heaven with abstraction. In that case there is another stage, an eighth, which is that of abstraction in its widest sense—the celestial world as a whole. The seven other stages belong to this world. To the world of time belong elementariness (the point), unity, negation, community, feasibility, arbitrariness, and sensation (the speck), while to the world of space belong extension, plurality, reality, causality, actuality, dependence, and consciousness (extensive manifold). The fact that the three worlds are three *celestial* worlds, as Peirce notes at the outset of MS. 916, means that the worlds of time and space unfold from within the celestial world in general. The celestial world "comes out of itself" and becomes particularized, but its differentiation is always guided by an underlying triadic isomorphism, and so it eventually returns to itself. But this still leaves the question of how the *It* becomes *Thou*. In Fig. 2a we are led to believe that the *I*, *It*, and *Thou* have a common source, and become more differentiated as the levels advance out of the center. The interpretation given here is that return to the center must be considered as well, and so Fig. 2a is misleading in that respect; it may have been more accurate for Peirce to have drawn a torus instead. The common source is most likely to be the celestial world, and the *It* becomes *Thou* once consciousness emerges in the process. In this case the three basic categories, the 'logic' of the particularizing process, exist only potentially within the celestial world.

At one point Peirce tried out his own diagrammatic representation of the modus of the *It* (found among the fragments of MS. 921 and dated 1 June, 1859). Although Peirce's own diagram differs from Fig. 3. in several respects, it suggests the viability of interpreting Fig. 3 in circular fashion. Peirce's own diagram consists of an octagon with the word "It" in the center and the eight groups of triads listed around the eight faces. There is an overall structural similarity between these two formulations, as well as between these and yet another formulation (MS. 923). Comparing the hierarchical categories of all these formulations, and beginning with what appears to be the most abstract realm, we get three lists, each to a significant degree with the same structure:

celestial world	expression	worlds
immense manifestation	intuition	logoi
total shape	quantity	existences
infinite quality	quality	forms of fact
influxual derivation	dependence	derivation
necessary form of fact	modality	qualities
absolute existence	degree	shapes
abstract revelation	stage	manifests
(MS. 916)	(MS. 921)	(MS. 923)

If the "worlds" of MS. 923 are placed at the bottom of the list, beneath "manifests," and the list is then reversed, it conforms to that of MS. 916. However, the order as given above in MS. 923 appears to be the one Peirce used most often, and for this reason shall also be used in what follows. Given the circular interpretation of the hierarchy advocated here, it would be permissible to place a top category at the bottom, or vice versa.

It now begins to become clear that Kant's four categories are merely starting points for a much larger scheme. We also note that in two of the lists the category of *quantity* is missing, and that there is an equivalence of *world* and *expression*. This equivalence follows from the argument of the "Analysis of Creation," where expression was considered the process whereby abstraction becomes realized in particular creations; the celestial world is itself what unfolds through expression.

The octagonal diagram mentioned above also differs from the argument of MS. 916 in listing eight further categories that are the results of a combination of the eight groups of triads. These are as follows:

formal intuitions of expression
total quantities of intuition
infinite qualities of quantity
influxual dependencies of quality
necessary modes of dependence
perfect degrees of modality
successive stages of degree
temporal expression of stage

A moment's thought reveals that these new categories result from a systematic combination of the previous triads. They are generated by taking the most abstract member of each triad (totality, infinity, influx, necessity, etc.) and first predicating it of its own level in the hierarchy, and then predicating this dyad of the level beneath it in the hierarchy.

In a paper entitled "An Essay on the Limits of Religious Thought written to prove that we can reason upon the nature of God," (MS. 858), probably written sometime between 1859 and 1861, Peirce illustrated to what use the above categories could be put in philosophical argumentation. If we think of a thought as an event, then every event involves one or more of three necessary modes— the necessary modes of dependence. In community there is no dependency and so no event can take place, as in the case, Peirce notes, of "two balls at the same instant of time"; in causality there is a dependence which "everything at each moment has upon things at the last moment"; and in influx the dependency is immediate as "substance to form, character to acts, things to qualities." But, Peirce continues, the necessary modes of dependence are but a part of the perfect degrees of dependence (modality); the latter, as degrees, are part of the successive stages of degree, and as stages derive from the temporal expressions of stage. The temporal expressions result from the formal intuitions of expression, and, being intuitions, are part of the total quantities of intuition; thus these quantities are part of the infinite qualities of quantity, and as qualities are part of the influxual dependencies of quality. Again we have come full circle and have connected the thought-event with the three categories of the final stage—negation, reality, infinity. "I have run through the categories," Peirce writes, "in this way in order to show precisely what infinity is and where in the scheme of conceptions it stands." Infinity is a predicate of quality, but as such plays a role in the qualities of *quantity;* for this reason we can speak intelligibly of adding two infinities, or of infinity as infinitely surpassing reality (limitation). Thus when a mind-event thinks the infinite, there is an extra-mental basis for the idea even if the mind does not comprehend fully its meaning. In this argument we see clearly how the categories were supposed to link with the previous speculations in the meta-physical essays on the cognizability of the infinite; the theory of categories supplies the link between the infinite as thought and as thought-of. We are not conscious of infinity, if only because consciousness is always a synthesis of two categories (nullity and perfection), and infinity is itself a member of the class of perfect categories.

Peirce continued to refine his categories in a paper entitled "SPQR" (MS. 923s). In this brief work he provides the first clear evidence of his turn toward idealism as the metaphysical interpretation of the categories. Quantities, he argued, when viewed 'transcendentally', are really qualities; for example, it is simply the quality of something that it weigh a given amount. This would explain his deletion of 'quantity' from some later accounts of the hierarchy of categories. Qualities, on the other hand, can be regarded as predicates, and predicates are really only relations when viewed 'transcendentally', that is, when "taken away from the quality so as to see their manner of affecting that quality." Qualities may be possessed negatively, particularly, or infinitely, and understanding them in this manner is to see them again, only this time as relations. Relations can be understood in terms of time; for example, in community there is only a single, encompassing time, in causality a specific change of time, and in influx an instantaneous change. It is interesting that Peirce appears to describe this process in almost cosmological terms:

Now how does the Amount of Time stand to the Relation? View the world first with the relations of things in it as all one momentary thing. How is it with the relations now? They are purely *formal*, forceless. Let us now introduce time. Now from one fact another follows in time; the relation is now *real* and *forcible*. The further we go back in time the more and more is the cause the origin of the effect, the greater and greater is the dependency through there being more and more Spiritual Exhibition, 'till we arrive at the *first* cause; this, since our faculty cannot think of a *first in time* (which, indeed, is not), becomes that which *sustains* this whole train of cause and effect—that from which all things *perpetually emanate*. Now the dependency is Absolute, exhibition being real. Now what is time that it should enable a spirit a-hold of matter and by it in connection with another spirit to communicate itself thereto? It is action-room, is it not?

Relations can be understood exclusively as temporal relations, and when viewed in this manner involve the three forms of fact: possibility, actuality, and necessity. If we accept the view that in time possibility becomes actuality, then there must be a character to time, a formal character, that makes this possible. This is the form of fact, which, when combined with matter, produces the 'matter of fact'. But how is this combination possible? What Peirce calls "spiritual exhibition" must contain an inherent rationality and must itself be guided by the set of perfect categories. Quantities must be infinite qualities, real predicates must be influxual relations, and times must be necessary forms of fact. But the process cannot end with forms of fact. For Peirce, the clue to what follows is found in the analogy between the categories as forms of fact of intellection and the categories as forms of fact of spiritual exhibition in general. In intellection the categories of possibility, actuality, and necessity are found in the processes of imagination, perception, and reason. And so necessary forms of fact must be guided by an inherent reasonableness:

> Give to the form of fact the reasonableness of [perception] and it has verity—positive, limited verity. Give to [the form of fact] the reasonableness of reason; it is necessary, it has a perfect verity. WHAT IS REASONABLENESS THAT IT SHOULD GIVE VERITY TO FORM OF FACT? This is the *Question!* Now you see we come to something *new*, new to the school of philosophy from which we have emerged. We have risen to a Cartesian, Platonic atmosphere—quite above the conceptions of Aristotle, Locke, or Hamilton. The identity of mind and matter, that they are the same thing from different points of view. Express the answer to this question how you please, you must give utterance to Idealism.

The picture of this new idealism begins to emerge even more clearly: as suggested previously, actuality is conceived as an unfolding out of abstraction; it is constructed from a series of hierarchical constituents according to isomorphic principles shared by each level in the series and guided by the ultimate reasonableness of abstraction. From this Peirce concludes: "Therefore the reason is at one in substance with all things. . . . [I]n common with the Pan, [each thing] stands in dependence of Influx on God. They all emanate from him. Reasonableness therefore signifies being of the Whole, which is simply Existence" (MS. 921). In the process there are two counteracting tendencies, that of *Expense,* which is the dissipation of forces, as in causality, and that of *Creation,* which is the coalescing of force into a formal pattern. Merely intellectual possibilities first become actualized in Expense, and then, through the inherent reasonableness of action-room, enter the realm of Creation. This takes place according to the following principle: "The amount of exertion requisite to make any Spiritual Exhibition in a given time is proportional to the Exhibition; and with the same exhibition is inversely proportional to the time" (MS. 919). Spiritual Exhibition takes time, and cannot be accelerated if not yet ready to 'exhibit'. Yet as time goes on it becomes progressively easier for exhibition to take place.

The evolutionary idealism beginning to emerge from these passages may be traced to Kant, at least in part. Around 1864 or 1865 Peirce wrote as part of his University Lectures:

> In a transcendental inquiry all conceptions of cause must be eliminated. Accordingly, Kant in his first essay on this subject, which was published twelve years before the Critic, uses form and matter for the effect of the material and formal causes. That which the world is (abstracted from how it is) is its elementary parts. How the world is (abstracted from its existence) is the coordination of those parts, or their relation to each other as parts, potential or actual. (MS. 349, pp. 19–20)

In the work to which Peirce refers, the inaugural dissertation *De Mundi sensibilis atque intelligibilis forma et principiis* (1770), Kant describes the relation of the form and matter of the world as *coordinatione, non subordinatione,* and speaks of the nexus that constitutes the essential form of the world as the ground of an *influxuum possibilium,* which constitutes the world as a collection of parts. This nexus itself must be changeless and based on a *rationem logicam;* its cause could not be attributed to an *Architectus* so much as to a *Creator.* Had Peirce been familiar with this work prior to its mention in the University Lectures he may have been inspired to interpret his system of categories from similar transcendental inquiry. It is but a short step from a purely formal picture of the world, based upon *a priori* ideas, to an evolutionary picture of that same world, now with categories as stages of development of the *rationem logicam.*

If Peirce did not borrow the notion of an influx into the material world from Kant, he may have done so from Swedenborg. But it is difficult to say precisely when he first read Swedenborg, though it is known that he took an interest in him from the mid-1860's and for many years thereafter. He may have known of such writings even before Henry James, Sr. published *Substance and Shadow* in 1866. In *The True Christian Religion* Swedenborg used the term 'influx' to describe the process of transition from spirit to nature and the control the former had over the latter. Against the natural philosophers he wrote: "They know nothing about the spiritual world and its influx into the natural. And so they confine themselves to the sphere of nature, ascending and descending, and soaring aloft therein like eagles in the air."[5] Swedenborg's use of the term 'manifestation' also suggests Peirce's use of the term. We may safely surmise that an assimilation of Swedenborg's system was no difficult feat for a young scholar already thoroughly familiar with Kant and Schiller. Swedenborg's message—that there are Two Worlds, spiritual and natural—reads loud and clear on first exposure, though Peirce probably had already been convinced of the necessity of yet another world, a *Thou*-world of Representability by the time he had read Swedenborg.

In these early years Peirce never produced a finished version of his system of categories; instead he experimented with several approaches, none of which resulted in anything like a complete system. And to make matters more difficult, he concerned himself less with what each newly generated category could mean in concrete experience than with simply locating its place within the overall scheme. Throughout his various efforts, however, the basic pattern persisted. At one point he postulated two hundred and sixteen individual categories, in three groups of seventy-two, the latter groups probably corresponding to the three basic categories of *I, It,* and *Thou.* Each of the three groups was divided into four subgroups of metaphysical, dynamical, mathematical, and physical categories; and then each of these subgroups was further divided into two groups of categories derived from the eight hierarchical levels. (The categories of the *I*, *It*, and *Thou*, as outlined by Peirce in MS. 923, will be found in Appendix 1, Figs. 1–3.) In order to produce the two hundred and sixteen categories, each of the twenty-four categories in each major group would have to be divided further into triads. How this is to be done Peirce unfortunately does not say; nor does he give any illustrations of what the categories meant in terms of the 'modus' of the basic triad, though the application of some is more obvious than of others.

Another problem that confronts the interpreter of these fragmentary writings involves finding that *regular system* of relations whereby Peirce combined and generated his categorial complexes. Among the early papers, but primarily in MS. 923, there are a series of diagrams suggesting how the categories could be combined. It is not clear, however, from such illustrations what Peirce's method of combination was; certain categories are missing, while others are crossed out without any indication why. In some additional diagrams presented in Appendix 1 (Figs. 4–6) an attempt has been made to reconstruct, as best as possible, Peirce's system of relationships by combining the results of several drafts. From such diagrams it will be evident that he indeed had a method, though its metaphysical justification is far from clear. A further complication, one already evident from previous lists, is that there is no consistent usage of terms throughout drafts. However, there is at least this rationale in the combinations: in the categories of the *I*, the first (*I*-like) category on the right of Fig. 5 of Appendix 1 qualifies the other two; in the categories of the *It*, it is the second (*It*-like), and in those of the *Thou*, it is the synthesizing third (*Thou*-like) category, that qualifies the other two. In addition, all three sets share the metaphysical triad of sensation, thought, and quality. This is plausible if we recall that these are the categories of 'world'. There is only one world divided into three sub-worlds, and only when differentiation increases does the *I*-ness or *It*-ness of the single world become apparent; in conformity with Fig. 2a above, the *I*, *It*, and *Thou* have a point of unification, namely, the central point, or world. The categories of *It* are perhaps the most intelligible. Peirce evidently devoted most of his efforts to their elaboration, and never formulated a 'modus' of the *I* or *Thou*.[6] But difficulties mount rapidly when we try to supply descriptions, not to mention justifications, for the complex categories. What precise sense could be given to an 'infinite quality of arbitrariness'? And are there also real and negative qualities of arbitrariness, which would help expand the list toward the anticipated two hundred and sixteen categories? Peirce gives us little or no guidance here, and we begin to suspect that it was at this point that he himself began to feel stymied. It would be a mistake, however, to dismiss this work lightly as exuberant adolescent philosophizing. While it may be near impossible to give a final clear reading of Peirce's first attempt to formulate a long list of categories, within the panoply of rich suggestions and insights some general features can be discerned as immovable foci. These features, or, more properly, *categories of categories,* seem to touch very close to the bedrock of metaphysical truth accepted by Peirce throughout his entire career as a philosopher. For just as he had attempted to formulate categories with which to organize the Kantian categories, so his own long list reveals an orderly array of unarticulated categories, which, I hope later to show, would appear continuously in his mature work, not only in metaphysics but in the other areas of philosophy as well.

3.CATEGORIES OF CATEGORIES

We may begin by noting that the metaphysical categories pertain to worlds and abstract *logoi,* such categories being influxes of negation. If we consider 'world' to be another way of expressing what we mean by a *universe,* in short, a Universal One, then according to Peirce, its differentiation into three categories occurs through immediate influx and negation; the One 'negates' part of itself in order to set up an opposition within the One, and so its universality is only of the most abstract kind. The first result of differentiation is the production of the abstract *logoi;* these are *abstract universals* within the Universal One. As infinities of unity they are both infinite in being abstractions and unities in being universals. Peirce may have thought of them as Platonic Ideas like 'goodness' and 'beauty'. They are stabilizing conditions set in opposition to influxual process. Thus within the metaphysical group of triads there is already an abstract/concrete opposition beginning to emerge. Condition limits, while exhibition seeks to transcend limits.

In the dynamical categories, the totals of internality pertain to "existences." On first reading this suggests that Peirce has made an abrupt plunge into concreteness, full particularity, and actuality, but from "The Modus of the It" we recall that for the abstract revelations to enter consciousness, they must first combine with 'absoluteness' or 'absolute existence' in the form of what might be considered *concrete universals,* specifically as sensible objective *logoi.* Such structures were postulated by the Scholastics as sensible and intelligible 'species', and more recently by Wilfrid Sellars as intermediate structures that 'guide' the material manifold into consciously perceptible form. Such universals are more concrete than the abstract universals, and are the most concrete 'entity' that can be thought without the assistance of the notion of relation-to-other; they are not infinities, but merely totals.

With the modes of time the first notion of relation enters, and these, being mere temporal relations, are the most *abstract relations* thinkable. In the Analogies Kant considered the three categories of relation in terms of the three modes of time—duration, succession, and simultaneity (A215, B262). For Peirce these are the three essential forms of fact, without at least one of which no 'matter of fact' could be possible. The totals of internality—the possible, actual, and necessary existences—combine with the modes of time to bring a further limitation on abstraction by restricting the possible relational form it can take.

The mathematical categories apply to derivations and qualities; but here again Peirce's choice of words can be deceptive. The influxual derivations are relations and dependencies, and the qualities are infinite qualities relating to quantity. If we assume, as seems plausible, that at this level further particularization is occurring, then the derivations are simply the more concrete forms of forms of fact; they are *concrete relations.* Negation is a more specific relation than community (reaction), reality more specified than causality, and infinity more specified than influxual relation. But why must they be considered derivations of sensation? Perhaps because for the first time the concrete relations require something more specific than the marking-of-time specificity of the modes of time. The qualities of arbitrariness are infinities that are subject to the abstract temporal relations; they are arbitrary in that the temporal form of fact determines their 'quantity', whether as unity, plurality, or totality. In this way these qualities—here understood as abstractions—acquire one of three abstract shapes or configurations. The qualities of arbitrariness, then, are the general forms taken on by the *logoi* when combined with the concrete relations.

Finally, in the physical categories, the absolutes of possibility refer to the three shapes, and the necessities of reaction to the three manifests. If the previous stage in the hierarchy was that of infinite quality, and if this stage is one of total shape, then another way of capturing the same distinction may be to say that the former are the *abstract shapes* and the latter are the *concrete shapes*. Elementariness is more particularized than unity; extension is more specific than plurality, and immensity more specific than totality. Unity must take on a total shape to become elementariness, and this it does, according to "The Modus of the It," by being considered a negative quality; similarly, plurality takes on the total shape of extension when considered a real quality, and totality takes on the total shape of immensity when considered an infinite quality. In general, concrete shapes are formed when concrete relations combine with abstract shapes. What then are the manifests? We note from Fig. 3 that heaven and abstraction, while appearing to be opposites, can be considered really one and the same, and if this is so, then the manifests must be somehow related to the Universal One once more. As concrete total shapes subject to the further qualification of the abstract shapes (unity, plurality, totality), we would expect them to be more abstract; however, if the trend of subsumption is to continue, they must also be more concrete. Here Peirce may have had in mind something that could be both. A 'manifest' was a necessity of reaction, so that as a necessity it belonged to the level of abstraction, and as a reaction, to the level of concreteness. Heaven is immensity as a total shape and so, to that extent, is concrete. Time as an immensity, that is, as a unified infinite quality, remains abstract whether looked at as abstract shape or as abstract relation. Space, as was noted in "The Modus of the It," results when time and heaven combine, and so has to be both concrete and abstract. But as total shapes all of the above have to be concrete. The Universal One, then, begins undifferentiated; soon it divides along abstract metaphysical lines, and then eventually recreates itself into a new unity once more, only this time containing greater specificity and concreteness; it becomes a Concrete One. The general scheme of spiritual exhibition can then be illustrated in the following manner. (Fig. 4.)

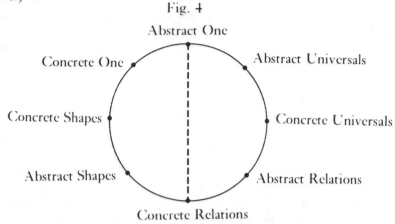

Fig. 4

With the aid of this schema we can detect yet a deeper underlying order in the categories of Appendix 1 (Figs. 4–6). We see that the abstract relations are farthest from the Concrete One and are mere modes of time, while the concrete relations are the farthest from the Universal (Abstract) One and so are concrete relations of sensation. Particularizing increases as the midpoint of sensation is reached, and then, as the midpoint is passed, generalizing begins once more in a return to the One. This interpretation also accords with the dialectic of Fig. 2b.

As for the categories of the *I* in the light of the above interpretation, we may note that these categories pertain to processes of creation and expression, just as those of the *It* pertained to entities and structures. As noted, however, the first triad of the metaphysical group is similar in all three lists, and these are the entities subject to creation. Similarly, in each list there are relations of sensation in the mathematical category. The triads of the *I* seem to follow an iso-morphic structure of *constancy, variation,* and *systemation.* Worlds are inflections of coordination within the One; as coordinates they are constant, but as inflections they are subject to variation. Their realization is found in the *logoi,* themselves variations of constancy. Sensation, thought, and quality are the three worlds, but language, expression, and meaning are the forms these worlds take in the creation process. As the process of 'inflection' proceeds from the abstract to the concrete, from worlds to manifests, the variations of constancy move from the abstract to the concrete to the abstract once more, making the abstract world and concrete manifest equivalent, though not identical.

The *Thou* categories appear to describe the possible *relations* between the categories of the *I* and *It*. Reticence and order on the one side is contrasted with commitment and sponateity on the other. Their synthesis is always a moderate or reasoned commitment—in line with the notion that reasonableness guides the overall triadic process—producing harmony, sympathy, cooperation, and friendship. 'Light' is a synthesis of the order of systemation and the vitality and variability of life; sympathy is the synthesis of an emotionless state and a persistently emotional state; and friendship (liking) is the synthesis of a strong passion (love) and a weak involvement (interest).

Given the scope of Peirce's undertaking, it is doubtful that he intended the *Thou* categories to apply only to human interpersonal relations; rather we suspect that they were conceived to pervade all of creation, with their anthropomorphic interpretation only one of several possible interpretations. Indeed, with respect to each of the three hierarchies, we should take Peirce seriously when he notes (in MS. 921): "It is obvious that much more than usual is meant by the words" used to describe the categories. And if so, we must conclude that such triads, along with their categorial systematization, represents one of the most involved and spohisticated attempts to produce a thoroughly rational metaphysics of nature and experience made to that time, and perhaps since. Even Hegel's *Encyclopedia* does not attempt to reveal how groups of detailed categories combine, but only how they are to be distinguished philosophically. What is also striking is that Peirce should have thought that a theory of categories could be recursive and dialectical in nature, rather than based simply upon a taxonomy of language, or on a table of logical judgments. The latter procedures interested him considerably in this early period, but the idea of a *systematic generation of categories,* at best only hinted at by Kant, seems to have been an original contribution of Peirce's early work.

As he was soon to realize, the categories pointed to idealism, and it was in this direction that his thought was eventually to move. Like Kant, he was concerned to explain how thought could represent its object, but he was not content with a simple picture of the blending of *a priori* categories with the material contents of experience.

He knew that for such a picture to be possible, a larger picture was required, just as in later decades he would come to the conclusion that if pragmaticism were correct, it would require an extensive metaphysics to show it. This view is found already in 1858 in an explanation of how the burning of a finger can produce learning in a child:

> Now the mere matter cannot have given him a notion since it had none to give; therefore, it must have been God who at the creation of the world put this thought into nature. Now this heat was a form, and all powers are forms. And matter we know nothing of.
>
> All forms are also powers, since to affect is to effect, and are therefore spiritual manifestations. If this is so, every form must have a meaning. But since all phenomena are forms, all things have meanings. The transparency of the drop of water must actually convey a meaning to our conscious affections as truly as the Whole Sea itself. (MS. 891)

The long list of categories can be seen as an attempt to produce a theory of the "Whole Sea" itself, with a drop of water containing the "meaning" of the "Whole Sea." Such a picture implies a thoroughgoing rationalism. whose main features were clearly emerging by 1861. Primary among these is the view that the "drop of water" we know as conscious, time-determined thought inadequately reflects, but does reflect nonetheless, the Whole Sea of Absolute Mind or God. Whatever is possible can be conceived, and whatever is conceivable is true (in some generalized sense of the term). However, to be able to reason upon something is not the same thing as being able to comprehend it fully, as in the case of the categories of perfection.

From such reflections Peirce was led to reject the claim that metaphysics could purify its own standpoint through critical reflection. If the philosophizing self is not the extent of the universe, and if the laws of the universe are not simply the exertions of cognition, then a tacit dimension remains around all reflection, and so logic cannot dispense with some form of faith. The task of the metaphysician becomes one of expanding the circle of logical clarity and defining, as best as possible, the nature of the interface between clarity and vagueness. We have seen that when Peirce spoke of 'faith' he had in mind something rather sophisticated and philosophical, the kind of faith that Kant or Mansel would endorse only after the most rigorous analysis. It may be that he was happy to embrace fideism for other reasons—reasons pertaining to the general climate of enlightened New England theism, with its respect for the philosophical import of mysticism and religious sentiment. It is important to keep in mind, however, that Peirce felt no tension between his qualified espousal of fideism and his 'logico-practical' method of analysis.

Chapter III
The New List of Categories

In the years between 1862 and 1869 Peirce turned his attention more to questions of logic and science than to metaphysics. Now a married man, and holder of the Sc. B degree *summa cum laude* in chemistry from Harvard, he began publishing and lecturing on scientific theory, and particularly on what he called the 'logic of science'. But the thread of metaphysical investigation was not broken. After putting aside the quest for the long list of metaphysical categories—though only temporarily, as we shall see in later chapters—he chose instead in those years to focus on a clearer formulation of the short list by seeking to uncover the logical kernel within the hitherto vague and somewhat psychologistic notions of the *I*, *It*, and *Thou*. This was not a turn to logic proper, though it was a philosophic utilization of logic for a larger purpose. In all of the new work the grand scheme of a complete metaphysics could never have been far from his thoughts. And it may be safe to say that by 1863 Peirce already had settled on the rudiments of his lifelong philosophic perspective—objective idealism. This is clearly evident in the address he gave on 12 November 1863 before the

Cambridge High School Association. Echoing earlier views Peirce announced, to an audience hardly prepared to comprehend the full meaning of his words, "It is only by means of idealism that truth is possible in science" (MS. 1638).[1] He continued:

> Human learning must fail somewhere. Materialism fails on the side of incompleteness. Idealism always presents a systematic totality, but it must always have some vagueness and thus lead to error. Materialism is destitute of a philosophy. Thus it is necessarily one-sided. It misunderstands its relations to idealism; it misunderstands the nature of its own logic. But if materialism without idealism is blind, idealism without materialism is void.

Materialism misunderstands its relation to idealism by assuming that it stands opposed to idealism, where in fact it exists only as a simple-minded form of human intelligence. Being "destitute of a philosophy," it does not match its philosophy against that of the idealists, but rather attempts to match common sense against transcendental sense. One of the ways to reveal this asymmetry is to show the materialist that his conceptual framework is a great deal richer than is allowable under the guiding pronouncements of his philosophy. For Peirce, this effort involved a detailed analysis of the logical structure of scientific explanation. Only then would the materialist cease misunderstanding the nature of his own logic.

Along with this task there was the task of displaying the fundamental logical forms, so that it would be possible to show how the very conduct of science, so prized by the materialist, is subject to the fundamental categories. In the Harvard University Lectures of 1865 and the Lowell Lectures of 1866 Peirce informed his listeners in a general and tentative fashion of the scope of this undertaking. One of the most important tasks would be that of convincing the materialist to accept an unpsychological view of logic. In the psychological view, most closely associated with the British empiricists, logic involved only actual mental processes, and it was held that a specific language is essential to thought. In the unpsychological view, logic concerns merely the *form* of relations between symbols and marks, even if such symbols and marks require an actual thought. Now while Peirce confesses that "there is no difference amounting to the slightest contradiction between the two views" (MS. 340), in his opinion the unpsychological view possesses definite advantages, the main being that a militantly unpsychological view of logic more easily reveals excessively psychologistic intrusions in logic, while its allowable psychological version would be less sensitive to such intrusions. Indeed, according to Peirce, an interest in logical fallacies has been one of the results of psychologism in logic. Yet if a psychological view is held, by what strict criterion can the processes of thought be considered fallacious? Only if we understand logic as a study of representation and symbol do we give the 'normative' question a rigorous standing as well. In fact, the normative question need no longer be separately posed and separately treated, but finds a natural justification in the notion of adequacy between symbol and symbolized. In this sense logic is *essentially* normative, and the problem of establishing separate normative laws that logic must obey is entirely eliminated.

The unpsychological view of logic, then, concerns itself with a *logical world*, and logic becomes "the formal science of the logical world" (MS. 340). This is no redundancy to Peirce. Recalling the earlier work on the categories, we may consider the logical world a world of archtypical *logoi* that have a mode of being independent of thought, and logic itself simply the endeavor to comprehend *as humanly as possible* these forms. To Peirce the latter qualification is important. For Hegel, logic is the science of the 'pure idea', but for Peirce it is "the science of the laws of experience in virtue of its being a determination of the idea" (MS. 340). We cannot begin with the pure concept, as does Hegel, but must analyze it out of the fabric of experience.

In a proposed treatise on his view of logic written around 1865 (MS. 726), Peirce distinguished three forms of representation: *marks* as simple denotata that denote with no connotation; *analogues* that connote without denoting by virtue of features similar to the thing connoted; and *symbols* that both denote and do so with connotation. Logic proper, he thought, would concern itself only with symbols, but a broader science of representations would encompass all three forms—the science of semiotic (MS. 802). The ability to represent was not something intelligible exclusively in a human context, Peirce thought at the time. This fact was perhaps the most telling objection for him against psychologism. A mirror has the capacity to reject an object through an image, and a written syllogism has the ability simply as written to display the connection between subject and predicate (MS. 769). Thus while it is true that everything that comes into consciousness can be taken as a representation, it does not follow that representability is a purely psychological act of particular persons. To establish the first point Peirce maintains that "if there were something which were not a representation it would not be represented, for an object represented is a representation of the same object in itself." (MS. 769). In this sense the sensation 'red' is a representation of 'red', for it can be taken as such, and this means that anything whatsoever can be taken as a representation of itself. "*Whatever is,*" Peirce concludes, "is a representation," though he should have added "to something else." Surely, he maintains, it would not be possible for us to suppose that something could not be a representation "since that which is supposed is thereby represented." He does not deny that something can simply 'be', but if all 'things' are representations they do not possess a wholly inner character. And to say that something merely 'is' is to say that it represents *only* itself, or that it is 'identical' with itself, so that unity always implies duality. At this point Peirce may have wondered whether he had stumbled upon an important, though subtle point, or whether he had uselessly confused the earlier distinctions between thing, representation, and abstraction. By 1865, in any case, he felt the need to clarify the issue once and for all.

Peirce made several starts toward his unpsychological theory of categories (MSS. 720, 732, 733, 734, 769, and parts of 921 and 922.). Kant had begun his theory of categories with the tables of judgment, Hegel with the notion of pure being. Peirce seeks now to combine both methods: "The method which ought to be adopted is one which derives the categories from the functions of judgment but which has its starting-point in pure being" (MS. 720). That is, we must first seek the condition that brings unity to experience, then, if necessary, seek the condition of that condition, and, so as not to generate broad, groundless theories to explain such conditions, guide the analysis from the start by a determination eventually to ground the ultimate condition of unity in pure being. Peirce, then, is choosing the *direction* of Kant's analysis—from judgment to categories—but with Hegel's starting point as its ultimate *goal.* It was perhaps for this reason that he chose to discuss his new theory of semiotic under the heading of "Teleological Logic" (MS. 802). We begin with the idea of pure being, and guided by it we arrive at its instantiation in experience. Then once we have performed this operation on a variety of judgments and sensations of consciousness, we can abstract the elementary processes involved and reveal the the essential categories.

Between 1865 and 1867 Peirce attempted to apply his method to both sensation and logical judgment. In the former case he sought the logical condition of sensuous intuition, and in the latter the logical conditions of judgment. These were not essentially different tasks for him, although it is not at first clear how his work on the categories and his work on the logic of the syllogism bear a common problematic origin. The point of unification is the *sign-relation*. While Perice was working on reformulating the short list of categories, he was also working on Kant's "Mistaken Subtlety" question of finding a common ground for the four figures of the syllogism. Eventually he came to the conclusion (2.792ff) that three distinct rules of inference were required to generate the first three figures, something Kant had not noticed in his seemingly successful argument to reduce all figures to the first. But whereas the quest for unity was frustrated in this direction, it was still possible in another. For at this point, if not sooner, Peirce realized that inference in general, regardless of its scope or specific form, involves a linking of sign and signified through a particular medium.

This result conformed with his earlier analysis of immediate experience as well. The immediate, in order to be brought to consciousness (be expressed), must take on a form not present in the experience itself. Thus whether we are considering sensation or judgment proper, we are at least talking of a *something represented*. But this implies a duality and a linking of *somethings*. Careful analysis shows that no such notion would be possible without a distinction between a something-in-itself and a something-for-another, and with the former we arrive at the core notion of pure being. In this sense pure being is not literally a starting point, but the end result. Peirce calls it "the final stroke which binds the elements of the judgment into unity" and "the result of generalization" (MS. 922).

Hearkening back to early problems on the foundation of metaphysical analysis, however, we might ask how the end product of analysis can be considered a fundamental metaphysical category.

Peirce's answer is that the concept of a *something*-in-itself is essential to the idea of a something-represented because "without it reference to a correlate is unintelligible." What we must do, then, is unfold the elements of cognition not found in, but implied by, our most fundamental intuitions. In the process it will become clear that what is first in the order of reflection (pure being as our starting point) is last in the order of reality.

Within the notion of representability Peirce distinguishes several features: (1) the notion of pure, unrelated self-reference, or inner being; (2) the notion of a *something* unrelated; (3) the notion of something related beyond itself to a yet-to-be-determined something; and (4) the notion of a determinate something related to a determinate something. These comprise the four fundamental conceptions, the first "without content" and the others with increasing degrees of determinateness. What must now be shown is how it is possible that the mind is both conditioned by these conceptions and capable of bringing them to awareness through analysis. The schema of Fig. 5 illustrates the connection between the conceptions and the basic forms of cognition as suggested by Peirce (in MSS. 922 and 720).

Fig. 5

FUNDAMENTAL CONCEPTIONS	ELEMENTS OF COGNITION	LOGICAL FORM
Self-Reference (Pure Being)		A is . . .
	Inference	
Reference to Character (Ground)		A (with character P) is . . .
	Generalization	
Reference to Correlate		A (given P) is B
	Comparison	
Reference to Characterized Correlate (Correspondent)		A (as B) is of kind-B
	Immediate Cognition	

Here "$A \rightarrow B$" should read as "A is the condition of B" or "B is the result of A." The schema makes clear Peirce's remark: "I hold that that which immediately justifies an abstraction is the next highest element of cognition" (MS. 922). And in MS. 720 he writes: "We have, then, a uniform chain of conceptions stretching from pure being to the intuition in general. Now the three links composing this chain, namely, reference to a ground, to a correlate, and to a correspondent afford the elements for a complete system of logic." Peirce begins with sensation and, with the idea of pure being as his goal, shows how sensation produces a specific correlate in consciousness, in this case a concrete noetic/noematic connection; from this we are led, by comparing various noemata, to abstract the notion of a simple reference to correlate. Then, generalizing upon the basic notion of reference to correlate, we are led back to a character of a 'something' that links with the correlate; and finally, seeing that it is inference or predicating that character makes possible, we arrive at the pure uncharacterized something—pure being. In most cases, Peirce's order of exposition is just the reverse of this, beginning with pure being and showing each step of the way the relation of each link to sensation.

But how do the three links generate a complete system of logic? If we focus now not on the fundamental conceptions, or on the noetic act, but instead on the nature of the 'thing' referred to by the conceptions, we notice that reference to a character is precisely reference to a *quality;* that reference to a correlate is reference to a *relation* between ground and correlate; and finally, that reference to a correspondent is reference to a correlate that contains character, or a *representation*. With these notions, then, we begin to build the science of semiotic. Indeed, as Peirce suggests in the fragmentary formulation of the fundamental conception (in MS. 921), the schema of Fig. 5 contains also the elements to generate an entire system of metaphysics. Each conception may be regarded either subjectively or objectively, that is, either noetically or noematically. The conception without content becomes objectively *pure substance;* the first with content, internal mark or quality, becomes objectively a general essence or *pure form;* the second with content, viewed subjectively as an act of comparing, becomes objectively a *relation* of two things. Now the ground becomes a full-fledged *object* or, when regarded abstractly and objectively, *matter*. In the third content the characterized correlate, now as object, contains *actual* relations with another object, its subject. Following Peirce's analogies here, we would say that the object now becomes a *concrete thing*.

With only the slightest elaboration we may see in all of this the earlier work on the three stages of perfection. In MS. 921 Peirce writes:

> In whatever relation anything is, it is for some purpose, effect, or actuality; if nobody should make a comparison the comparison would not be made . . . . What is, has a *ground*, [and] since it has also an *object*, has in the third place a *subject*. This *subject*, which must not be supposed to be in a mind though it may be a human representation, and which is only that which is determined by the representation to agree with it in its reference to the object on that ground,— this subject is an abstraction which philosophers have left too much out of account.

To call this embodied object or correspondent a *thing* is not to deny its essential dimension of relatability, its ability to suggest comparison. But Peirce is not saying that its subject is a mind that makes the thing its object. Because the thing is a correlate with character it also is a representation, and its subject then is simply that thing *taken as a representation* in some manner, though not exclusively through the manner of human representation. Earlier Peirce suggested that mirror-representation was capable of turning the correspondent into a subject. Thus there is no thing that is without character, no character without correlate, no correlate without character, and so no correlate-with-character without the ability to be taken as a representation.

Is there a thing that is also a pure representation, that is, something whose being is simply to be represented? At once we think of Berkeley's *esse est percipi*. MS. 732 completes the picture by emphasizing the importance of impressions in the above analysis. In pure sensation to say that A (as B) is of kind-B is to say simply that A is A, and this is as well as to say simply that A *is*. As a pure impression something is an 'ultimate fact' and *as such* does not admit of being something of a kind. But then this means that impressions cannot be known, for to know them is to represent them. Observing this Peirce writes, "Whether there be any such ultimate premisses is a difficult question. It amounts, however, merely to this; whether the boundary of consciousness is in consciousness or out of it." But this is a moot question for us representing-humans, for "it is the only way we have of expressing that most important conception [of presentative character]." As is evident from Fig. 5, immediate cognition stands at the boundary of knowledge, and does not enter knowledge unless in a represented form through the work of the elements of cognition.

It is also in MS. 732 that Peirce suggests for the first time that this process of unfolding the relational implications of immediate cognition follows the logic of hypothesis, so that hypothesis and conception are one and the same. He then notes: "*Being* introduces nothing into thought; for 'A griffin is or would be' means nothing. Hence, this conception is not materially hypothetical—It is rather the end of all hypothesis—the accomplishment of that unity for which hypotheses are established." This affords another way of looking at Fig. 5. The line from immediate cognition to being via hypothetical inference can be considered circular, with immediate cognition, when objectively viewed as impression, one and the same in conceptual structure with pure being. It is perhaps for this reason that Peirce can both begin and end with pure being. Consciousness lies between these extremes, in the realm of conception or hypothesis proper. In being we have pure undifferentiated subjectness with no predication considered, while in impression we have a pure un-differentiated objectness with no subject considered. And in between these we have *substance, matter,* and *thing* (moving from subjectness to objectness) and *quality, relation,* and *representation* (moving from objectness to subjectness). If we identify being and impression, then, while substance stands next to being as the next most determined level of subjectness, we can see that they are actually poles apart, and so Peirce tells us: "The substance and being are the two poles of thought. Substance is the beginning, and the *end* of all conception. Substance is inapplicable to a predicate, *being* is equally so to a subject."

To an almost uncanny degree the earlier conceptual structure of the long list of categories of *I, It,* and *Thou* begins to emerge once more. Fig. 5 now recasts Fig. 3 in a shorter form, with abstraction and heaven in the latter becoming being and impression in the former. And much as the earlier long list of categories could be recast in the form of Fig. 4, the same can be done with the short list as well if we keep in mind the unity of impression and being. Now pure being is the Abstract One, while impression is the Concrete One. Rephrased, Fig. 5 then becomes:

Pure Subjectness	Being	Inner Being
Subjectness with Character	Substance	
Subjectness with Object	Representation	Outer Being
Objectness with Character	Interpretant	
Pure Objectness	Impression	Inner Being

In §8 of MS. 732 Peirce discusses the relation between interpretant and impression. An interpretant or correspondent is a medium that links subject and object (relate and correlate) in the form of representation. But if substance is a qualified inner being, then to maintain symmetry, so must be the interpretant. Yet how could this be possible if the interpretant is to have a representing capacity, that is, if it is to be a subject-with-object or outer being? Pure objectness is objectness without reference to a subject, making it also a pure inner being, and so the interpretant is both qualified outer being and qualified inner being. We may explain this by saying that its function contains both an inner and outer dimension. As something that generates representation, the interpretant has an outer being, but as something that remains merely a suggestive medium, a catalyst, so to speak, of representation, it retains an inner reality. All of this Peirce may have hoped to capture in his characterization of it as a "mediating representation." The problematic nature of the interpretant did not elude him even in this early formulation. Something is an interpretant if it is made to function as one by some representing system, in this case, human beings:

> Reference to an interpretant, is simply, the *addressing* of an impression to a conception. To *address* or *appeal to*, is an act we, in fact, suppose everything to perform, whether we attend to the circumstances or not. It is unanalysable, I think . . . . Now [impressions] are not brought to unity until we conceive them together as being *ours*, that is, until

we refer them to a conception as their interpretant. Thus the reference to an interpretant arises upon the holding together of diverse impressions, and therefore it does not join a conception to the substance, as the other two references do, but unites directly the manifold of the substance, itself. It is therefore the last conception in order in passing from *being* to *substance*.

An interpretant is unanalyzable because to analyze it is to regard it as a representation and to employ another interpretant in the process. And it is the last conception in passing from being to substance in the sense that it is the last object with an inner character prior to the wholly inner being of pure being and impression.

It might be objected that 'impression' is itself precisely objectness with character. However, for Peirce the term is used to refer to the pre-reflective dimension of immediate cognition, again as an 'ultimate fact', and not in the sense of, say, the 'impression of red'. Against such usage he writes: "Colour is sometimes given as an example of an impression. It is a bad one, because the simplest colour is almost as complicated as a piece of music" (MS, 732).

While it should be noted that Peirce's own list is slightly different from the one given here, their underlying similarities emerge on closer inspection. He writes, for example (§9 of MS. 732), that the three forms of reference—to ground, to correlate, and to interpretant—generate three prescindible objects: *quality, relation,* and *representation.* These are not in conflict with the initial triad—substance, representation, and interpretant—but can be seen as characteristics of the latter. In fact, Peirce himself calls them "characters" of three more fundamental objects—*quale, relate,* and *representamen.* Perhaps these latter terms come closest to expressing the sense of quality, representation, and interpretant as used in the above list. It is the quale that gives quality to substance; it is the relationship between subject and object that makes actual representation possible; and it is the quality related, the representamen, that makes possible the function of the interpretant.

We might wonder at this point whether Peirce considered the fresh attempt to reformulate the short list of categories a significant departure from the pre-1863 work. Evidence would seem to indicate that he had simply put the larger questions on the back burner, and that it was his intention to revive them once the revised short list was refined. His 'new list' categories, then, were formal in nature, but would eventually acquire real import as well. In one of the 'new list' drafts (in MS. 921) he notes, for example, that the three fundamental conceptions have three phases: grammatical, logical, and rhetorical (real), and that these conceptions "in their transcendental (or rhetorical) transformation, appear as quality, event, and purposeful act." This is surely an indication, early on, that the new list was intended to be used to clarify the nature and relations of non-logical subjects.

2. The Logic of Science

In his Lowell Lectures of 1866 Peirce devotes most of his attention to an account of the logical implications of the above conceptions. From the three forms of reference he derives the logical notions of *term, proposition,* and *argument,* and *connotation, denotation,* and *implication.* Yet these lectures are also part of the logic of science, and because he considered part of the purpose of logic to be that of making thought processes intelligible to thought, the short list had to generate epistemological implications as well. This result may have been unavoidable insofar as Peirce began his treatment of the conceptions with epistemological remarks on the nature of impressions. But he had in mind an even grander project than merely to correlate the three references with impressions, conceptions, and ideas. For to him they also suggest implications for the involved and systematic process of *acquiring* knowledge we know to be science itself.

In the final three Lowell Lectures Peirce introduces his audience to some broader applications of the three forms of reference. In the ninth lecture (MS. 357) he takes up the classification of the sciences. The necessity for such an undertaking is justified by an argument that the sciences cannot be classified according to the subjects they treat, since they usually treat the same subjects but in different respects. The sciences consider the function of objects, not objects proper, and so ask different questions of these objects; this means that a classification of questioning procedures is what is necessary to classify the sciences. But a questioning procedure is a way of constructing answers in the form of premises and deriving conclusions sought by the questions; here Peirce describes three such procedures and some of their sciences:

> Deductive: *mathematics, law, political economy*
> Inductive: *zoology, botany, mineralogy, morphology, descriptive astronomy, chemistry, logic*
> Hypothetic: *mechanics, acoustics, optics, heat, electricity, history, geology, physiology*

In the final two lectures (numbers ten and eleven) of the series (MSS. 358–359; 7.579–96) Peirce elaborates somewhat on the epistemological and metaphysical implications of the theory of categories first suggested in the ninth lecture. This is not surprising, for if the interpretation of the three references given above is correct, this work should reveal similarities with the earlier, more grandiose speculations. But even now such implications appear only as an afterthought, and when, on 14 May 1867, he introduced to his audience at a meeting of the American Academy of Arts and Sciences the final version of the new theory, "On a New List of Categories," the metaphysical strain is altogether lacking. Instead, the categories, presented as they were in a series of papers in logic, are seemingly employed only to elucidate some interesting connections in logical theory. More, however, lies beneath the surface.

In the eleventh lecture Peirce makes clear his view that philosophy unavoidably concerns metaphysical questions, and, recalling his early view—that all men are metaphysicians—he argues that "since, then, everyone must have conceptions of things in general, it is most important that they should be carefully constructed" (7.579). Once more it is the business of metaphysics carefully to construct the basic conceptions out of the commonly understood conceptions of things in general. But it is also the business of metaphysics to construct metaphors of parts of reality, linking them to other parts and to the whole of reality, if by 'metaphor' is meant "broad comparison on the ground of characters of a formal and highly abstract kind" (7.590). In a sense, then, the 'new list' itself is a *metaphor* of the metaphysical structure of all of reality, just as the *I, It,* and *Thou* were in the previous system.

To see that Peirce himself believed this to be the case at the time we might turn to the tenth and eleventh lectures just mentioned, but unfortunately nearly all of the tenth has been lost. All we know of it is that in it Peirce had argued the view that all cognition is inferential. Fortunately, however, a summary of the scope of that lecture is given in the eleventh lecture. Among the results of the previous lecture noted there, we find the conclusions (1) that logic supplies a classification of the elements of consciousness, (2) that all modifications of consciousness are inferences, and (3) that there are no invalid inferences. Inferences, we find, are of three general kinds:

Mediate ("Intellectual"): Deduction, Induction, Hypothesis
Immediate ("Sensation, Emotion, Instinct"): Hypothesis
Habitual: Induction

The senses of 'hypothesis' and 'induction' differ in the second and third inference from those implied in the first. In the first we have hypothesis and induction as the mediative process of thought with which we are usually concerned. But in the other inferences a more specialized sense must be understood. Immediate inferences are hypotheses "whose predicates are unanalyzed in comprehension" (7.580). If, as Peirce suggests, hypothesis has the form:

Q_1, Q_2, Q_3 instantiate P
S is also an instance of Q_1, Q_2, Q_3
$\therefore S$ is a case of P with reference to Q_1, Q_2, Q_3

then an instinct is simply an inference in which the intensionality of P, its logical depth, is ignored in the judgment 'S is P'. The connection is *immediately* made without considering whether Q_1, Q_2, and Q_3 actually belong to P. In habitual inference we have inductions "whose subjects are unanalyzed in extension." Again, if induction has the form:

Q_1, Q_2, Q_3 are taken at random from the S's
Q_1, Q_2, Q_3 are P
$\therefore$ any S is P,

then a habit is an inference in which the extensionality of *S*, its logical breadth, is ignored. If an inference is made on the basis of habit, what is ignored is whether the present case comes under the inductively-formed general rule. If by induction I know that 'If I leave my pipe for more than eight minutes it will go out', I may habitually strike a match to light it after eight minutes without first seeing if the pipe remains lit in this case.

This suggests that in mediative inference a judgment results when the breadth and depth of terms of two or more propositions are analyzed with reference to each other. In the final paper presented to the Academy on 13 November 1867, "Upon Logical Comprehension and Extension," Peirce shows how deduction, induction, and hypothesis can be understood in terms of *breadth*, *depth*, and their logical product, *information*. Consequently, all three kinds of inference can be understood in those terms as well. But certain gaps remain to be filled in. If the logical terms are to have epistemological and even metaphysical implication, a *basis* for such analogies must be established; a correspondence rule must be enunciated. Although no such clear correlation is indicated in the paper, something close to it is encountered in Peirce's discussion of *informed* breadth and depth. There he characterizes information as a combination of some breadth and some depth, the former being all those things of which a term is predicable and the latter all characters of which it is predicated. He continues:

> The informed breadth and depth suppose a state of information which lies between two imaginary extremes. These are, first, the state in which no fact would be known, but only the meaning of terms; and, second, the state in which the information would amount to an absolute intuition of all there is, so that the things we should know would be the very substances themselves, and the qualities we should know would be the very concrete forms themselves. (2.409)

Here is the missing link in the 'new list' argument that unites with it the previous system of categories. Now Fig. 5 can once more be rephrased in the comprehensive form given in Fig. 6:

Fig. 6

	ESSENTIAL	INFORMED	SUBSTANTIAL
BREADTH	Ideal Substances	Reference to Object	Real Substances
DEPTH	Pure Meanings	Reference to Ground	Real Concrete Forms
INFORMATION	Immediate/Ideal	Mediate	Immediate/Real

Essential breadth involves all "those real things of which, according to its very meaning, a term is predicable" (2.412). Peirce does not name such 'things'; indeed, he cannot, for knowledge of meanings alone would rule out being able to know the denoted object *except by the pure meaning.* Given the meaning, we know that such 'things' *would be* referred to by the term; hence they are termed here 'ideal' substances, though Peirce himself leaves them unnamed. Depending upon the "extensive distinctness" (2.408) of the term, its essential breadth will be more or less ideal and abstract. As Peirce notes, with a term like 'being' we have as a meaning "that which can be predicated of whatever you please" (2.412), and so its breadth is the most general character of all possible objects—that they be something or other. In this sense "the essential subjects of being cannot be enumerated" (2.412) and are for this reason 'ideal', while still subjects of predication.

The state of essential information is immediate and ideal simply because meanings are 'given'. This is second-intention knowledge of definitions, and for this reason Peirce does not qualify information in terms of truth. Substantial information, on the other hand, is both immediate and *real,* and so involves "absolute truth" (2.414). In the former case a term has a ground, its meaning, but predication does not take place; instead, information involves simply the intuition: S(with character P). In the latter case predication occurs immediately in that S(with character P) is seen as identical with the object, O(with form P). There is no subject, S, left behind; the thought is at once the object, emptying itself into the object in a manner suggestive of Hegel's dialectical transitions. In the intermediate case predication takes place as normally considered. Here S(with character P) is seen to share its attribute with an object, O(with form P). As in the substantial case, a relation is established here as well, and so truth is possible, but only "logical truth," where by "logical" Peirce means something broader and richer than is usually meant.

Mediated information also involves a breadth and depth that may be "certain or doubtful, actual or potential" (2.408). If the 'informed' state is an intermediate stage between the 'essential' and the 'substantial' states, then it may be plausible to interpret the middle state as a mixture of extremes. In the essential state we have complete certainty, but only on a terminological level, and. consequently truth is purely potential; in the informed state we have a combination of certainty and. doubt, actual and potential knowledge; and in the substantial state we have factual certainty and a purely actual knowledge, absolute truth, the "absolute intuition of all there is." To know everything literally is to leave nothing outside of knowledge, so that no medium remains to re-present our knowledge. Inference and judgment are not required, if by judgment is meant the act of predicating some but not all features of something to something. Absolute intuition sees all features at once, and so judgment is unnecessary.

How, then, does the schema of Fig. 6 tie in with the three kinds of inference? Peirce distinguishes "three elements of consciousness" (7.580) in the following manner:

1. *Feelings*, or Elements of Comprehension
2. *Efforts*, or Elements of Extension
3. *Notions*, or Elements of Information

These elements lie between the extreme, 'imaginary' states of knowledge, but are themselves isomorphically related to the three states. Feelings are as close to pure meanings as reference to ground could be; efforts necessarily involve reference to objects; while notions are as close to real forms as reference to an interpretant could be.

By now Peirce must have been convinced that the forms of representation, of inference, of logical intension and extension, and of cognition could be linked into one system. That he had already clarified the issue to such an extent was surely, in the words of Murray Murphey, "an extraordinary feat of ingenuity."[2] But more remained to be done. A problem that required a great deal of further clarification was that of establishing a priority for the various triads. This problem may be enunciated in a variety of ways. One way is to ask how it could be possible for consciousness to 'imagine' *proto-* and *hyper*-states of consciousness, that is, to pose the question of the boundary of consciousness once more. This problem is tied in with the more general problem of establishing a priority among the logical and psychological forms. Clearly, the drift of Peirce's reflections, now for more than a decade, gives the place of pride to the former. But this now necessitates a clear statement on the relation between mind and the general categories. No doubt Peirce himself realized this, and, perhaps for this reason, treated his audience to some provocative reflections on the subject in the final Lowell Lecture of 1866, where he takes up the question 'What is Man?'.

3. THE SIGN THEORY OF COGNITION

The argument presented in the final Lowell Lecture is now familiar to us in the form of the answer 'Man is a sign' (7.580-96). Here Peirce not only rejects the Cartesian view of man as an indivisible and autonomous center of consciousness, but also dismisses the prevalent materialistic–Darwinian view as nothing but "a heterogeneous hodgepodge of the most contradictory theories" (7.580). A major obstacle to getting a clear view on the nature of human life results, according to Peirce, from the failure to subject such life to both inductive and hypothetic explanation. Induction gives greater breadth to the term 'man', while hypothesis gives greater depth; both are needed. Hypothesis involves "the causes or necessary antecedents of the phenomena of human life" (7.581). But such an analysis can go foward only as a result of guidance from the inductive task, which investigates what sorts of things share attributes with human life.

Human life as commonly understood is animal life, but Peirce prefers to extend the breadth of 'man' by considering all those things that might display qualities similar to human feelings, actions, and conceptions. If other things have such characters, then they are to some degree man-like and men are to some degree like them. Here then is a clear illustration of the analogical extension of the categories mentioned above. The core of Peirce's argument is perhaps too simply stated (7.583):

We have already seen [in lecture ten] that every state of consciousness [is] an inference; so that life is but a sequence of inferences or a train of thought. At any instant then man is a thought, and as thought is a species of symbol, the general answer to the question 'What is man?' is that he is a symbol.

In the extant fragments of the tenth lecture we find very little by way of a clear defense of the view that every state of consciousness is the result of an inference. Instead, Peirce suggests (in MS. 358) three reasons why it is most probable that there are no non-inferential states of consciousness:

> 1st that the reasons for supporting ultimate sensations are futile, 2nd that all the sensations now supposed to be ultimate, are more probably inferences, 3rd that no sensation can possibly be known to be an ultimate premise and that consequently no error of *fact* is involved in saying that there is no ultimate premise, since *fact* refers to a possible experience only.

In the first case we are reminded of the earlier arguments against dogmatism in metaphysics. What reasons, after all, could be adduced for supposing sensations to be ultimate? If we deduce the conclusion 'X is an ultimate sensation' from other premises, these premises must not contain equivalent notions such as 'givenness' or 'intuitiveness'. The second reason turns on Peirce's view that our ordinary sensations are actually quite complex when reflectively scrutinized, so that their ultimacy is of an uninteresting psychological sort, one not revealing an important metaphysical distinction. The third reason is very much like the first, except that Peirce adds to it a 'pragmatic' dimension, which looks something like this:

> Whatever is a fact, is a source of possible (future) experience.
> An ultimate sensation would be wholly actual and present.
> ∴No ultimate sensation could be a fact.

And from this Peirce concludes that nothing turns on the claim that 'X is an ultimate sensation'. As formulated, the argument appears at first to be rather weak, depending as it does on a specialized interpretation of 'fact'. After all, it seems perfectly reasonable to say that something is both an ultimate sensation and a fact of consciousness. Then while it would be true that this particular sensation would not be repeated, others of its kind may be future, possible experiences. This seems to accord with ordinary uses of the word 'fact', but it also suggests that what Peirce may have had in mind in saying that no sensation could be known to be ultimate is that particularity and incorrigibility must go hand in hand. And as long as we consider not 'sensations' in general but 'this sensation', no ultimacy can be established for the reasons given. Then to say that *kinds* of sensation are ultimate is to engage in sign-making, and so to move away from immediacy altogether.

Peirce's arguments here also revive the view he held in his college days that consciousness is essentially relational, and that states of consciousness are therefore relational (dyadic and triadic) rather than monadic. Such a view made possible a rejection of solipsistic phenomenalism by overturning the claim that there had to be an 'intended' reality beyond the boundary of consciousness. Without ultimate and incorrigible states of consciousness, the life of the mind does not grow from a single foundation, from the simple to the complex, as Descartes had suggested. Instead it is an ongoing sequence of signs. The fact that it is a sequence by itself does not mark a departure from Descartes, for his *cogito* can also be thought of as a sequence of states of mind. It is the fact that life itself is regarded as a symbolic, or semiotic, enterprise that makes the difference here; if life is a semiotic process, those things that 'live' must be semiotic entities in some sense. What, then, does it mean to say that man is a symbol? Is each man a specific symbol or are all men part of one symbol? Peirce speaks of man as a "species of symbol," sharing the attributes of symbols with other semiotic entities, and then suggests the following attributes which are, for example, shared between man and the symbol *six* (7.584–90): self-reference, external reference, unity of consistency, increase in information, conformity to norms, self-creation. A word is always an index of itself, as is our conscious self-reflection; it refers beyond itself, and so does the attentive act of consciousness; a word maintains a consistency of self-identity; yet a word can change its reference (breadth and depth), and so can a man by learning; a word is subject to grammatical norms, while a man is subject to moral norms; and finally, a word can make a new word in definition and a man can make a new man in procreation.

It would be a mistake, however, to take these 'analogies' (7.591) as amounting to an argument proper. Peirce does not deny any of the obvious differences between persons and words; what he is saying is that they are a great deal more alike than is usually thought, and so such analogies make possible a continuing expansion of the inter-pretation of the three forms of reference. The general schema of Fig. 6 was used to characterize three elements of consciousness, and now other important aspects of human reality can also be understood in this light. Reference to object can be found in *attention;* reference to ground, in *feeling;* and reference to interpretant, in some future experience which recounts in some fashion an experience of the past, in *thought.* Man, then, is an evolving semiotic system with a twofold complementarity as both symbolizing and symbol-ized. Thus it is more correct to say that persons are *in* symbols as their species than that symbols are in them. We are not "shut up in a box of flesh and blood," but instead have an "outreaching identity" (7.591), which we experience in communication with others. When someone else reflects upon what I think and express to him, he does not only take what is mine into himself; my soul itself becomes extended into his as well. Each soul is a combination of novelty and convention, just as in the earlier writings expression was seen as a combination of determination and indetermination, language and meaning. Something utterly novel could not be expressed, while something utterly conventional requires no expression. The same applies to all human communication. The individual soul is but "a special determination of the generic soul of the family, the class, the nation, the race to which he belongs" (7.592).

But is there no personal soul? The word *six* refers to an "eternal truth" and so if man is a "true symbol" (7.593) he too must be immortal. The truth of man is a symbolic truth. This means that a man must be something that exercises symbolizing consciousness, and the more intense the exercise the more truthful he is as a symbol. However, to Peirce, this exercise is at odds with the contingent animal nature of man. The personal soul is but an abstract unity of symbolization—the 'I think'; the "generic soul is true and eternal, but its specific and individual soul is but a shadow" (7.594). Immortality depends upon the transcendence of the animal state and the subsequent contemplation of truth. Yet we may still wonder *what* it is that is immortal. A truth? A personal soul? This is not clear in the text of MS. 359. Nor is it likely that it was clear in Peirce's own mind at the time. Perhaps to distinguish the impersonality of truth from the attestation of that truth by some spiritual entity, he saw fit to note that "truth, it is said, is never without a witness" (7.593). But then he is confronted with the problem of characterizing that 'witness' in terms of personality in order to avoid the circularity of characterizing personal immortality in terms of truth and truth in terms of personal immortality. Again, it is not clear how this can be done.

Peirce's speculations in this closing Lowell Lecture do not end here with the question of the nature of personality. An even larger implication is suggested:

> There is another important corollary which may be drawn from the law of symbols. As each thing has its symbol, so everything has its symbol. I do not mean the empty conception of *being,* the interpretant of absolutely undetermined feeling, whose comprehension is *nought* [text unclear], nor the blind conception of *substance,* the interpretant of absolutely undetermined attention. But that symbol whose information is all-embracing, which signifies every fact about everything, not contingently but necessarily.

We are at once reminded of the earlier speculations on Worlds and Manifests, and perhaps of something like Spinoza's Substance. But it is to no abstract, metaphysical entity that Peirce now refers. Rather it is to "the Creator of the World since all is necessarily conformed thereto" who was "a personal being for the same reason that all symbols are personal." In this case, reference is exclusively self-reference, and both ground and interpretant are identical to the symbol itself. As a symbol, reference to the three dimensions of symbolizing is still required, but as the all-embracing symbol the three references are to a single object. Nor does this mean, according to Peirce, that the three references are three points of view of the infinite symbol, for since the latter is all-embracing, nothing lies beyond it to have a point of view. Peirce then suggests a connection with the Christian doctrine of the Triune God, though he cuts short this speculation "as it may be offensive to the prejudices of some who are present" (MS. 359).

The task of reconciling philosophy and theology, a task already evident in his earliest writings, now reappears in a somewhat modified form. But it may be a mistake to conclude from this that Peirce was putting metaphysics at the service of Christianity. Instead, it may be more accurate to say that he had hoped to reveal the metaphysical kernel within the picturesque core of traditional religion. This course, however, is a treacherous one. We humans are *persons* insofar as we are symbols. Yet can there be an ultimate symbol which can be, in Peirce's words, "the well-spring of all personality since only by virute of the Law does the unity of consistency become part of the finite symbol" (MS. 359)? In what sense is such a Law of Symbols a person as well? My personality is provisionally abiding, and yet ultimately epiphenomenal. What of the Whole itself? Should it be or contain a personality, a self-reflection, a thought-thinking itself, it must be of a nature wholly unlike symbolizing personality as found among finite symbols. No doubt Peirce was aware of the difficulties, for he asked his audience to ponder "whether such a God would be a God of Prayer." For him this could be so only in the sense that prayer involves a request that the universe be according to God's will, and not that it be according to the will of the person who prays. In the former case the prayer would be answered "through the proper chain of material necessary antecedents," in the latter case only if the prayer requests what is in accordance with the divine interpretant in the first place. Once more we are reminded of Spinoza and a Spinozistic prayer to an eternal, changeless Substance, but Peirce gives us no further clues at this point as to how such a divine symbol might be interpreted.

As was the case with the 1867 series on logic, Peirce tried out more of his speculations in 1868 on the readers of the *Journal of Speculative Philosophy*. Again the method used was to present a seemingly simple question and answer it with suggestive and widely ramified argument. Little could the St. Louis Hegelians have known at the time that this young Cambridge logician, while eyeing with suspicion the heady speculative enthusiasms of their journal, had already labored a decade in architectonic construction and had assimilated the spirit of the new German philosophy as well as had Hedge, Henry, and Hickok before him. What they would see was only the tip of the iceberg. A case in point is Peirce's somewhat puzzling confrontation with William T. Harris, the journal's editor, on the question of Hegel's dialectic of *Being, Nothing,* and *Becoming.* In his review of Paul Janet's *Essai sur la dialectique dans Platon et dans Hegel* Harris argued against Janet's claim that Hegel had not derived Becoming from Being and Nothing, but had gratuitously added it to some otherwise trivial logical remarks about the identity of Being and Nothing. We can imagine Peirce reading with interest Harris's argument, prefaced as it was with the claim that "psychology should not be dragged into Logic."[3] In the argument Harris wrote:

> Being is the pure simple; as such it is considered under the form of self-reflection. But as it is wholly undetermined, and has no content, it is pure nought or absolute negation . . . . The negative is a relative, and a negative by itself is a negative related to itself, which is self-cancelling. Thus Being and nought, posited objectively as having validity, prove dissolving forms and pass over into each other. Being is the *ceasing* and nought is the *beginning,* and these are the two forms of *Becoming.*

On 24 January 1868 Peirce wrote to Harris, and the latter published portions of the letter in the second volume of the journal as "the most profound and compendious statement of the anti-speculative standpoint as related to the Science of Pure Thought" (p. 57). In his letter Peirce noted that if an abstract term such as *Being* is considered "according to the doctrine of modern times" (6.620) to be a way of expressing concrete predicates, then in no way could Being and Nothing be mutually coextensive, for there is a clear difference between the circumstance whereby 'Being' and 'Nothing' are predicated of a hundred dollars in my pocket. To this Harris replied that by *Being* he meant not something *possessed* by a thing, namely a determinate quality of existence (*Dasein*), but pure being (*Sein*). But Peirce had already noted such a distinction (6.619), and had dismissed it as not what he took Harris to be saying. Clearly, to say that 'Being is No-thing' is not to touch on Harris's point, and Peirce realized this full well. What then was the issue?

In his letter (6.621) Peirce asks Harris to justify the claim that if something is undetermined, it is a negation of all determination. This to Peirce seemed to imply "that to abstract from a character is to deny it," and if so, Peirce wanted to know why. He also wanted to know why Harris claimed that 'nothing' *had* no determination, in short, that it was a 'relative' of some sort. In the paper on logical comprehension and extension, Peirce had concluded that *being* was by nature indeterminate and had essential breadth, while *nothing* had only essential depth (2.411–12), but also concluded that negation and the character of indetermination were not derived from these distinctions. He then suggests in the letter to Harris, that what the latter may have assumed is that determination is simply a character of *difference,* so that an indeterminate being is a being with no difference from anything, and thus no difference from nothing as well. But this argument rests upon an equivocation of two senses of 'indeterminate', one pertaining to the meaning of terms, the other to the characterization of objects. Being *is* indeterminate in the sense that there is no predicate with more depth than the term *being* itself, which can be predicated of all beings, but beyond this it makes no sense to say that the abstract Being is indeterminate, and so *is* Nothing.

In effect Peirce appears to be raising some healthy doubts about the Hegelian method of dialectical reasoning, and at the end of his argument he asks Harris whether logical contradiction is at odds with the Hegelian system, implying that if one must be sacrificed it should be the system (6.624). To this Harris replied that "the maxims of formal logic are *prima facie* true, for the *prima facie* mode of viewing things always gives validity to the immediate phase of things" (p. 60), but added that such a view had to be constantly subject to reflective analysis in order to penetrate beyond immediacy. What was at issue, Harris noted, was whether there were only concrete things of common sense, in short, whether nominalism was true, or whether there were relations, mediations, and the "generic" as is maintained in Scholastic Realism. No doubt this reply must have struck Peirce close to home, for while Harris may have been stating a flawed case, he was doing so for the right reasons—at least according to Peirce's way of thinking—and this is what very likely aroused his curiosity at the outset.

In a follow-up letter, printed in a later issue of the second volume (pp. 190–91), Peirce further elaborates on his idea of determination, recalling the earlier remark that determination can be thought to apply either to things or to words. In the latter case the determination is of some general nature, in the sense that 'some one horse' is determinate relative to 'horse' but indeterminate relative to 'Dexter'. The former is an indeterminate individual, the latter a determinate individual. Now *being*, Peirce observes, is indeterminate in the sense that it refers to no particular character of one or more individuals, but it is an indetermination of predication of terms, not of an *object* denoted by *being*. Here, I think, we come to Peirce's underlying contention. It was not his intention to refute the Hegelian dialectic after all, but to correct what he saw to be Harris's misapprehension of it. He was arguing that one cannot simply derive the identity of Being and Nothing from the meaning of these terms, for logic can give a clear and mutually exclusive definition of each. What is missing in such an acount is the context of *human reflection*, and Peirce appeals to Hegel himself to back him up on this issue:

> Hegel teaches that the whole series of categories or universal conceptions can be *evolved* from one—that is, from *Seyn* [sic]—by a certain process, the effect of which is to make actually thought that which was virtually latent in the thought. So that this reflection which constitutes *Daseyn* lies implicitly even in *Seyn*, and it is by *explicitly* evolving it from *Seyn* that *Daseyn* is evolved from *Seyn*. (6.626)

The dialectic, in other words, is a dialectic of reflection, which, when further reflected upon, comes to be seen as a dialectic of *Sein* into *Dasein*. Without reflection, the implicit does not become explicit, and *Sein* and *Dasein* are not able to be seen as related. However, it is not always clear that Hegel would indeed back Peirce up on this. While the former notes that Being must "yield to dialectic" to pass into Nothing, he also observes:

> If it be replied that Being and Nothing are both of them thoughts, so that thought may be reckoned common ground, the objector forgets that Being is not a particular or definite thought, and hence, being quite indeterminate, is a thought not to be distinguished from Nothing.[4]

Peirce would deny the latter point as a confusion between the first and second intention senses of the term *being*. A logically precise characterization of *being* can be given even if it is not possible to specify a character of everything referred to by the term. And we must assume that he thought he had already given such a characterization in his 'new list' paper and in related papers. Had Peirce wished, he could have defended his point using Hegel's *Science of Logic* instead, particularly where the latter speaks of Being as "what is there before us" and as "an expression of reflection," and makes similar remarks with respect to Nothing.

We might still wonder why Peirce provoked Harris with views "according to the doctrine of modern times," views he himself did not hold (see 6.627). Was it merely his penchant for playing devil's advocate learned during many long evenings of intellectual sparring with his father? Perhaps more likely is the fact that this new journal devoted to German metaphysics dealt with issues very close to Peirce's own philosophical heart, and yet its early papers showed none of the logical rigor he thought essential to the grand enterprise of metaphysical architectonic. We can only wonder how Peirce must have felt when his 1868 papers on intuition were introduced in that journal as essays having "a psychological basis" (2, iv), when it is clear now, and was so to Peirce then, that the metaphysical theory of categories alone served as the basis of the papers (see, for example, 5.223). In these papers—"Questions Concerning Certain Faculties Claimed for Man," "Some Consequences of Four Incapacities," and "Grounds of Validity of the Laws of Logic: Further Consequences of Four Incapacities"—we can find Peirce's fuller reply to Harris on the issue of how an idealistic metaphysics had best be carried out. These papers might also be considered Peirce's official debut as a philosopher, presented to the audience he must have hoped would be the most responsive to his ideas.

We notice at once that the topics of the papers follow closely those of the 1867 series on logic, except that now there is greater emphasis on defending the application of the theory of reference to areas not directly logical. Specifically, it is their purpose to show that the categories can be used to elucidate the activity of mind by demonstrating that the mind, or mental action, operates according to a general principle of inference, and that in this principle can be found the workings of the categories. Although Peirce returns to similar themes in all three papers, for the most part, and not surprisingly, the order of exposition reverses the order of architectonic. In the third paper the principle of syllogistic inference is defended in general; in the second its relevance to the categories is explained; and in the first the relevance of the categories to cognition is revealed. Peirce begins with thought and consciousness, and from this takes his reader on a long journey to the foundations of inference, stating its general principle as follows: "In a system of signs in which no sign is taken in two different senses, two signs which differ only in their manner of representing their object, but which are equivalent in meaning, can always be substituted for one another" (5.323). Inference is, so to speak, the ticket permitting the movement from premise to conclusion. As stated, however, this notion raises some problems of interpretation. How, for example, should we interpret Peirce's distinction between the meaning and manner of representation? If we are to be able to substitute one sign for another we must understand the former extensionally and the latter intensionally, thereby making the manner of representation the meaning. But even this assumes that the substitution is carried out for the purpose of describing what is the case. 'The morning star' may be substituted for 'the evening star' in any statement about their extension, that is, involving truth, but may not be substituted if their intension is of foremost concern. From the context of the discussion, however, it is clear that this presented no problem for Peirce inasmuch as it was his intention to elucidate the conditions of inferences leading to knowledge.

To uncover the general principle of logical inference is one thing, to show its relevancy to mental action is another. Here Peirce required a link between such a principle and the workings of mind. The major portion of the third paper comprises a refutation of objections against the view that the syllogism is the underlying form of knowledge. Against the objection (5.328) that all syllogisms involve a *petitio principii,* and so must contain all knowledge at the outset, Peirce maintained that the function of the syllogism was to be demonstrative, and its effect in the mind was to render confused thought distinct by a process that simply happens in the mind by the very operation of the syllogism. But is thought, we might ask, simply a 'remembering' of previous unconscious, confused thought, or is it constituted out of the syllogistic process itself? If the former, then it may be necessary to defend a sort of Platonic Realism independently of the theory of cognition. If the latter, we may wonder what could justify the distinction between distinct and indistinct thought, except a comparison of the two, a comparison itself subject to the very syllogistic process it seeks to investigate. Peirce clearly accepted the force of this problem (see 5.327). In answering the next objection (5.329) he draws back from a literal interpretation of the mind as a syllogistic process. It is objected that a syllogism is a purely mechanical relation and so could never comprise something as dynamic as mental action. Against this he argues that the form of a syllogism only *represents* the form of mental inference, not that it is identical with it:

> There is reason to believe that the act of the mind is, as it were, a continuous movement. Now the doctrine embodied in syllogistic formulae (so far as it applies to the mind at all) is, that if two successive positions, occupied by the mind in this movement, be taken, they will be found to have certain relations.

Here, then, is the missing link of the argument, one unifying the logical principle of 'substitution' (5.323) with the theory of mental inference. No doubt such a 'doctrine' would require justification, but Peirce leaves that for another occasion.

A more formidable objection concerns not deductive inference, but probabilistic inference. Up to now Peirce had been content to specify conceivable states of affairs in mind and nature that could make possible syllogistic inference. But now he confronts "a paradox of the greatest difficulty" (5.347). For no conceived state of the universe could be such as to give credence to both the successes and the failures of probabilistic inference. On the other hand, neither could a logical principle be adduced as the foundation of such inference. And so upon what is this "magical" (5.347) process based? Peirce is not prepared to reject such inference, calling it an "intellectual intuition" and a "second avenue of truth" (5.341). In this case we somehow *know* something about what we have not yet experienced—something we have no grounds to know in the light of previous experience. In the case of deductive inference, logically considered, all judgments are analytic; but with probabilistic inference the conclusion is not logically contained in the premises. The judgment is synthetic, and so Peirce concludes:

> There can be no doubt of the importance of this problem. According to Kant, the central question of philosophy is 'How are synthetic judgments *a priori* possible?' But antecedently to this comes the question how synthetical reasoning is possible at all. When the answer to the general problem has been obtained, the particular one will be comparatively simple. This is the lock upon the door of philosophy. (5.348)

It becomes evident that to unlock the door of philosophy is to justify the 'doctrine' of the relationship between successive positions of the mind. And it was to begin such a justification that Peirce wrote the first two papers of the series.

In the second paper (5.264–317) Peirce presents the most unified elaboration of the relevance of the categories to mental activity attempted so far. There he argues that all mental action involves valid reasoning, since it is exclusively inferential and all inferences are valid; and from this he shows that even in logical fallacies a form of valid inference must be assumed (5.280–82). As the third paper shows, all such reasoning comprises "one genus" (5.278) and "one general form" (5.279). It was at this point that he began to nudge open the door of philosophy by characterizing the "certain relations" (5.329) of mental events as *sign*-relations. This means that "whenever we think, we have present to the consciousness some feeling, image, conception, or other representation, which serves as a sign" (5.283). But this means that we ourselves must be given to ourselves as a sign, since there is no self except as self-consciousness. And so to elucidate upon the nature of thought-signs is to reveal as well the nature of the self-sign. If each sign contains the features of quality, relation, and representation, so too must all mental action. But constructing mental activity according to these categories is no small feat. We shall nevertheless attempt a reconstruction based upon Peirce's piecemeal remarks on the subject (5.283–310).

Suppose a person to have three thoughts in the temporal sequence from *A* to *C:*

A: Toussaint is a Negro
B: Toussaint is a man
C: Toussaint is a general

Suppose further that we must investigate thought-*B* as a sign. Its quality or ground is simply the thought of Toussaint as present to consciousness; its correlate or relation is both the extensional object *and* the previous thought-*A;* and its interpretant or representation is the subsequent thought-*C*. In the last case *C* is the interpretant of *B* for me, but might also be for some other thinker if I speak my thoughts to that person. It is important to see that for Peirce these are not three freely associated thoughts, but are part of a logical structure. *A* suggests *B*, and so *A* is a sign of *B*, and *B* interprets *A* (5.284). In accordance with his rejection of intuition, Peirce rejects the possibility of a first thought. To have a thought is to have had a previous thought. This may be interpreted as meaning not that a person cannot change the subject of thought, but that for him to do so he must turn to a subject previously thought. Upon leaving the house I may be surprised and think 'It's cold now', but to be able to do this I must have thought similar thoughts previously. In other words, for *A* to suggest *B*, *A* and *B* must be related as part of a formal 'language-game', so that on the occasion of one the other can result. But *need* it result? To this Peirce would reply: yes, but only if no other factors contribute to the formation of cognition. In fact, however, there are many such factors—bodily states and external conditions—and these interrupt the flow of thought-signs. Had we a pure mind, however, thought would be continuously unfolding the logical relations of fact. For us thought begins in "the ideal first, which is quite singular, and quite out of consciousness. This ideal first is the particular thing-in-itself" (5.311). Rather than assuming a pre-existing abstraction which combines with sensation to produce thought, Peirce now seems to be assuming that thought emerges out of pure determinateness. However, he still denies that a thing-in-itself exists *as such* insofar as there is nothing not in relation to mind, though he now holds that having such a relation does not preclude something's having an independent existence as well.

The general structures of the man-sign suggested by Peirce are presented in Fig. 7. It should be noted that while he did not use the early categories of simple, human, and perfect relations, there is evidence to suggest that he retained at least a rudimentary notion of these in his arguments here. He speaks of degrees of sensation and emotion, of some material quality being more prominent in some cognitions than in others, and he also notes that some relations are real, while others are rational as well (5.294). To tie in the three sign-categories with mental action he describes the first as "material quality" and the second as "pure demonstrative application." If we consider that each sign-structure can take a form between the extremes of simplicity (the incomplex) and complexity, then we can understand why distinctions can be made within each of the structures.

Those categories given in brackets in Fig. 7 are missing in Peirce's

Fig. 7

	SIMPLE		COMPLEX
QUALITY	Feeling	Sensation/Emotion	Thought-itself
RELATION	Attention	Habit	Action [Inquiry]
REPRESENTATION	[Inference]	[Interpretation]	Understanding

own account, and are suggested partly in the hope of extending the analogy in an acceptable direction, partly to shed light on later notions. Any noematic structure considered in itself is comprised of mere quality, though the degree of that quality may range from a vague mood to a complex thought. In spite of this, "every thought, however artificial and complex, is, so far as it is immediately present, a mere sensation without parts, and therefore, in itself, without similarity to any other, but incomparable with any other and absolutely *sui generis*" (5.289). A thought may *have* parts, or, more precisely, its content may, but only when these parts are compared is this content cognized. Consciousness itself is only a sensation (5.313) and, like sensation, is more than a simple feeling in that it takes a more determinate form than feeling. However, whether material quality is to be simple or complex depends upon its role in mental action. If simple, it is only 'pure experience', and this hardly so, while if complex, it rises to "intellectual value" (5.289) in its ability to serve as a sign of subsequent thought and an inter-pretant of previous thought. Sensation and emotion enter the realm of representation and meaning; they are cognitions *of* something, and have the ability to generate interpretants.

The second dimension of signs is pure demonstrative application ("Relation" in Fig. 7). The sign-relation is at the least a *real* relation between the sign and signified, whether that relation be established in the world (a weathercock or tally, 5.287) or in the brain (5.287). In either case the relation must be in some manner physical. Attention is such a relation-generating power (5.295-96); without it inferences could not begin, for no matter how the content of a sign suggests a later or earlier sign, no connection would be made without attention. This conclusion parallels the earlier idea that the mind is not a sign-generating machine. From attention the train of mental action may move either to the realm of quality or to that of representation, and may then return to the task of application in a more developed form–habit (5.297). Now attention is systematized to the point where it no longer requires a feeling of consciousness. The habit itself makes the connection (inductively) between signs. Finally, voluntary action is born: "Voluntary actions result from the sensations produced by habits" (5.297). Habits also have an influence on quality and representation, but when application is taken up again it takes a more complex, fulfilled form in action, or, to anticipate later notions, produces *inquiry*.

Representative function is the relatedness of quality. Here Peirce's remarks are scantest of all. In part the triad proposed in Fig. 7 is suggested from the following remark: "We have thus seen that every sort of modification of consciousness—Attention, Sensation, and Understanding—is an inference" (5.298). But where should we place 'Understanding' in the triad? It is assumed here that Under-standing is more than mere simple representation; it is the making of sign-relations with comprehension and complexity. A less complex sort of comprehension would be interpretation in which only a few signs are related in a representative ensemble, as is found in the case of something being interpreted in light of a specific interpreting framework. And the most restricted comprehension is that which links just two signs in a inference. This, in any case, seems to be close enough to what Peirce may have had in mind to be worthy of consideration. No doubt other interpretations are possible.

We come finally to the first paper (5.213-63), of which the latter two are 'consequences'. Although it is the first paper that is a consequence of the expanded theory of the latter two, Peirce presents it first because it is perhaps the most effective opening argument for his theory. After all, the plausibility of his later proposals, for the most part, stands or falls on whether he can convince the reader that his theory best explains the facts about cognition established in the first paper. If it cannot be established that there is a first cognition, generated *ab ovo* from intuition, then the view that there is not such an intuition, advanced later, cannot be ruled out.

Peirce begins by asking how we could know if a cognition is a first cognition, and then argues as follows (with subscripts added here for clarity): no $cognition_2$ of a $cognition_1$ is part of the content of $cognition_1$ (in the sense of "material quality" given above); hence the determination of $cognition_2$ on $cognition_1$ cannot be cognized from such content alone, and so if a given cognition is proposed as being without determination, we cannot know (i.e. cognize) this to be the case. As in cases of unquestioned belief, in experiences of magic and dreams, and in sensory knowledge generally (5.215-23) what seems 'given' may be actually inferred. Secondly, if there is no first cognition, then there is no first cognition of the self, or, in other words, our knowledge of ourselves is inferred as well. This follows from the first argument, but Peirce takes special note of it to emphasize the connection. It is not entirely clear, however, whether he is speaking of an empirical or transcendental self here. Our cognition of an empirical self slowly grows out of our childhood experiences and, as Peirce suggests, in this sense it is true to say that with 'I was wrong' the 'I' is born inferentially. This growth of self-awareness is a matter of increasingly taking into account that experience is a personal, contingent affair and part of learning. Yet there is another sense in which we must imagine a self that does the growing and learning, one that exists in the barest sense of the absolute self. Does the "absolute *ego* of pure apperception" (5.235) inferentially grow out of a non-self as well, or is it *sui generis*? On this question Peirce is content to argue that our knowledge of our self is no more certain than our knowledge "that there is another fact" (5.237), that is, that there is a non-self. This, of course, does not show that the self derives from the non-self. We cannot know that the self is *sui generis,* and while we also cannot know that it isn't, we do know that we know the non-self (whatever it is) with as much certainty as we know the self. From this we are at least able to conclude that "there is no necessity of supposing an intuitive self-consciousness, since self-consciousness may easily be the result of inference" (5.237). It is interesting that in this argument Peirce characterizes the certainty of the knowledge of self and non-self as based not on an equal argumentation, and naturally not on intuition, but on the equal absence of doubt about both, a theme that runs through all three papers (5.237, 5.264, 5.319). This theme would be amplified more fully in the decade to follow.

Peirce next eliminates the possibility of an intuitive introspection of *modes* of cognition—noetic acts. All noetic distinctions, such as those between sensing and imagining, or believing and conceiving, result from a comparison of features of noematic content. But because the intuitive cognition of such content "implies no intuitive recognition of subjective elements of consciousness" (5.242), those elements cannot themselves be intuitively known. This raises the further question of whether it is possible to have any knowledge, intuitive or otherwise, of a mental world not derived from knowledge of external facts. This question involves a comparison of two kinds of knowledge, not of knowledge and the world, and as such follows the approach of Kant's 'refutation of idealism' in the second-edition *Critique*. Such knowledge could not be intuitive for reasons already given, for whether or not it was subjective in nature would concern the noetic mode of knowledge and this itself cannot be intuitively known. If such knowledge were inferential, it could only derive from an internal inspection of the noematic content of mental experience; however, such content is not self-explanatory, that is, we can legitimately ask why such contents and not others are 'given'. But if noemata are predicates of some undetermined sort, of what subjects are they predicated? At this point Peirce must compare the noema with 'external' subjects and not with an 'internal' subject, the mind or ego. But how can this be done short of introspection of the noetic dimension of the experience? If I cognize 'red' I must be able to discern that I am not imagining it, that in short the noema is not a predicate of my mind. Descartes found no ground whatsoever to justify such a procedure, and, to further complicate matters, suggested the possibility of a secret mind of which the noema could be predicated. To illustrate this point Peirce chooses what is perhaps a more convenient noema—anger—noting that while it is I who am angry, it is about something that I am angry. And so if a man is angry, "a little reflection will serve to show that this anger consists in his saying to himself, 'this thing is vile, abominable, etc.' and it is rather a work of returning reason to say 'I am angry' " (5.247). But such a reflection must be able to distinguish among the experiences of anger, pretending anger, love–hate feelings, and the memory of anger, for, as argued previously, there is nothing in the 'anger' noema to indicate in what particular mode it is being experienced. To this Peirce might reply that he wishes to characterize the intentionality of anger, not as reflectively analyzed into noesis and noema, but as presented to consciousness in pure experience. Such a distinction seems to beg the question, however, for it is open to question whether or not direct experiences can be distinguished from experiences reflected upon, and surely Peirce has already given us reasons for doubting the standing of the former. He is willing, in any case, to maintain that in the act of abstracting there must be noemata that 'intend' extra-mental objects and only later are seen as mental noemata: "Hence, the knowledge of the power of abstracting may be inferred from abstract objects . . . " (5.248).

The main hurdle he must now face is that of showing how such noemata intend objects that are external facts. Even if we grant the force of the intentionality argument, we are still left with the problem of showing that the noemata are 'derived' from external facts. He has shown that there is no noesis without noema, and no noema not intentionally connected with an actual or would-be subject, but he has not shown that these subjects are external facts. In the refutation of idealism Kant admits that to prove that inner experience depends upon outer experience is in no way to prove the reality of the latter (B279), and so we must conclude that if Peirce thought that he had proved more than this he was mistaken. It is plausible, however, to think that he made no such mistake and intended that his discussion be taken in no sense broader than Kant's. Perhaps the best evidence of this can be found in the fact that he thought it necessary to redefine the concept of reality in such a way as to preclude a naive understanding of a noema based directly upon an external fact.

At this point, Peirce was ready to present the cornerstone of his reflections of the past several years—that there is no thought except in signs (5.250). Having shown that all knowledge of cognition requires reference to external facts (of some sort), he now argues that whatever is of the sort of an external fact is a *sign* to thought—hence all knowledge of cognition requires reference to signs. But to make reference to signs is to think of signs, and so to think of a sign is to use a sign to refer to a sign. It is here that Peirce's previous rejection of an incognizable thought, that is, a thought once had yet impossible to re-cognize, comes into play. For if such a thought were possible, it would be a thought that itself could not be thought, and so would be a thought not a sign at the same time. But Peirce rules out such a possibility, and from this goes on to show (5.253) that "every thought must address itself to some other, must determine some other, since that is the essence of a sign." A sign must have relation and representation, and out of this comes both the intending of one thought by another and the interpretation of the former by the latter.

If all cognitions are in signs, are there also signs of the incognizable? Such a sign would amount to a cognition of the incognizable. Naturally, such a possibility is eliminated if it is held that all actual and possible cognitions are in signs, and that all signs are cognized further in signs, *ad infinitum*. But perhaps Peirce found such an argument by itself a bit facile. Something more was required, namely, to establish that *reality* was exclusively comprised of what is cognized or cognizable, and this he did by showing that the idea of the incognizable was self-contradictory (5.257); the idea of the not-cognizable is like '*A*, not-*A*' in the sense that if the incognized is even thought-of it must be cognized. It becomes clear how Peirce's treatment of cognition in terms of signs facilitates this argument. A sign, in the simplest sense, need have only the slightest material quality and yet must still have full demonstrative application. Thus, cognition need not be comprehension, and Peirce is not committed to the view that the incognizable need be known fully in order to be cognized at all.

But perhaps there is an incognizable reality in the fuller sense of comprehension, a reality we cannot fully know. The postulation of such a reality would have to be at best hypothetical, but even here, Peirce holds, we are faced with a contradiction. For if the business of a hypothesis is to delineate an *explanans* it must do so with some *explanandum* in mind, but it must do so in a manner in which the *explanans* is more intelligible than the *explanandum*. But in the case of the hypothesis that there is an incognizable reality, clearly the latter condition is not satisfied, and the former may only be vaguely met, if at all. What, after all, is the *explanandum* of the hypothesis that there is a thing-in-itself? The existence of error is not sufficient, for this could be explained by assuming that not all of reality has been cognized.

The theoretical groundwork of the new sign-oriented revision of the older metaphysical system has now been laid. We have seen that in the course of his arguments Peirce has been forced to open up new areas of research, his own thought—like that of sign activity itself in general—growing and developing in breadth and implication. It may be worthwhile, then, to pause and note in what manner the 1868-69 papers on intuition either sharpen older notions or present new ones.

We find in these papers a reconfirmation of Peirce's idealism, which, in this context, involves the view that all reality is mediatable and entails the rejection of the view that there could be something ultimate and unanalyzable (5.265). The rejection of Cartesian foundationalism leads directly, in his view, to this idealism (5.310), which in turn sheds light on the operation of the relation between probabilistic inference and reality (5.353). With the theory of reality we find Peirce breaking new ground. If all reality is cognizable, then it follows that if something is real, it is increasingly likely to become known *as long as knowledge grows*. The latter assumption, new to the argument here considered, hearkens back the earlier notion of time as 'room' for new experience. Now Peirce directly relates time and thought: "There is no exception, therefore, to the law that every thought-sign is translated or interpreted in a subsequent one, unless it be that all thought comes to an abrupt and final end in death" (5.284). Thought is an isomorphism of time in that it is a "continuous process" and a "growing process" (5.284). But growth implies a time's arrow, one supplying a criterion of growth through time. This larger question is noted by Peirce in these papers (5.330) as not directly related to the central question of the inferential nature of cognition. Assuming, then, that knowledge does grow, it follows that one way to characterize the real is to say that it is whatever is or will be an object of knowledge. This systematic cognizability of reality pushed Peirce yet further into newer areas. Reality need only be cognized by minds in an aggregate sense, by a *community* of knowers (5.265, 5.311), and does not depend for its knowability on the action of this or that mind. Nothing in the definition of reality as cognizability restricts cognizability to any particular mind.

Peirce was led to the notion of a community of knowers from yet another direction. Perhaps the inferential process not only fails to make contact with reality, but distorts that reality by its very action, with the result that it is never reality that is cognized, but only some distorted shadow of it. Now if this is possible, then either this distortion itself is discoverable, and so reality is still cognizable, or else the distortion cannot be detected. But if the latter, then all men do and will continue to suffer systematic illusion, and so all men will come to agree as a community upon this illusion as what they mean by 'reality'. But this is precisely what Peirce considers reality (5.352). Cognizability of reality by a community, then, allows him to meet this difficulty by a redefinition of reality. And yet almost at once he began seeking a stronger guarantee that the community come in contact with reality as normally understood.

It is important to note at this point that Peirce was saying more than that minds seek truth because of curiosity or wonderment. In attempting to establish a link between the logical and psychological, he was attempting to argue that minds are teleologically disposed toward knowledge of reality. It is on this point that the systematic cognizability of reality must stand or fall. This view forced Peirce to speculate about the structure of mind. It is not enough to hold that the mind involves mental action, and that thoughts are temporal events of mind (5.288). Teleology also requires *guided* activity. In one sense "the mind is a sign developing according to the laws of inference" (5.313), but in another it is something wider and deeper than consciousness (5.284). No doubt Peirce considered this a topic for later consideration, but the assumption is there nonetheless, and at the very outset of the series: "Now it is a known law of the mind, that when phenomena of an extreme complexity are presented, which yet would be reduced to *order* or mediate simplicity by application of a certain conception, that conception sooner or later arises in application to those phenomena" (5.223). By itself this is no defense of teleology, but it indicates that in these arguments Peirce was already assuming the existence of such a 'law'.

Another important feature of the teleological view is the manner in which Peirce linked mental action with other forms of action. If the pursuit of knowledge involves more than quiescent contemplation, then the teleological view requires such a link as well. The result is an action theory of belief (5.242, 5.268), which Peirce presents as part of the argument, but which again represents a new dimension in this thought. Beliefs are to be acted upon in such a way, both internally and externally, as to remain open to the influences of the community (5.354). This enriched notion of the community has grown from that which served to define the simple aggregation of minds, and this only for the purpose of rendering a general account of reality, to that of something guided by a *telos*. But nothing Peirce had claimed about the nature of the community in these papers justified this view, and he no doubt knew this. For the papers close on a melancholy note, referring to the extinction of community and of all mind whatsoever. The problem of extinction "is single and supreme, and ALL is at stake upon it." And so the "hope of success" is a sentiment "rigidly demanded by logic" (5.357).

Peirce was hardly likely to have been satisfied with such slim hope. Even in these papers, in his defense of Scholastic Realism, we can see a halting attempt to establish a deeper congeniality of mind and reality. "Since no cognition of ours is absolutely determinate," Peirce announced, "generals must have a real existence" (5.312). He may have reasoned that if what is not completely determinate involves generality, then cognition does involve generality, inasmuch as it is not completely determinate. But whatever involves cognition can itself be cognized; therefore generality can indeed be cognized. But this is only one part of the solution. The problems before him grew vaster with each reformulation of his metaphysical theory. Although Peirce was still a young man of thirty, now setting out to make his way in the world, he would find less time in the coming years to devote himself to more than scattered fragments and implications of his overall vision of reality and of the mind that knows it.

Part Two
(1870-1884)

The Metaphysics of Experience

Chapter
IV
Teleological Thought

It is indispensible that a metaphysician be a person of many talents, but it is also likely that the possession of many talents eventually deflects the zeal for metaphysical architectonic. Such was the case with Peirce between the years 1869 and 1885 or so. Unlike the previous fifteen years, during which time he devoted himself fairly continuously to metaphysical theory and to closely related issues, the next fifteen or more years were to be primarily devoted to experimental science and to logic proper. These were also to be years taken up with the concerns of love and family and with the pressures from those around him to set about to make something of himself. By 1887, however, he was ready to give up any plans for an orthodox career and so retired to his newly built home in Milford, Pennsylvania.

It may not be far from the truth to say that during this period Peirce added very little, with respect to problems of philosophical foundations, to what he had achieved hitherto. And it may have been that the often celebrated fertilization of ideas of the Metaphysical Club in the early 1870's were for him very much less than that. The doubt–belief theory of inquiry, which is often singled out as the major contribution of this period, had already been articulated several years earlier, primarily in the form of asides within the papers on intuition. It is thus more likely that Peirce tried these ideas out on the members of the circle—Chauncy Wright, Nicholas St. John Green, William James, Oliver Wendell Holmes, and others—than that he developed them out of the encounters of the group. And having now followed the course of his speculations from early youth, we can be assured that Peirce had much to share with the members of this literate circle.

1. Thought and Manifestation

Between 1869 and 1876 Peirce wrote comparatively little on metaphysics. What we find instead are some of the early speculations peeking out at us from the book reviews written for *The Nation* and other periodicals. In the review of Noah Porter's *The Human Intellect*, for example, we find the suggestion that one result of a unified theory of cognition would be to show that there is no distinction between the activity of mind proper and a reflection upon that activity for the purposes of studying mind.[1] It is clear, then, that to Peirce one of the reasons for the unified theory of inference was to establish the possibility of metaphysical speculation without resorting to intellectual intuition, while taking care at the same time not to undermine the legitimacy of his own argument from within—as in the case of the materialistic psychologists, whose philosophic method should have been rendered impossible by their very conclusions. Here we are reminded once more of the early speculations on the foundations of metaphysics. In the earlier writings he had concluded that the threefold nature of metaphysics, and the irreducibility thereof, derived from the transcendental nature of the categories of *I, It,* and *Thou;* now the unity of metaphysics could be established if a theory unifying the fundamental conceptions with the processes of thought justifying them could be established. And this is what the sign-theory of thought was supposed to accomplish.

Peirce used a review of James Mills's *Analysis of the Phenomenon of the Human Mind* to argue against nominalism by showing that the associationists had not given a clear, non-question-begging account of the notion of resemblance in their theories of mind.[2] "The doctrine that an idea is the copy of a sensation," he wrote, "has obviously not been derived from exact observation."[3] And in his review of Henry James, Sr.'s *The Secret of Swedenborg* for *The North American Review*, we have evidence that Peirce was increasingly convinced that questions of reality raised earlier could be settled by assuming cognizability to have as its complement a non-ideal feature in reality itself, a feature he called *manifestability*. There he wrote:

> But if an underlying being is essential to existence, no less is manifestation essential to being. It can make no difference whatever whether a thing is or is not, if it is never to any mind to give any sign of its being. Hence, to *be* without being manifested is a kind of being which does not differ from its negative, but is a meaningless form of words.[4]

Here already is the pragmatic maxim clearly stated, and in such a manner as to display its role in the overall metaphysical project.

In his lengthy review of *The Works of George Berkeley*, also published in *The North American Review*, Peirce continued to refine his notion of reality and his understanding of the realist/nominalist controversy.[5] We can see in this review his increasing awareness of the necessity of a pervasive teleological force influencing the universe generally and the workings of cognition specifically: "To assert that there are external things which can be known only as exerting a power on our sense, is nothing different from asserting that there is a general *drift* in the history of human thought which will lead it to one general agreement, one catholic consent" (8.12). Also strongly pronounced in this review is the opinion that cognition emerges out of particularity and determination, the 'ideal' first of the earlier papers, but now already containing generality within it. Sensation sets mental action in motion, but only so that generality as *habitualiter* becomes *actualiter* (8.13, 8.18); and this generality in the form of intelligible conceptions is genuinely real, if by 'real' we mean what is to be known in a final unanimous opinion by a community of minds. Even more striking is Peirce's interpretation of this theory of reality as "a highly practical and common-sense position" (8.16). For having once settled upon the definitions of reality and truth, we can have a good idea of how to realize them. If generality depended upon this or that consciousness for its reality, it could not be truly general, and so must exist independently of consciousness. But scientific research is precisely the study of the manifestation of being in light of the influence of generality, so that the theory of reality depends upon science as the manner by which questions of truth come to be settled and the real comes to be fully known. The 'practical' dimension of this method involves the process of reaching a consensus among opinions. If generality is to be expressed, it must be formulated in language for the purpose of communication; experience must become externalized to be shared, and only then is anything like a final opinion possible. For this reason Peirce rejected Berkeley's suggestion that abstractions have no reality unless they can be *internally* experienced. In its place he suggests an *external* criterion for attaining consensus, a pragmatic maxim in yet another form designed to overcome "the deceits of language." He writes, "Do things fulfil the same function practically? Then let them be signified by the same word. Do they not? Then let them be distinguished" (8.33). We should note that this method of making our ideas clear was designed for the purpose of attaining truth *only in light of the previous ensemble of problems and theories.* It was never intended to stand by itself, something he would continually insist upon in the last decade of his life (see Chapter VII below). In its original context it had nothing to do with operationalism or conventionalism, and certainly nothing to do with nominalism. These interpretations have generally derived from extrapolations of writings taken out of context, and in some cases from imprecise wording in the pivotal essay "How to Make Our Ideas Clear," an imprecision for which Peirce would later "damn" himself. He had remained on course in his quest for an answer to the riddle of the sphinx, except that he had come to realize that "a difficult question cannot be expected to reach solution until it takes some practical form" (8.38). And so he turned more of his attention to logic of science, and, within that, to the logic of action and inquiry.

In his earlier writings the criterion of communal consensus was not clearly articulated. We must assume that he never would have considered truth to have been settled by majority vote, though he was sure that however it was settled upon, the majority would in sufficient time attest to it. In the Berkeley review he observes without elaboration that Berkeley never realized "that *an object's independence of our thought about it* is constituted by its connection with experience in general" (8.30). This is not at all the same thing as saying that independence is what a generally held opinion settles upon, for that opinion may be plainly false. The community, it would seem, becomes linked to truth, not because it is a community, but because as a community it is best suited to attaining "experience in general." The question of numbers of minds is not what is crucial here. One man may just as well be a 'community' if he lives long enough, converses with himself, and is curious enought of the time. In an unpublished notebook (MS. 587) Peirce wrote around 1870: "By truth concerning a thing we do not mean how any man is affected by a thing. Nor how a majority is affected. But how a man would be affected after sufficient experience, discussion, and reasoning." This result would have to follow from the realistic theory of inquiry Peirce was setting out, and from the "magical" influence of probabilistic inferences upon the attainment of truth. Simply by having a sufficient amount of experience, the chemistry of cognition is set into motion, and over a period of time, during which idiosyncrasy is extirpated, truth is the result.

A comprehensive statement of his various theories of cognition and reality was begun, but soon put aside, in 1873 in the form of a logic text, one of a number Peirce set out to write during his lifetime. He probably decided upon such a work on the basis of his encounters in the Metaphysical Club, and evidently read portions of the work to its members.[6] Four methods of achieving consensus are described in these fragmentary chapters: the method of *obstinacy* (the refusal to criticize one's beliefs); the method of *persecution* (the refusal to let others criticize your beliefs); the method of *public opinion* (the refusal to criticize beliefs of a group); and the method of *reasoning* (the refusal of any refusal to criticize any belief). The first three methods thwart the *telos*, or now "Fate" (7.334), of truth and so no matter how predominant, in the long run can produce no lasting knowledge; the last method is geared for the long run, and so gives investigation the time required to test questions and to make the requisite number of inferences. What is of greater interest in this work, however, is Peirce's attempt to come to grips with the question of the automatic nature of inferential reasoning. He had previously rejected the idea that a logic machine could as well satisfy his theory of mind, and now attempted to say why. Any inference requires not simply two or more signs related through some mode of signification; it requires an awareness of the inferential process itself. In fact, even when two ostensibly similar thoughts are merely compared, the comparison itself is not involved in the noemata compared; yet the comparison must be known of itself in order that comparison take place, and this means that "there is a possibility of some mental process besides observation" (7.332).

We might wonder at this point whether Peirce had abandoned his view of only a few years earlier that there is no knowledge of noetic acts except by reference to noemata. Now it seems as though the discredited Cartesian subjectivity is reemerging. How could there be control over the very process of investigation (7.346) if that control is not separate from the canons of investigation and is apodictic and intuitive instead? Either the normative comments about the "best" method of investigation are entirely unnecessary, and the law of mental action works of its own accord, or else it does not; and if it does not, then the whole theory of cognition requires a meta-theory of cognition to justify it not only more fully, but also more along traditional psychologistic lines. In order to overcome this "paradox" Peirce decided that consciousness must take place over a duration of time and not at once (7.350–51). The investigative process, then, could be guided by a conscious watchful eye as it unfolds. But he had already considered this guiding element in his discussion of *attention* as the factor that completely links the elements inferred with those inferring.

The most obvious objection to the importance of this sort of knowledge of mental processes as providing a guiding element in inquiry is that those who use distorted methods of inquiry are just as aware of these processes as those who use rational inquiry; indeed, in many cases they are highly aware of them in order to be in a position to effectuate their goals. Even in obstinacy there may be an awareness that reasoning of some sort has taken place, even while there is an unwillingness to let it continue. In the earlier papers Peirce evidently did not think such distortions were relevant to a general theory of mental action, being content at the time to show that the general form of inference could not be violated even if one wished. What he should have realized was that it was not control he was seeking, but continuity. If a logic machine possessed continuity it would be no different from the 'alive' thought of mental action. When Peirce finally described how consciousness could exist through time, he did so in terms of noemata:

What is present to the mind during the whole of an interval
of time is something generally consisting of what there was
in common in what was present to the mind during parts of
that interval. And this may be the same with what is present
to the mind during any interval of time, or if not the same,
at least similar—that is, the two may be such that they have
much in common. (MS. 377)

Unfortunately, such a continuity does not establish the continuity
of an inference whereby different *relata* are linked in a continuous
inference; it simply describes the continuity of a consciousness of
some single noema, and it also does not establish how one can discern
the similarity at issue here. Peirce's goal might have been better
served had he characterized notions such as 'control', 'awareness',
and 'consciousness' as epiphenomena explained by the theory of
thought-signs. He did not require a thought *behind* thought to explain
it, but he did require a theory of continuity of thought-signs, and,
if the work of later years is any indication, he eventually realized
this. The law of the mind postulated earlier should have required an
explanation in terms of general metaphysical categories, not in
terms of more features of mind itself. Instead, he took consciousness
to be the "matter of thought" (7.352), that which was held in common
by similar thoughts, and, by implication, must have considered
the theory of thought-signs to concern the form of thought only.
But if there was any tenet close to his heart at the time, it would
have been that there is no quality of reasoning thought, but only of
cognitions of a lower grade; thought comprised only relations, and
so was exclusively formal. Hence all that was required for an account
of it was a formal continuity established through the sign function,
in short, a *semiotic causation* which Peirce himself noted in the Logic
of 1873 (7.353). Why he thought on some occasions that another
source of continuity was required must remain open to conjecture.

The revival of the early notion of manifestation, evidenced in the
Swedenborg review, is continued in the Logic of 1873. Here it is
argued that to say that something is real is to say that it can manifest
itself as real (MS. 372). This is what is implied in the process of
scientific experimentation, where circumstances are contrived in
order to have something reveal itself in a certain systematic fashion.
All cognition, then, may be looked upon as a form of experimentation

producing experience and oriented toward some future result. But if we model cognition generally after experimentation, thereby assuming that it too has a telic dimension, we are forced to explain how sensation (as cognition) is also experimental in nature. Any cognition has a future orientation, a role it plays in a larger context of thought and action. But this does not mean that there is a single course to follow, a single result from the experience of any given sensation. Instead, Peirce postulated two orientations or directions of the stream of thought (MS. 368), one to the past and one to the future. A given sensation, no matter how novel, is measured by the conceptions of past experience, and it is the *combination* of past conceptions and present sensations that establishes an interpretation of possible future experience.

The cognitions of a tyrant have as their interpretant the unshakeable conviction that all obey him, and so all experience becomes measured by him in such a fashion. To a "logical mind" (7.358), on the other hand, the interpretant of experience is a unity of consistency manifesting truth. In both cases habits are formed, but only in the latter are the habits close to the model of science; in both cases the actions and habits are rational in the light of the accepted interpretants, but only in the latter is their rationality capable of modification in light of new experience. For this reason, Peirce requires a reality independent of personal thought. Without it there could be no practical difference between the methods of persecution and reasoning. Each would be subject to certain *idola* determined by the nature of the interpretants accepted in each case, and would amount to dogmatism in either case. When Peirce makes this point—writing, "thought is rational only so far as it recommends itself to a possible future thought. Or in other words the rationality of thought lies in its reference to a possible future" (7.361)—he does not distinguish between the future of a tyrant and of a scientist, unless it be that the future has in store for the tyrant something he is not prepared for, while the scientist is prepared for any eventuality. For this an uncontrollable reality is required to serve as a basis for distinguishing methods of mental action. And here once more is a vector pointing beyond the theory of cognition, one incapable of explanation short of metaphysics. Reference to a possible future by itself cannot serve to distinguish which method is "better" unless there is a normative character to the very events of history. An inductive approach to this character is plainly unsuitable, for that would be to test the claim in question, that the rationality of thought lies in its reference to the future, by reference to the past. There must be something in the future, then, that guarantees the success of the method of reasoning and the long-run failure of all other methods. But Peirce had not yet taken up this question in any detail.

During the mid-1870's Peirce put aside metaphysics almost altogether; only some brief notes on idealism (MS. 935) have been found among his unpublished papers. Instead, he wrote and published on mathematics, cartography, chronometry, astronomy, and the physical sciences. He had been to Europe as the first American delegate to the International Geodetic Conference in 1875, spending the winter in Paris and returning in July of 1876. At some time during this period his attention turned to the subject of political economy. In his Berkeley review he had briefly remarked that the law of natural selection had a "precise analogue in another realm of law of supply and demand" (8.36). In September 1874 he was trying out such ideas on political economy, relating "three categories," which in this case were dependence of demand on price, dependence of cost on demand, and dependence of price on demand, cost, and other circumstances (MS. 1569). While the remaining portions of this brief essay investigate these relations in mathematical and econometric terms, what is of interest to us here is the fact that scant as the work is, it fairly clearly indicates Peirce's continuing interest in extending his triadic metaphsyics beyond logic, semiotic, and psychology, applying it in the social realm as well. Subsequently, of course, he would do just that.

2. The Logic of Probabilistic Inference

By late 1877 the first of the six-paper series, "Illustrations of the Logic of Science," appeared in *The Popular Science Monthly*. The first two papers of the series, "The Fixation of Belief" and "How to Make Our Ideas Clear" were probably not looked upon very highly by Peirce himself. While they no doubt seemed exciting and well-written to his readers, they may have seemed rather discursive to him. We can only speculate that he had been encouraged about the importance of this unsystematic approach through his encounters in the Metaphysical Club, and he might have thought of these papers as first steps in introducing a wider audience to the rigors of triadic metaphysics. It is far less likely that these papers, cut off as they are from the categories, could have signaled a rejection of the triadic approach or even a lapse into psychologism. In the remaining four papers of the series—"The Doctrine of Chances," "The Probability of Induction," "The Order of Nature," and "Deduction, Induction, and Hypothesis"—Peirce supplies several new pieces to this unfolding logic-of-science puzzle, now in its third version, and fits others more tightly into place. The general theme of the papers is the logic of probabilistic inference, but this theme is taken up within the context of the following overall question: What conditions in mind and nature make possible inferences from the known to the unknown? We recall that the door of philosophy is to be unlocked by the answer to this question; and here Peirce adopts Kant's answer to the question of how synthetic *a priori* judgments are possible for the explanation of synthetic judgments *a posteriori* (2.690). A synthetic inference is possible only on the grounds that the conditions necessary for the formation of the inference are necessarily related to the conditions that constitute the fact inferred. The very formation of an inference, in this view, is evidence that reality operates upon mind in some systematic fashion. In order for the inference to be drawn in the form 'All beans in the bag are purple' on the basis of having picked two handfuls of purple beans, perception must be able to identify the beans according to color, memory must recall the sequence of samples, and muscles must extend, grasp, and contain the sample. Now the same organizing conditions must operate in nature as well: colors must not change, nor the beans themselves, nor must the bag fail to hold them. Such an illustration (from 2.691) seems hardly enlightening on first reading. For Peirce it was a first step in finding a way to unlock the door of philosophy, which for the first time he tells us requires nothing less than "a general philosophy of the universe" (2.690); only this can solve the "strange paradox" of probabilistic inference.

We can see how the other problems considered in the series, those centering around chance and order, tie in with this main question. In a universe of pure chance no unifying conditions would be possible, while in a universe of pure order no inferences would be made from the known to unknown. Instead, our universe must be a combination of order and disorder, the latter sufficient to create uneasiness and inquiry, the former sufficient to satisfy it. Rather than begin with some *a priori* principles upon which to base his proposed general theory of the universe, Peirce chooses instead to search the processes of synthetic inference (science in general) for the evidence of the unifying conditions. That evidence, we are told in "The Doctrine of Chances," can be found in the way science investigates *continuous quantities* (2.646). Rather than beginning with an *a priori* configuration of descriptive categories into which all physical phenomena are to be placed, the scientist chooses certain interesting characters of a subject and then seeks to extend their application into other areas; guided by the notion of continuity, he seeks intermediate cases of his subject and in the process comes to modify his original characters in light of the insights afforded by them. And so the scientist "builds up from the study of Nature a new general conception of the character in question. He obtains, for example, an idea of a leaf which includes every part of the flower, and an idea of a vertebra which includes the skull. I surely need not say much to show what a logical engine is here" (2.646). In this manner the idea of continuity is "a powerful aid to the formation of true and fruitful conceptions" (2.646). It ties in with probabilistic inference in two ways. First, probability itself is a continuous quantity that varies by degree, and second, a 'logical mind' that embraces probabilistic inference is always willing to entertain the possibility of a revision of an inference in order better to approximate the truth. Analogous to the notion of a fixed species, which threatens a continuity of forms, mental obstinacy threatens the continuity of arguments. Part of the commitment Peirce requires to an unlimited community of investigators implicitly involves a commitment to a systematic revision of arguments. One of the logical sentiments— hope in the unlimited continuation of intellectual activity (2.655) —requires that intellectual activity be carried on continuously. This means that for any argument, there will be some mind pondering it critically. It would destroy the notion of such a union of minds if by a community Peirce only required that there be a continuity of despots, each dogmatizing without cessation. In short, the notion of continuity guides not only the individual logical mind, but the mind of the community as well.

According to the criterion of clarity set out in this series of papers, a clear idea is one with conceivable sensible effects, and so a clear idea of continuity must be possible in terms of specific operations. Such clarity becomes possible if "synthetic inference is founded upon a classification of facts, not according to their characters, but according to the manner of obtaining them" (2.692). If a set, P, of operations (p_1, p_2, p_3, ... p_n) is employed to discover a given fact, F, then whenever P is employed, those facts with characters relevantly similar to F will be discovered. Thus in order to investigate an analogue of F, what is required is that the operations of P be modified in some continuous manner. In the sampling of beans from a bag the number sampled can be modified by the selecting process of grasping one, a few, many, or all. The formal study of the manipulation of scientific operations would be accurately called the 'economy of research', and it is not surpising that by early 1877, if not before, Peirce's attention had already turned to this question (7.139–57). From his experimental work on determining the gravitational constant he conceived of the problem of having to decide the most economic direction of the manipulation of operations:

> The doctrine of economy, in general, treats of the relations between utility and cost. That branch of it which relates to research considers the relations between the utility and the cost of diminishing the probable error of our knowledge. Its main problem is, how, with a given expenditure of money, time, and energy, to obtain the most valuable addition to our knowledge. (7.140)

The earlier question concerning the direction or *telos* of knowledge once more emerges, though in a different form. The economy of systematic research is but one facet of the overall economy of a cognizing being. It attempts to recreate in a conventional manner what is already highly institutionalized in the structures of organized entities. The utility of knowledge is saved from subjectivity by the fact that it is to be measured by its "capability of being combined with other knowledge so as to enable us to calculate how we should act" (7.142). Out of successful action comes habit, and with this, belief. Hence utility is not a whim of choice, but a measure of what we believe to be valuable in knowledge. If beliefs were cut off from action, there would be no way in which action could correct the process of research by bringing about a redesign of the program. Obstinacy would prevail and experimentation would be fruitless. "That belief gradually tends to fix itself under the influence of inquiry is, indeed, one of the facts with which logic sets out"—so Peirce concludes (2.693).

The economy of research, then, returns us to the question of the conditions unifying the world and the inquirer, or, in other words, to 'the philosophy of the universe'. This is the topic of the fifth paper, "The Order of Nature," where Peirce argues that a world entirely governed by chance would be one in which neither the occurrence nor non-occurrence of characters could be prohibited, and consequently would be a totally systematic world. No logically possible combination of characters could be prohibited unless there were some uniformity continuously prohibiting it; without such a uniformity all possible combinations would be not only possible, but actual as well. Furthermore, no precise combination of characters would be repeated in two or more substances, and so a purely chaotic universe would contain only monads. But, Peirce continues, not only is such a pure-chance universe very much unlike the universe in which we live, with its uniformities and natural kinds, but it can be shown on purely logical grounds that for any two (or more) objects there is always some character they share in common (6.402).

Such an argument is a provocative anticipation of statistical mechanics as first formulated by J. Willard Gibbs, whereby the universe is seen to consist of elementary particles each possessing all possible degrees of freedom. The difference, however, lies in the fact that the degrees of freedom in the latter case are restricted to those subject to the constraints of physics, while in Peirce's argument the 'characters' can be of any logical nature, including negations. This presents a problem, namely, how to establish that the merely possible is necessarily actual, a problem not unknown to possible-world logicians even today. In a pure-chance world there need be no sufficient (uniform) reason why a given character does not appear; it is just as possible that it does not as that it does. As Peirce assumes, in an orderly world the non-occurrence of a character could be construed as the result of order, but it does not follow that if a character does not occur, then an orderly process indeed prohibits it. A disorderly process may produce the same result. In general it cannot be stated that "every case of the non-occurrence of a combination of characters would constitute a uniformity in Nature" (6.400) unless it be further assumed (1) that any non-occurrence has only one specific prohibition (which acts uniformly) and (2) that in the long run a pure-chance world must turn up all combination of characters. Appropriately, Peirce may then reply that when speaking of the order of the universe the second assumption is not unreasonable to make. As for the first, however, there may be many chaotic prohibitions to a non-occurrence, prohibitions in no way amounting to a uniformity, and so not every case of non-occurrence would constitute a uniformity. It would only be a sequence of prohibitors of similar character that could lead to such a uniformity, and so uniformity would have to be assumed at the outset.

The upshot of Peirce's argument is to establish the plausibility of conceiving of our world as an interplay of order and disorder:

> When a quantity of letters are poured out of a bag, the appearance of disorder is due to the circumstance that the phenomena are only partly fortuitous. The laws of space are supposed, in that case, to be rigidly preserved, and there is also a certain amount of regularity in the formation of the letters. The result is that some elements are orderly and some are disorderly, which is precisely what we observe in the actual world. (6.401)

Order, then, is required as a condition for the possibility of a judgment that something is disorderly. While Peirce does not explicitly note this, such a notion is implicit in his argument that a mind must be orderly enough to categorize an event as disorderly and that this can only be possible if there are some features of the event which facilitate categorization. The letters cannot scatter too far or too fast, for example. And the mind must retain a description of the event from start to finish. This orderly interlocking of mind and nature is more accurately the implication of Peirce's analysis, at least with respect to its metaphysical implications. In this respect he notes that "so long as we regard characters abstractly, without regard to their relative importance, etc., there is no possibility of a more or less degree of orderliness in the world, the whole system of relationship between the different characters being given by mere logic" (6.405). Relative importance is importance to some mind, and from such a relation can come the degree of orderliness in a contextual sense. Consider two worlds, one highly disorderly but known by a highly orderly mind (a Maxwellian Demon), and another highly orderly but known by a highly disorderly mind. Both worlds may contextually contain the same degree of order for the mind residing in it. From the fact that any world must seem organized to some degree if there is some mind to know it, it would follow that a world of total chance or total order would not conduce to mental activity (6.406). It would be a world, to recall earlier work once again, "too much a system to be systematic."

The degree of orderliness, then, can be translated into a degree of mental orderliness. As the latter increases, so does the orderliness of nature itself. At the "very vanishing-point of intelligence" the world becomes total disorder, and so "the actual world is almost a chance-medley to the mind of a polyp. The interest which the uniformities of nature have for an animal measures his place in the scale of intelligence" (6.406). The 'interest' of an organism results when its intelligence is more highly organized than its simplest experiences, its sensations. Out of this interest, induction, hypothesis, and inquiry in general is provoked. But in making inquiry a contextual response of organism to environment, Peirce is both arguing the now familiar theme that cognition has an automatic dimension and raising the problem of having to explain how, if this is so, cognition can be misled. Induction can be erroneously carried out, as when we choose the characters investigated after a sequence of events has been observed. Peirce does not attempt either to explain this away or to explain why there is such error. But he does argue that certain inductions "present an approach to universality" (6.416) in that they result from operations of inquiry that cannot be thought of as accidental, that are, in short, automatic. The continuity of space is both something inferred and yet something not explainable in terms of the simple mechanisms of cognition. Such a mechanism, including the physiology of the eye and central nervous system, is comprised of discrete entities having discrete functions, and could not explain the perception of the continuity of space unless it were predisposed to produce the inference automatically. Without assuming such an inferential disposition in perception there would be no way to explain spatiality, so that we must conclude that "certain relations subsist between the excitations of different nerve-points, and these constitute the premises upon which the hypothesis of space is founded, and from which it is inferred" (6.416).

How are these relations to be explained? Peirce's answer invokes the fact that the mind is "strongly adapted to the comprehension of the world" (6.417), a fact itself explained by natural selection (6.418). In the series of papers previously considered Peirce had suggested natural selection as the cause of the mind's capacity to employ probabilistic inference (5.341). Now it becomes clear that if the key unlocking the door of philosophy is to be found in a general philosophy of the universe, then general philosophy will be in some sense evolutionary in nature. In "The Order of Nature" Peirce takes the first steps in this direction. He is clearly not satisfied with an explanation exclusively in terms of natural selection, however, for natural selection may adequately explain instinctive reactions, but is less enlightening when it comes to what appear to be adaptive reactions, reactions in which an organism actively adapts to its environment rather than being 'selected' by it. It is to the immense advantage of an organism not only that it be able to obtain the source of its continued existence, but that it come to realize the connection between force and the relations of time, space, and mass, or, in other words, that it develop the science of physics. In this light the hypothesis of natural selection is inadequate and "there is some secret here which remains to be discovered" (6.418).

From Peirce's remaining speculations in "The Order of Nature" we can be led to believe that the secret must be found in some rather pervasive character in the construction of the universe. But at this point, and in the format of the series, he was not prepared to take up such an issue. Instead we are told (in seeming contradiction to earlier remarks) that we ought to presume the universe too vast to possess an all-embracing character (6.422) and that a presumption in favor of scientific principles ought to be made in any treatment of this question (6.423). And we are also told that while science and religion are at odds (6.425–26), any metaphysical theory of "the mode of being of the perfect" would not destroy "that aspiration toward the perfect which constitutes the essence of religion" (6.427). How, we might wonder, can a general theory of the universe be subject only to the mechanical principles of physical science if that theory is to be in a position to explain scientific inferences in the first place? To do this would be to base metaphysics on physics. On the other hand, Peirce is also telling us that metaphysics is a danger to religion because it cannot comprehend the full scope of reality sensed by the human heart. We may then wonder how a general philosophy of the universe could be possible in such an intellectual climate. Again, the format of the series—the fact that the papers were directed to an audience of "popular scientists" and not to fellow philosophers—may account for the lack of rigor in such articulations and in the rhetorical nature of Peirce's remarks, though to some degree, Peirce himself may have had sympathy with such objections, knowing as he must have what such a general philosophy would require. Curiously, no mention of semiotic notions is made in the series. Without the semiotic framework he would be in the circular difficulty just noted, but with the framework serving as a bridge between physics and metaphysics the circle could be broken, and a premature appeal to faith prevented.

In the final paper of the series, "Deduction, Induction, and Hypothesis," we find a clearer formulation of the relation between the three forms of inference and the isomorphism between the logical and psychological realms. Each form of inference is now a "logical formula" of a physiological and psychological process. Habits are formed inductively, sensations and feelings hypothetically, and attention and volition deductively (2.643). And from a combination of all three cognitive capacities in the form of inquiry, the three formulae determine the three procedures of science and so afford a means of classifying the sciences as well (2.644).

By 1878 or so Peirce must have been more aware than ever of what would be required to construct a fully developed theory of the universe based on his theory of categories. In this respect the *Popular Science* series, although not presenting a conceptual advance over previous work, must have made clear to him that the work on categories of the late 1860's required a framework of the sort he had speculated upon in his college years. A general theory of nebular evolution, noted by Peirce in the paper on the order of nature (6.420), was advanced by his father, Benjamin Peirce, in six Lowell Lectures delivered in early 1879. Peirce probably heard these lectures either at that time or when they were given again a year later—the year of his father's death—at the Peabody Institute in Baltimore. Later printed as *Ideality in the Physical Sciences,* these lectures present an evolutionary theory of the universe, beginning with undifferentiated chaos and culminating in spiritual individuality. In them the elder Peirce argues (1) that the evolutionary process is mathematically structured through a "law of continuity"; (2) that the process of science is both a result of evolution and a determining agent in further evolution, the former through a natural occurrence of "unconscious induction," the latter through the transition from induction to hypothesis; and (3) that a pre-established harmony governs the entire process. Thus

> the nebular theory is, pre-eminently, a grand ideal organization of all the phenomena of the celestial universe, and embraces a complete ideal history of the inorganic world. The universe, according to that theory, commences with an all-pervading substance, in which there is no apparent structure nor division into parts, but the same monotonous uniformity throughout. Passing through innumerable transformations, it terminates in a system, whence disoganization has been wholly eliminated, and where vast multitudes of individuals, each a perfect organism in itself, are combined in indestructible harmony. In the beginning, it has the unity of monotony; in the end, it has the unity of complete organization.[7]

In general outline the younger Peirce must have concurred with his father's suggestions, but it must also have been clear to him that between the nebular hypothesis proper and the theory of spiritual evolution there was a formidably wide chasm. In effect, Benjamin Peirce's contentions, like those of Fisk and Spencer, amounted only to a suggestion that a physical theory be given normative import, and are based on a vague Pythagorean interpretation of physical laws. What is lacking is a precise conceptual apparatus sufficient to give even a rudimentary intimation of the law of continuity. This Charles Peirce had been laboring on for some time now, but it must have been clear to him, as he reflected upon his father's cosmogony, how far he had yet to go.

3. The Logic of Psychophysics

In late 1879 Peirce accepted a position as lecturer in logic at Johns Hopkins University, and had the opportunity to become part of yet another Metaphysical Club. Among its members was George Sylvester Morris, who had studied philosophy in Germany, and had returned a Hegelian modified with Aristotelian voluntarism. The speculations of Morris were but one of several stimulating influences Peirce must have encountered during the next four years. This was a period in which he might have thought that the work of the community of investigators could get well on its way. Papers on Kant, Hegel, Fichte, and Hickok were presented during this time in meetings of the club. Peirce himself presented a version of "Questions Concerning Certain Faculties Claimed for Man" on 11 November 1879; in March 1880 he discussed the relation between Kant's *Critique* and modern logic, and in 1881 he read a paper on sensory discrimination. The latter paper provides a good illustration of how Peirce took some of his earlier speculative ideas and developed them in an academic setting. The result was an article entitled "On Small Differences of Sensation" (7.21–35; see also MS. 1104), published in the *Memoirs of the National Academy of Sciences* in 1884.

With the assistance of one of his students, Joseph Jastrow, Peirce proposed to investigate the question of whether or not there is a minimum threshold below which two sensations of similar quality could no longer be distinguished one from the other. He chose for the experiment the tactile sense (pressure) and constructed an apparatus to subject the investigator's finger to differing pressures in the order of ratio of 1.005 to 1.100; he also devised a randomizing method of selecting pressures, using playing cards to guard against the mind's being able to devise hypotheses extraneous to the experience open to test (7.29). The sensory organism, once left to a 'state of nature' would, if Peirce's guess was correct, be able to tell in a surprising number of cases which of two situations involved the application of greater or lesser pressure. To Jastrow, Peirce might have appeared to be investigating a purely psychophysiological question, but to Peirce the implications of the experiment were much broader. (Twenty years later he would indicate in a draft letter to M. M. Curtis, L–107, the importance of the experiment in relation to synechism). If, as Fechner and other physiological psychologists had argued, there was a fixed ratio beneath which two sensations, though still differing in intensity, could not be discriminated, then it might appear that the basis of any discrimination at or above the fixed ratio was purely the result of a fixed intuitive grasp of the difference. Peirce had already been inclined to suspect this conclusion on the basis of his view that sensation was a form of hypothetic inference. The experiment showed by the statistical method of least squares that the probability of error of a discrimination followed a standard continuous probability curve and that even when the sensations appeared the same, the subject was still able in a majority of cases to guess correctly the greater or lesser of the two. The threshold of tactile discrimination was evidently lower than that of conscious discrimination. Peirce also found that with practice, the subjects' discriminating ability increased (7.27). From this he concluded that no fixed ratio existed, and that instead discrimination was a continuous process built into cognizing systems even beneath the threshold where it begins to be subject to the control of consciousness, attention, and concentration. He also concluded that the feedback effect of attention pushes the threshold of consciousness ever closer to an ultimate limit where no discrimination can be made because no difference exists to be discriminated. Had he wished, Peirce could have put the results in terms of a theory of signs where the series of interpretants becomes increasingly richer, "growing" as it were, and so making comparison of material sign-qualities easier.

Peirce did suggest a "highly important practical bearing" of the experiment (7.35); evidence for the possibility of a telepathic influence of one mind upon another. For if sensations and thoughts are both signs, and if the former can be cognized, reasoned upon, and discriminated—though we are hardly conscious of the process— it may be possible that the same can be said about thought-signs as well. This possibility can also be placed in the context of Peirce's previous speculations about man as a sign having an essentially inferential and 'outer' being.

While at Johns Hopkins Peirce also introduced his students to some of his long-standing views on the forms of inference and the logic of relations. The result was a work called *Studies in Logic* (1883) containing papers by Peirce and some of his students. In one of his own contributions to the volume, "A Theory of Probable Inference," we can sense a conflict between his view that nature goads cognition automatically and teleologically, and his view that in scientific investigation our inferences must be formed in such a way as to assume as little as possible of the uniformities of nature and to suspect as much as possible the instincts of mind. If we accept the latter, we may find it tempting to conclude that "nature is a far vaster and less clearly arranged repertory of fact than a census report" and that as a result "man has thus far not attained to any knowledge that is not in a wide sense either mechanical or anthropological in its nature, and it may be reasonably presumed that he never will" (2.753). This is hardly the view that the categories of nature and mind are ultimately the same, or that through the workings of a community of minds, knowledge more closely approximates truth. Such a tension, however, may be resolved, at least in part, by observing that Peirce was seeking to make the formation of scientific hypotheses as free from unnatural (dogmatic) influences as possible *precisely in order to allow nature the greatest possible influence upon mind.* The methods of sampling and defining he suggests are designed to minimize human distortion, and to check the tendency to fix belief along gratuitous lines.

It is likely that Peirce had concluded by this time that the problem with any general theory of the universe, of the sort presented by Hegel, for example, is that it corrupts the scientific process in a way that leads to self-fulfilling predictions. In a review of F. E. Abbot's *Organic Scientific Philosophy: Scientific Theism,* written for *The Nation* a few years after *Studies in Logic,* Peirce criticized Abbot's rendering of metaphysics according to foundationalist principles. Such an approach, he must have felt, left no room for a continually elaborated relation between science and theism, and he noted that "everything like uniting the members of his main distinctions by insensible gradations, by a deeper underlying unity, or by any mediating cause, except the Divine Mind which creates the relations but not the related things, is foreign to his idea."[8] In *Studies in Logic* (2.750) Peirce was clearly prepared to depart from his father's opinion that a higher power is required to understand the workings of nature. But did this mean that no general metaphysical theory could be acceptable as a framework within which to speculate upon the workings of science? Logic had always been to him the sacred ground upon which the concrete and the universal could impartially meet, but now we find him departing from an unpsychological view of logic, saying that "formal logic must not be too purely formal; it must represent a fact of psychology, or else it is in danger of degenerating into mathematical recreation" (2.710). "Very, very few are the new problems," he wrote in his review of Jevons's *Studies in Deductive Logic,* "which have ever been solved by the regular application of any system of logic."[9] Was this Peirce the Professor, grown cautious by virtue of his present responsibilities as an educator? It is not likely that, given his temperament, he would have encouraged his better students to accept a single unified theory of formal logic, and along with that an entire metaphysical theory, to which they would be subject in later years; he did not want to generate a scholasticism based on authority alone (5.517). More likely he sought to counter a simplistic view by contending that no place of pride be given any of the notions of formal logic (2.710), even though he had done just that with the categories of sign-structure years earlier. The implications of these views of logic would soon enough have sent Peirce directly into the English School, and only if he had been prepared to repudiate three decades of work in philosophy would he have accepted that.

For a number of years Peirce had been impressed by the mathematization of logic into a 'new logic', the logic of Boole and De Morgan, as a mediating logic that included a notion of continuity. It is not so much that the earlier work of the 'new list' of categories, based as it was on the subject–predicate logic, had to be abandoned,[10] as that the copula of inclusion had to be understood in the broadest possible way. De Morgan's logic of relations, then, not only allowed for 'insensible gradations', but when clearly stated could reveal an 'underlying unity' of whatever was subject to such logic.

To be able to say that two things *in any way whatsoever* related to a third are related to each other is a considerable improvement over the syllogism, wherein the copula is taken in the sense of identity or class inclusion. It is true that identity may be implied in speaking of a *something* in two or more respects, as is required in relating two things to a third, but this is the self-identity of being, not the identity of the copula of the syllogism. The copula of predication or of the sign-relation generally may take a variety of forms in the logic of relations and is not restricted to any one or few such forms. But it was not only for its generality that Peirce appreciated De Morgan's logic. "The universe," he notes (2.696), "might be all so fluid and variable that nothing should preserve its individual identity, and that no measurement should be conceivable; and still one portion might remain inclosed within a second, itself inclosed within a third, so that a syllogism would be possible." In such a situation a sufficiently general theory of relations would be able to categorize the relations possible in a fluid universe even when these relations are continually changing. For such a general theory Peirce may have had in mind a theory of relations based upon simple numerical relations. If logic *per se* does not solve new problems, the same may not be said for mathematics, and particularly for algebra. Algebra could be a system of symbols entirely independent of the meanings of the symbols involved, and for this reason alone would have been most suited to a theory of relations. Of significance to the present work is Peirce's growing interest in extending the formalist notions of De Morgan, Boole, Sylvester, Cayley, Kempe, and others from algebra, geometry, topology, the algebra of logic, etc., to a general 'algebra of metaphysics', so to speak. But before this could be done it would be necessary to establish the connection between logic and experience in a manner more precise than that of a one-sided relation between the modes of inference and psychological states.

4. THE PSYCHOPHYSICS OF LOGIC

What Peirce attempted in his 1880 paper, "On the Algebra of Logic" (3.154–251), was to present a unified picture of cognition in terms of a logical algebra. There he argued that all forms of cognition involve a process of transmission and modification. This takes the physiological form of the stimulation of the ganglion, the irritation resulting therefrom, and the relaxation resulting from the transmission of the stimulation to other ganglia. The entire process is guided by two rules: (1) that stimulation be abated, if not in some routine fashion, then by a continual modification of a nerve-structure until the circumstance is found bringing about attenuation (3.156), and (2) that the repetition of a stimulation produce a systematic method of achieving attenuation. Out of these facts a physiology of logic emerges, providing an outward expression of the modes of transmission and modification by a process Peirce would identify decades later as *hypostatic abstraction* (5.534). Modification of experience takes place, necessitating the task of linking the old with the new, the clearly known with the vaguely known, and out of this we get the study of inference. Peirce had set down at the time the fundamental guidelines of an experimentalist theory of cognition that would be given fuller expression only much later in Dewey's *Logic: the Theory of Inquiry* (1938). In Peirce's case, however, it became clear that the purpose of his approach was to discover a unified theory of logic, psychology, and metaphysics, and to present it in some sort of logical form.

The most elementary transmission relation is the logical relation of implication symbolized by $-\!\!\prec$; identity itself was composed of such a relation in the form $A -\!\!\prec B$ and $B -\!\!\prec A$. It was only, Peirce notes, the fact that in our experience the relation of identity enables us to think of reducing two things to one that leads us to think of such a relation as ultimately simple. "Accordingly," he continues, "it is more philosophical to use the copula $-\!\!\prec$ apart from all considerations of convenience. Besides, this copula is intimately related to our natural logical and metaphysical ideas; and it is one of the chief purposes of logic to show what validity those ideas have" (3.173, n.2). To the question of how the copula could assist in metaphysical analysis, we get a reply in Peirce's use of the notion to elaborate upon certain remarks of Kant on the regulative employment of the transcendental Ideas. In the "Appendix to the Transcendental Dialectic" Kant had argued that Reason postulates a systematic unity of all knowledge and, in striving to achieve it, operates on the assumption that any collection of things contains a generic property and any individual thing comprises a group of still more specific properties. The former assumption comprised a *principle of homogeneity* and the latter a *principle of variety* (A657, B686). But from these principles yet a third becomes evident—the asumption that between any genus and species other continuous genus/species relations can be found. For without a *principle of continuity (or affinity)* linking given genus and species, there could be no grounds for claiming to be guided by a systematic unity of knowledge. It follows, then, that any two concepts must have a point of overlapping application, or, in other words, must be mediated by a third concept; but to be able to say this is to be able to say that they share a relation through some third concept.

Kant, of course, denied that such a principle could ever be transcendentally deduced, for it could not be shown that such a principle was necessary to the formation of the concepts of the Understanding. Perhaps Peirce was of the opinion that while he was occupied with the problem of unlocking the door of philosophy by an analysis of inference in general, he could establish in the process a necessary ground for the principle of continuity as well. What Kant lacked, he might have thought, was a precise way of formulating the principle of continuity in unpsychological terms. However, using the notation of a logic of relations (and later, of existential graphs) it becomes possible to show that just as any two items share a common character, so any single item, even a putative 'logical atom', is further divisible. As a result there is nothing that is completely determinate. Interestingly enough, Peirce supported this contention with an appeal to psychophysics, wherein every form of stimulation contained a dimension of uncertainty (3.93). But by using logical conventions, individuals and single atoms could at least be defined, and then so could the general processes whereby they come to be related. Thus of three things related, it may be possible to establish a priority where two become related first (an "*interior* operation") and these in turn become related (an "*exterior* operation") to the third. (3.251).

Between his 1880 paper on the algebra of logic and his 1885 paper of the same title (3.359–403) Peirce became increasingly disposed toward attempting a formulation of the logic of relations so as to generate metaphysical, and not simply logical, implications. The semiotic apparatus is now once more introduced, this time in the language of *token*, *index*, and *icon*. And Peirce enunciates more clearly than ever the importance of mathematical reasoning to questions of fact:

> All deductive reasoning, even simple syllogism, involves an element of observation; namely, deduction consists in constructing an icon or diagram the relations of whose parts shall present a complete analogy with those of the parts of the object of reasoning, of experimenting upon this image in the imagination, and of observing the result so as to discover unnoticed and hidden relations among the parts. (3.363)

In Kant's system there is no possibility of finding an element of observation in the postulations of Reason, but in Peirce's system deductive forms educate the deducer, just as earlier he had held that men create words and are subsequently educated by them. This is possible only on the assumption that a unified view of nature and reason is possible. Reason is already externalized in nature in the form of organized entities, and the reasoning of such entities continues the externalizing process. If psychophysics follows a logic, this is only because logic is ultimately an affair of psychophysics. But as a result this unified view cannot be described in the traditional one-sided concepts of logic and psychology; a new vocabulary is required, one involving a logic of relations and a refined formulation of the short and long lists of categories. At this point, although Peirce had made great advances in logical theory and application in cross-breeding the system of Boole and De Morgen, he had not come much farther than he had come in the early years when he had conceived the long list of categories to have the form (A of B) of C.[11] But even so, his Johns Hopkins period of intense work in logic and mathematics rekindled his earlier confidence in the possibility of constructing the general philosophy of the universe—the theory of the Whole Sea—upon a foundation of critically examined elementary categories formulated with mathematical precision. And, fortunately for future generations, Peirce was soon given his leave from the university, freeing him finally to pursue his continually postponed metaphysical project.

Part Three

(1885-1913)

Objective Idealism

Chapter
V
Tychism and Synechism

During his Johns Hopkins years and shortly thereafter Peirce's metaphysical speculations were running in two directions at once. He had begun a fresh start toward a characterization of the short list of categories once more, and he had begun a more detailed probing of the question of the relation between evolution and the categories. In January 1884 he read a paper on "Design and Chance" before the Metaphysical Club. From what are probably fragments of the paper (MS. 875) we find him enunciating a form of thoroughgoing evolutionism:

> But I maintain that the postulate that things shall be explicable extends itself to *laws* as well as to states of things. We want a theory of the evolution of physical law. We ought to suppose that as we go back into the indefinite past not merely special laws but *law* itself is found to be less and less determinate. And how can that be if causation was always as rigidly necessary as it is now.

Twenty-five years earlier Peirce had entertained the same notion in his reflections upon Spiritual Exhibition. Now it was his hope to be able to give a more precise account of the way a time's arrow governs the process. He had already concluded that, paradoxically, a chaotic universe was highly systematic in that without positive or negative uniformities, everything that could happen was already happening. In a chance universe, on the other hand, whatever was subject to chance would change in the long run. But then it is just as plausible to say that the conditions of change themselves will also be subject to change in the long run. In short, in a closed system such as is the universe (by definition), there will be fluctuations from the pure chaotic state as long as the system does not receive fresh influxes of chaos from outside. There is no one around to reshuffle the deck in such a universe.

From such reasoning Peirce was led to conclude that "change must act to move things in the long run from a state of homogeneity to a state of heterogeneity." The problem, however, is that a fluctuation does not amount to a time's arrow unless a constraint is introduced to prohibit the backward slide of heterogeneity, if not in individual cases, at least aggregately. If it could be shown that certain forms are inherently resistant to degradation, then while any of those forms might lose their integration under sufficient pressure, their prevalence and lifetime would be such as to provide a metric for a time's arrow. But while Peirce was none too clear at this point about what might provide such a metric, he was committed to the view that one was required. In an unpublished review of Royce's *The Religious Aspect of Philosophy* he observed that "a tendency toward ends is so necessary a constituent of the universe that the mere action of chance upon innumerable atoms has an inevitable teleological result" (8.44).

It is at this juncture that a treatment of the categories can be of assistance. What sort of language, we may ask, would be required to describe the evolutionary metric? A language capable of giving proper names to all objects would not suffice, for we would also require concepts allowing the objects to be ordered. Even a simple (atomic) language, containing a vocabulary describing the most elementary items shared by all objects in the universe, would leave us with an ordering problem. With such a vocabulary we would remain restricted to a substance-oriented language and would have to espouse a reductive materialism rather than an evolutionary ontology. It would be preferable initially to develop ordering categories on an elementary (mathematical and logical) level, and then test them to see if they can assist in the formation of a physically meaningful metric. Assuming the task of finding a method of ordering relations, we would turn almost at once to the logic of relations. And this, as we have noted, is what Peirce had been doing for some time.

Among the problems that stand in the way of establishing universal, developmental categories is that of avoiding a Kantian subjectivism. How, it may be wondered, can *universal* categories of mind and nature be discoverable by mind alone? If mind is a category-discovering apparatus, how can it be established (by mind) that the mechanism of discovery is governed by the very categories discovered by the mechanism? In Kant's system the categories were necessary conditions for even the possibility of experience as we know it, and so were transcendentally deducible upon that ground. But to Peirce the elaborate transcendental method is unnecessary and even worthless. If there were indeed a short list of categories, one would not require an Archimedean standpoint to be able to discover them. For if one part of the universe had the ability thoroughly to analyze the structure of any other part of the universe, no matter how minute, then its analyzing structure would have to contain all members of the short list, and if so, it would be possible to discover the categories in what is analyzed *provided the categories were of such a nature as to make analysis possible in the first place.* Such a restriction would not guarantee a discovery of the long list, for categories in that case could conceivably appear there beyond the range of mind, but it would guarantee that even the most complex member of the short list would not be missed. But, it might be asked, doesn't this make the short list mind-dependent after all? In response to this it may be said that if the categories of comprehension and analysis can be described in a manner independent of the structure of mind *per se*, this would afford indirect evidence for genuine universality. Such categories could then be said to operate *in* mind, but not to be produced *by* mind. Kant's categories had an alien quality to them; there was no way to link their formation with their justification except through transcendental analogy. In the case of the short-list categories, which could account both for the process of their discovery and for the fact that what can be discovered need not be mental in essence, we would have some grounds for believing that a genuine short list had been discovered. We could not be certain of such a discovery, but we would have some ground for claiming that a fairly good guess had been made about them. Sometime around 1885 Peirce remarked concerning Kant that

> he drew too hard a line between the operations of observation and of ratiocination. He allows himself to fall into the habit of thinking that the latter only begins after the former is complete; and wholly fails to see that even the simplest syllogistic conclusion can only be drawn by observing the relations of the terms in the premises and conclusion. His doctrine of the *schemata* can only have been an afterthought, an addition to his system after it was substantially complete. For if the *schemata* had been considered early enough, they would have overgrown his whole work. (1.35)

What Peirce seems to be saying is that if it is possible that we must be able to cognize relations in order to cognize at all, then it can just as well be possible to discover the relational dimension of cognition even while applying them. But this could only be possible if the structure of cognition can become externalized—and this structure is precisely what mathematics and formal logic reveal. In this vein Peirce wrote in 1890: "Reasoning is strictly experimentation. Euclid, having constructed a diagram according to prescription, draws an extra line, whereupon the mind's eye observes new relations not among those prescribed quite as surprising as new metals or new stars" (6.568). Hence Kant was right in looking to logic for clues to the categories, but wrong in thinking that no manner in which the categories could be directly cognized could be found. The schemata are not only to be applied, but are also to be analyzed, and with this it becomes possible to investigate the variety of cognizing structures (deduction, induction, hypothesis, sign-relation, etc.) with an eye to similarities and differences. In this sense the whole project of a critique of pure reason is rapidly overgrown and instead we enter the realm of *Naturphilosophie*. Needless to say, the effectiveness of such a procedure would depend to a considerable extent upon how convincing the categories chosen for the short list were.

In his paper on "Logical Machines," published in 1887, Peirce rejected the notion that a formal inquiring system could discover relations it was not previously programmed to discover. Then in extending the analogy to human inquiry he observes:

> When we perform a reasoning in our unaided minds . . . we construct an image in our fancy under certain general conditions, and observe the result. In this point of view, too, every machine is a reasoning machine, in so much as there are certain relations between its parts, which relations involve other relations that were not expressly intended. A piece of apparatus for performing a physical or chemical experiment is also a reasoning machine, with this difference, that it does not depend on the laws of the human mind but on the objective reason embodied in the laws of nature.[1]

As in the case of the other remarks from this period, we find the requirement of externalization, but on a larger scale. Now any organization can be regarded as an externalized incarnation of reason. In this light the discovery process is very much like a process of growing self-awareness; it is the problem of a computer being given not only a program, but also the task of discovering what that program is independently of reference to input. The computer must first create a language for externalizing its usual tasks in a general form, then generalize upon those previous categories, create in the process a theory of the import of future input, and finally begin making generalizations about all possible worlds. Then if it is in essential harmony with its environment the program should slowly begin to emerge. Throughout it must be assumed that the means whereby the computer categorizes its data are essentially the same as the program itself, otherwise to discover those means would not be the same as to discover the program. This latter assumption, then, commits one to some form of monism, or at least to the view that there is no systematic prohibition keeping the computer from generalizing upon its generalizations. It becomes clear that the problem of *what* the categories are is inextricably connected with that of *how* they are to be discovered. Increasingly during the 1880's this point must have been impressed upon Peirce. The study of logic was part of the story, but much more was required. It became time for a major effort to unlock the door of philosophy. And time was something he probably had at his disposal. By 1887 he had left his longstanding job with the U.S. Coast Survey for good, and, pooling his own inheritance with funds of his second wife, Juliette, he retired to his home to begin the most productive metaphysical period of his life.

Between 1890 and 1895 Peirce conceived of, and partly executed, a plan to produce a giant metaphysical *opus*. He began a project called "A Guess at the Riddle" around 1890, followed in 1893 by a "Grand Logic" and "Short Logic" and what surely would have been the *magnum opus* of his life, had he completed it "The Principles of Philosophy: or Logic, Physics, and Psychics, considered as a unity, in the Light of the Nineteenth Century." This latter work was to comprise twelve volumes involving his entire lifework. In a prospectus of the work for publishers he wrote:

> The principles supported by Mr. Peirce bear a close affinity with those of Hegel; perhaps are what Hegel's might have been had he been educated in a physical laboratory instead of in a theological seminary. Thus, Mr. Peirce acknowledges an objective logic (though its movement differs from the Hegelian dialectic) . . . .

In brief outline the plan of the work took the following form:

> Vol. I *Review of the Leading Ideas of the Nineteenth Century* [industrial revolution, social structure of ideas, idealisms, objective logic, statistical methods in science, evolution—all unified in the idea of continuity]
>
> Vol. II *Theory of Demonstrative Reasoning* [formal logic: ordinary and relative]
>
> Vol. III *The Philosophy of Probability* [theories of inference]
>
> Vol. IV *Plato's World: An Elucidation of the Ideas of Modern Mathematics* [theories of calculus, functions, geometries, infinities, continuities]
>
> Vol. V *Scientific Metaphysics* [theory of cognition, external world, nominalism and realism, evolution, necessitarianism]
>
> Vol. VI *Soul and Body* [law of association, sense experience,

evolution of matter]

Vol. VII *Evolutionary Chemistry* [Mendeleev's law and the chemical evolution]

Vol. VIII *Continuity in the Psychological and Moral Sciences* [formal theory of economics, utilitarianism, psychology of action]

Vol. IX *Studies in Comparative Biography*

Vol. X *The Regeneration of the Church* [relation of science and religion]

Vol. XI *A Philosophical Encylopaedia* ["something like Hegel's Encyclopaedia"]

Vol. XII *Index raisonné*

None of these works were ever entirely completed, or even readied for publication, but to a significant degree they exist nonetheless in something more than merely fragmentary form. Their foundation is the formal theory of categories, now with detailed application. Here Peirce returned, as he notes (1.300), to his early triads, *I, It,* and *Thou* and *simple, human* and *perfect,* in a more highly refined form.

1. Firstness, Secondness, Thirdness

In describing the fundamental categories one faces a problem we have already noted: that of constructing a language of description in such a manner as to avoid implying that the defining characteristics are more fundamental than the categories defined. Peirce signaled this problem in a number of ways, calling the categories "tones or tints upon conceptions" (1.353, 1.356), "three grades of separability" (1.353), or "thin skeletons of thought" (1.356). By 1892 he had begun to present them as "three distinct and irreducible forms of rhemata" (3.422). And it was becoming increasingly clear to him how it might be possible to know the categories even while being subject to them, that is, by holding that all cognition is not only in signs, but is diagrammatic as well (1.54). This process specifically involves abstraction as a particular method of subjecting something to scrutiny or, even more specifically, the asking of a question about something that has already been given as an answer to the very same question. "Thus," Peirce notes, "the mathematician conceives an operation as something itself to be operated upon"

(1.83). From the answer 'X is the form of Y' I ask 'What is the form of X?'. Eventually I may ask 'What is the form of forms?' and arrive simultaneously at semiotic and relative logic. But it is necessary that these sorts of questions avoid the kind of logomachy Wittgenstein warned against, and this is only possible if our answers retain a fact-like character. Only a creative imagination can guarantee the success of such an outcome.

Peirce felt that the mind was capable of grasping the abstract shape of a diagram—its skeleton-set (7.427–32)—and consequently the process of abstraction is capable of revealing real features of the world. We may wonder whether in arguing this Peirce was returning to intuitionism. To a large degree he continued to adhere to his earlier views (see 7.420, 7.426), stating flatly at one point that "there are no data" (7.465). And so how does abstraction reveal the fundamentality of the categories? The only answer is: by inferences we ourselves make about diagrams. If a diagram is to have metaphysical implications, those implications must somehow be drawn. Peirce was well aware of this distinction, and did not think that because there could be a logic of relations there had to be a metaphysical theory based upon it (1.301). But if it could be shown that the very process of inference involved use of the same categories as were inferred upon, then their fundamentality would take on a new dimension—a transcendental dimension. Not surprisingly, then, Division II of the "Grand Logic," called "Transcendental Logic," concerned itself with the non-cognitive conditions of cognition (6.278–86), in such a manner as to reveal the similarities between them. Unfortunately, Peirce seldom made this point clear. In "The Logic of Quantity"—Chapter 17 of the "Grand Logic," and one of Peirce's most satisfying papers (see L–387)—he describes the process whereby abstractions come to be formed:

> It is not by a simple mental stare, or strain of mental vision. It is by manipulating on paper, or in fancy, formulae or other diagrams—experimenting on them, *experiencing* the thing. Such experience alone *evolves* the reason hidden within us and as utterly hidden as gold ten feet below ground—and this experience only differs from what usually carries that name in that it brings out the reason hidden within and not the reason of Nature, as do the chemists' or physicists' experiments. (4.86)

In order to be able to apply the formal categories to reality as a whole, there must be a mechanism under which the categories come to be revealed and which is also governed by the categories. Recalling the earlier Platonic period, Peirce suggests the unfolding-of-Reason model for the former process, even while insisting that psycho-logical investigation was the source of our knowledge that cognition conforms to the categories. Here once more we encounter the "two streams" of cognition, one emerging out of the particularity of experience (feeling) under the governance of the categories, and the other subjecting previous experience to iconic and rhematic analysis (generality). The problem of how the latter stream becomes possible remains, however, and it was this problem that prompted many of the post-Kantian idealists to resort to the primacy of intellectual intuition—an answer Peirce himself seemed disposed toward at times (5.341). This problem is truly the lock on the door of philosophy. Surely some non-intuitive hypothesis is required to establish the claim that if something is an elementary abstraction of cognition, it is also an elementary abstraction of reality. Converting the formal categories to metaphysical categories requires this leap.

This issue emerges most clearly in Peirce's reaction to A. B. Kempe's paper, "A Memoir on the theory of Mathematical Form," published in the Royal Society's *Philosophical Transactions*, 177 (1886), 1–70. In this paper on the formal foundations of mathematics, Kempe generated a theory of relations using only two items—spots and lines. That Peirce had high regard for the paper is not surprising, but that he considered it a "formidable objection to my views" (3.423) is somewhat puzzling, particularly since he understood very clearly in what respect Kempe's remarks did not undermine triadicity:

> Having examined this analysis attentively, I am of the opinion that it is of extraordinary value. It causes me somewhat to modify my position, but not to surrender it. For, in the first place, it is to be remarked that Mr. Kempe's conception depends upon considering the diagram in its self-contained relations, the idea of its representing anything being altogether left out of view; while my doctrine depends upon considering how the diagram is to be connected with nature. (3.423)

Kempe's paper drove home to Peirce the fact that he could not capture *ultimate* mediation, the mediation of a fundamental category, in a mere diagram. This still required that abstraction be performed by a *mediator*, specifically by applying the rheme '——represents——' to the rheme '——is the form of——'. Only through this "living" mediation (to use a term increasingly sought to carry the weight of his insights) could the categories have metaphysical application. Rather than undermining Peirce's logic of relations, Kempe's paper strengthened it. For example, in Kempe's retranslation of '*A* gives *B* to *C*' as

> In a certain act, *D*, something is given by *A*.
> In the act, *D*, something is given to *C*.
> In the act, *D*, to somebody is given *B*,

it becomes obvious that the rheme '——gives——to——' is contained in *D*, and Peirce does not fail to notice this. His objection, however, is that Kempe's translation is deficient in that it

> fails to afford any formal representation of the manner in which this abstract idea is derived from the concrete ideas. Yet it is precisely in such processes that the difficulty of all difficult reasoning lies. We have an illustration of this in the circumstance that I was led into an error about the capability of my own algebra for want of just the idea that process would have supplied. The process consists, psychologically, in catching one of the transient elements of thought upon the wing and converting it into one of the resting places of the mind. (3.424)

The metaphysical question for the basic categories, then, does not lie ultimately with immediacy, but it cannot dispense with it either. Using a hierarchical searching technique, and guided by an algorithm of rhematic forms, the process of abstraction brings to awareness candidates for further metaphysical speculation. But it is only when these forms have been applied to areas not previously subject to them that they can take on a mark of independence.

The category of *Firstness*, corresponding to the *I*-simple, serves as a name for the common characteristics of freshness, life, freedom, immediacy, feeling, quality, vivacity, and independence (1.302–3, 1.337, 1.357; 6.32), of being or being-in-itself (1.356, 1.329), and of mere potentiality (1.328), something that is both concrete and yet undifferentiated; that of *Secondness* involves action, resistance, facticity, dependence, relation, compulsion, effect, reality, and result (1.337, 1.356, 1.358). As reference to fact, Secondness implies stability and yet dependence; it "suffers yet resists" (1.358). Something dead and without the activity and novelty of life is preeminently a Second (1.361) because it surrenders to all relation (decomposition) and yet remains for a time still something to have relations. But the *Secondness* of something consists in the vitality of the relation of dependence, just as the Firstness of something consisted in the vitality of independence. When the vitality is lost we have a *degenerate Second*, a relation of mere otherness, negation, coexistence, resemblance, contrast, and comparison—a relation of reason that links but does not bind (1.326, 1.358, 1.365, 1.372; 6.32). *Thirdness* is evident in mediation, synthesis, living, continuity, process, moderation, learning, memory, inference, representation, intelligence, intelligibility, generality, infinity, diffusion, growth, and, now completing the triad of Fig 7, conduct (1.337, 1.340, 1.356, 1.359, 1.361, 1.362, 1.366; 6.32). It possesses *two degrees of degeneracy* by virtue of its dual relational possibilities. In the first degree we have an inadvertant unification of a Third to a First and Second by the unification of the latter two (1.366, 1.372, 1.386). A mixture of two items is possible only because each item is confined (Secondness) by the container; then each is confined with the other. Something pinned to a wall is confined by a Second-relation of the pin in the wall. In second-degree degenercy not even the dual relation occurs, and instead we have a situation analogous to degenerate Secondness, a mere collection of singularities unified by a mental Second such as resemblance, comparison, similarity (1.372, 1.383, 1.387).

The basic structures of the categories can be represented in rhematic form:

Firstness   '——————'
Secondness
    genuine   '——interacts with——'
    degenerate   '——is related to——'

Thirdness
   genuine   '——mediates between——and——'
   degenerate
      first degree   '——connects——and——'
      second degree '——is related to——and——'

Once the fundamental categories have been suggested, it must be shown how they operate in nature and how such operation makes their being known possible. The first task concerns the origins of nature, the second, its direction and perhaps destiny.

2. THE EVOLUTIONARY SCENARIO

Given the structures of the basic categories, it is possible to think of them as stages of development and accretion, much in the manner of the simple, human, and perfect stages of the early reformulation of the Kantian list. This involves something of an extension of a biological theory of evolution, where ontogeny recapitulates phylogeny, to the metaphysical level in general; in this case, the part always reflects the whole. And if the triads govern many of the specific processes of nature and mind, it is plausible that they govern the entire cosmological process. These ideas Peirce presented in developed form for the first time in five papers in *The Monist* of 1891–93: "The Architecture of Theories" (6.7–34), "The Doctrine of Necessity Examined" (6.35–65), "The Law of Mind" (6.102–63), "Man's Glassy Essence" (6.238–71), and "Evolutionary Love" (6.287–317).

If it was not enough to defend the need for an evolutionary hypothesis simply in terms of the spirit of the leading ideas of the nineteenth century, Peirce may have added the following argument, as indicated previously: the search for general categories of relation, unlike that for general categories of substance, commits us to an investigation of the general structures of *process*, for either the relating conditions are not part of the process of describing the basic triad, or else they are. If they are not, then the categories are not fundamental; but if the categories are fundamental, then they characterize all possible relating conditions, including those governing how the categories are formed and come to be known, and this means that they are categories of process also. Peirce made this point very nicely in a review of Spinoza's *Ethics:* "Let the predicates [categories] be relational, and generalization means organization, or the building up of an ideal system."[2] Given the high generality of the categories, it follows further that if they imply categories of process they imply categories of all processes, and so "philosophy requires thorough-going evolutionism or none" (6.14).

A process is one thing, evolution is another, or so it seems. But this Peirce denies. A reversible process is one in which evolution has occurred in one direction and then is reversed to 'return' to the previous state. The entire process is governed by laws, and with a suitable choice of boundary conditions any process, if it is a process, may be seen to have directionality. Peirce does not deny that there is a sense in which we can speak of reversible processes, though he could see no grounds for claiming that reversible processes alone governed nature. It is no less plausible to suggest that irreversible processes exist as well on the basis of the observed heterogeneity and complexity of nature. Indeed, the categories themselves require directionality: there can be no Thirdness until there is Secondness, and no Secondness until there is Firstness. Hence the categories afford a measure, a vague one to be sure, of a time's arrow of evolution. The *rate* of development, however, is not captured in the categories. We cannot be sure that a universe containing Thirdness is older than another containing Secondness and Firstness, but we can be sure that if a universe contains genuine Thirdness it previously contained Firstness and Secondness. Even if Thirdness follows instantaneously after the others, mediation still requires something to be mediated in respect to something else.

The actual developmental scenario Peirce suggested as being no better than a 'guess at the riddle' can be briefly described as follows: in the beginning there was a universe of pure chance, without a tendency to the creation of any specific determination, and in which no uniformities could be detected. This constituted an indescribable state of *pure indeterminacy* because there was yet no thing to describe. Even the so-called chaos of the kinetic particles of a perfect gas is far from chaotic in this sense, for they display regular rectilinear motion and perfect elasticity. Instead, the state of pure Firstness is a "dreamy" (1.175), spontaneous (6.59, 6.553), and undifferentiated (6.132) state, a free living in immediacy (6.585). This would be a state without time, for no regularities could be observed and no clocks could be constructed. The next step is the most troublesome—how to get order out of disorder. It was mentioned that no tendency to promote a specific determination can operate in a universe of pure Firstness, but if such a general tendency were possible, then under appropriate circumstances that tendency might lead to a coalescing of order. Here Peirce introduces a "principle of habit" (1.412), a "principle of growth of principles" (6.585), and the germ of a generalizing tendency (6.33). Under what conditions might such a general tendency operate? We might conceive of a circumstance whereby two states of the primal chaos elicit a reaction from their environment simply by virtue of some chance novelty resultant upon their creation. Then that novelty might further deflect the 'normal' course of chaos and produce a reaction provisionally preserving the two states, now in some form of degenerate Secondness. This imbalance produces further imbalance and sorting, and so degenerate Secondness becomes genuine Secondness.

Among the numerous difficulties with such a model is the fact that it implies the coexistence of Secondness and Thirdness. For something to have a real effect upon something else, it must be directed toward it, and this involves Thirdness. But then Thirdness must exist at the outset as well, as a 'principle' or 'tendency' or God–*logos* or whatever. After a lifetime of denying the incognizable, Peirce may have finally arrived at a situation where the incognizable would have to be allowed. If cognition and intelligibility involve Thirdness, then in no manner could the transition of Firstness to Secondness be intelligible. For mediation to be possible something must serve as a mediator, and nothing of the sort is allowed in the transition of Firstness to Secondness. Explanation is mediation and cannot mediate the unmediated:

> If we were to find that all the grains of sand on a certain beach separated themselves into two or more sharply discrete classes, as spherical and cubical ones, there would be something to be explained, but that they are of various sizes and shapes, or no definable character, can only be referred to the general manifoldness of nature. Indeterminacy, then, or pure firstness, and haecceity,

or pure secondness, are facts not calling for and not capable of explanation. (1.405)

Absolute particularity and indeterminacy cannot, then, be explained, and in conjunction with this, neither can absolute chance—for to explain it is to deny it. On the other hand, absolute generality and lawfulness also cannot be explained, for again to do so implies the use of law and generality and the violation that the *explanans* be more general than the *explanandum*. What must be explained are circumstances involving mixtures of particularity and generality, chance and lawfulness, in relation to other mixtures of particularity and generality or in relation to the pure categories. Laws are subject to explanation only because chance continues to operate in them (1.407; 6.148, 6.612–13).

With the emergence of contextual order the tendency for its repetition begins to form, and with each repetition the tendency strengthens itself (1.409; 6.585). Chance continues to operate on all features of the universe, but some features become more resistant to it. Habit-breaking chance and habit-taking order interact with each other and as one diminishes the other increases, so that evolution becomes a limitation of possibility (6.132) and an increase of systematicity and of the other forms of Thirdness (6.33, 6.265).

From a global perspective, three forms of motion may be distinguished (6.581–82): *elliptic* motion, which is microscopically reversible (directionless) and homogeneous throughout; *parabolic* motion, which is globally reversible (cyclical) and heterogeneous within cycles; and *hyperbolic* motion, which is irreversible and heterogeneous throughout (developmental). The latter, according to Peirce, best characterizes the global evolutionary process in light of our empirical evidence concerning speciation and intelligence. However, the processes that determine the other two forms of motion also operate in hyperbolic motion, and so three forms of evolution can be distinguished: *tychastic* evolution, in which fortuitous variation operates, *anancastic* evolution, in which mechanical necessity operates, and *agapastic* evolution, in which the coalescent tendencies of desire, interest, and love operate.

3. Chance and Continuity

The defense of tychism and synechism depends to a large degree on a clear notion of chance and continuity. Upon this task Peirce expended no small effort. In "The Doctrine of Necessity Examined" (6.35–65) and "Reply to the Necessitarians" (6.588–615) he defended his view that regularity is compatible with inexactitude. A determinist (necessitarian) argues that any event must be the result of necessary and sufficient conditions which themselves have necessary and sufficient conditions, and so on. Against this Peirce argued that even if there were a high degree of uniformity between events and conditions, it need not be the case that actual determining conditions must be entirely governed by law. Given certain boundary conditions, the laws may hold even while the boundary conditions are subject to chance (6.55, 6.613). But against this the determinist may deny that even boundary conditions are subject to chance, being themselves events subject to yet other conditions, and from this it follows that all events must be *pre-determined*. The determinist is then committed to the notion of a block universe: "You think all the arbitrary specifications of the universe were introduced in one dose, in the beginning, if there was a beginning, and that the variety and complication of nature has always been just as much as it is now" (6.57). Peirce prefers to entertain the hypothesis that chance variation is possible. This is absolute chance, in the sense of being unconditioned, but its effect is such as to increase order. This means that the spontaneity of chance is "to some degree regular." In a universe subject to hyperbolic motion, something would have to free events from previous determining conditions in order to make new arrangements possible; but this is precisely the sort of universe we observe, with chance the only mechanism for this that we can imagine. Naturally, to suppose a divine orchestration of hyperbolic evolution is at once to deny that form of evolution, unless it be that God himself 'freely associates' the thought of his creatures-to-be. It is easy, of course, to suggest that whatever happens had to happen, and had to happen in some deterministic way, but Peirce would find that claim a part of a metaphysics too rarefied even for his tastes. Instead, our world seems demonstrably pliable, allowing for counterfactuals and a variety of responses to given conditions.

As part of his defense of tychism, Peirce rejected the grounds for accepting the law of conservation of energy. As long as the notion of 'potential energy' is accepted in the form of positional states alone, then it trivially follows that the sum of potential and kinetic energy remains unchanged, for the resultant positional energy is *defined* as the remainder not expended in kinetic form (6.601). In any process familiar to the scientist, total energy is conserved only if the loss of energy to friction or heat is considered, but this is energy which is lost or 'degraded' and which would take energy to reconvert to work. Hence the law of conservation of energy properly qualified is not incompatible with chance, and appears even to suggest a basis for it. The fact that energy is degraded indicates a randomizing factor most prominently considered in thermo-dynamics, where energy degradation is most acutely studied. Chance, Perice notes, is precisely how we could account for the fact that energy anti-degradation does not naturally take place (6.613). It appears, then, that when he speaks of *tychism* he means to characterize an entropic factor and when he speaks of *synechism* he means the opposing negentropic factor. Both factors are required for an understanding of nature, and with such an understanding, deterministic (Newtonian) mechanics must turn into statistical mechanics with its concern for aggregations and trans-atomic properties. In his review of R. M. Thurston's *The Animal as a Machine and a Prime Motor, and the Laws of Energetics* (1894) Peirce concurs with the author that negentropic processes, of the sort suggested by Maxwell, are possible in nature and that biological organisms are able to effectuate such processes.[3] Maxwell's Demon could create order out of disorder by utilizing an array of randomly moving particles to produce work. This it did by using its superior knowledge to isolate individual particles with the desired properties. In the case of organisms, aggregations are broken down by the ordering tendencies of physical structures. Such organisms require an ordering negentropic (habit-taking) tendency as well as an entropic (habit-breaking) tendency in the way they operate.

If it had not been clear to Peirce during the period in which he denied perfect order (i.e., since 1868) that absolute chance, in order to help explain evolution, must ultimately be subject to order, it became so to him in the early 1890's. He was sensitive to the criticism that a hypothesis of absolute chance could block the road of inquiry unless it were part of a larger hypothesis which itself opened up new avenues of inquiry. As a result he observed: "I make use of chance chiefly to make room for a principle of generalization, or tendency to form habits, which I hold has produced all regularities" (6.63, 6.606). Habit-breaking requires chance so that habit-taking activities may become increasingly subject to habit.

The next task was that of characterizing the negentropic tendency itself. How is this to be done, short of postulating a pre-established harmony or a divine intelligence? Here Peirce found the answer in synechism and in the notion of continuity. To counter chance, systematicity must be possible. But systematicity is possible only if coordination occurs, and this, only if communication occurs. Communication results from a transmission process, and transmission requires continuity and a "logic of quantity." Continuity involves some aspect of mutiplicity and arrangement (4.121); specifically, it involves infinite divisibility, or what Peirce called *Kanticity*, as well as a limit-tending concatenation, or what he called *Aristotelicity*. But no metaphysical theory could be based entirely upon such formal definitions. Peirce's views of how best to characterize continuity may have changed, but his metaphysical employment of the subject did not.[4]

Continuity was, aside from a mathematical notion, an experience of living systems, one best exemplified in our consciousness of a temporal duration. Without such a consciousness no idea of time would be possible, for any putatively mechanistic account of time-consciousness would require a generalization about temporal properties (6.110). Time-consciousness must be *sui generis*, for an inference could not produce such a continuity. In some way it must be directly experienced: "In an infinitesimal interval we directly perceive the temporal sequence of its beginning, middle, and end—not, of course, in the way of recognition, for recognition is only of the past, but in the way of immediate feeling" (6.111). The latter qualification enables Peirce to avoid inconsistency with his earlier views on intuition. The proposition 'time is continuous' is an inference based upon the character of our (past) experience, but the experience itself is not the result of an inference; as a feeling it is not an inference, though its recognition leads to an inference that 'feeling is continuous'.

Yet if we have a consciousness of a continuous interval and that interval is continuous with the one previous to it, do we not then have direct perception of all time in which we have been conscious? Clearly we do not have such a direct apperception, and so the interval must be infinitesimally short and both continuously divisible and discontinuously limited. Peirce explains a discontinuous continuity in the following manner: "My definition of a continuum only prescribes that, after every innumerable series of points, there shall be a *next* following point, and does not forbid this to follow at the interval of a mile. That, therefore, certainly permits cracks everywhere" (4.126). Even so, we are still left with the problem of explaining under which circumstances a *next* is or is not allowed. And this, it would seem, would require a continuum behind the continuum. If, as Peirce holds (1.168), all inference is of the past, how could we 'recognize' the experience of a continuous duration except by a process of inference which contains continuity itself? I must reflectively examine the character of time-consciousness and see its continuity as a predicate, and this requires a continuity in *attention.* The continuity of time-consciousness requires a deeper continuity, and so, it would seem does the 'law of mind' that ideas tend to spread continuously so as to affect other ideas (6.104). No amount of logical clarification could have circumvented this difficulty. Instead, what was required was a metaphysical interpretation of continuity, or rather, a logical formulation with a metaphysical interpretation.

It is likely that Peirce understood this difficulty, and its resolution must have been no small concern to him. "Time," he writes, "with its continuity logically involves some other kind of continuity than its own" (6.132). If time-consciousness is evidence of continuity it must be because some other continuity exists as well, and for the 'logical' reason just referred to. At first Peirce appeared satisfied to characterize the continuity behind time-continuity as "a continuous range of intensity in feeling" (6.132); yet if feeling is Firstness it is unclear how it could be continuous, that is, how it could generate a *next.* For this, Thirdness is required, but a Thirdness not based on personal consciousness. It must somehow be an objective Thirdness. Increasingly, then, Peirce comes to characterize feeling in terms of generality (4.172) and general ideas (6.143, 6.152), and observes that synechism requires besides objective idealism and tychism, *logical realism* (6.102–103, 6.163).

Around 1893 Peirce considered preparing a critical edition entitled *The Treatise of Petrus Peregrinus on the Lodestone* (MSS. 1310, 1311). In a prospectus of the proposed work he defined an *occult property* as a property only brought to light by experiment (7.392, n.7). Meanwhile, the use of the term "occult" began to appear elsewhere in his writings around this time. For example:

> Resemblance *consists* in an association due to the occult substratum of thought. (7.394, 7.467)

> Mathematics brings to light results as truly occult and unexpected as those of chemistry; only they are results dependent upon the action of reason in the depths of our own consciousness, instead of being dependent, like those of chemistry, upon the actions of Cosmical Reason, or Law. (6.595)

What is this 'action of reason' but a form of transcendental reflection, wherein we are led back to a leading principle unifying continuity with generality through an abstract *logos?* Then if evolution occurs through continuity, it must be because it is subject to a *logos,* which itself cannot be said to evolve. But once more we are confronted with the prospect of a block universe, one allowing only parabolic evolution. And we are back to the problem of cognizing the emergence of Thirdness, though in a slightly different form: now Thirdness is established and evolution itself becomes problematic!

One approach to this problem is to admit that the general form of Thirdness never changes but that its concrete manifestations do. The action of reason penetrates to the form itself, while nature moves away from the form and toward the particular. This point of view, however, necessitates the complete idealization of nature and the rejection of mechanistic mathematics, something Peirce appeared reluctant to do even up to 1890 (6.559). But this was to change. Two tasks now clearly emerged: (1) that of describing the categories in the most abstract manner possible (to be considered in the next chapter), and (2) that of showing the hidden isomorphism of the features of nature and mind.

4. THE LAWS OF NATURE AND MIND

We recall that in fragments of some of his earliest writings Peirce had come to the conclusion that mind and matter differ only by virtue of being two points of view of the same thing (MS. 923s). In the intervening thirty years he attempted to explain how a chance world could turn matter into mind. After 1890, however, he appeared to think that the problem was really that of explaining how mind turns into matter. It is not enough to say that mind and matter may continuously act upon one another in a synechistic world. Some underlying unity of the two must be granted for this possibility. In "The Law of Mind" Peirce announced his view that tychism led to "a Schelling-fashioned idealism which holds matter to be mere specialized and partially deadened mind" (6.102: see also 6.158, 6.277, 6.301, 6.605). In a mechanistic world subject only to conservative principles there is no room for the growth of feelings: "Mechanical causation, if absolute, leaves nothing for consciousness to do in the world of matter; and if the world of mind is merely a transcript of that of matter, there is nothing for consciousness to do even in the mental realm" (6.613). Again we recall the earlier "Analysis of Creation," where consciousness results from a combination of the generality of abstraction and the particularity of sensation, and represents a departure from rigid determination. When determination and uniformity predominate consciousness disappears; when they diminish, consciousness ascends to spread itself and its influence and to produce new forms of determination. This leads to a biperspective view of mind and matter:

> Viewing a thing from the outside, considering its relations of action and reaction with other things, it appears as matter. Viewing it from inside, looking at its immediate character as feeling, it appears as consciousness. These two views are combined when we remember that mechanical laws are nothing but acquired habits, like all the regularities of mind, including the tendency to take habit, itself; and that this action of habit

is nothing but generalization, and generalization is nothing but the spreading of feeling. (6.268)

The unity of mind and matter is required if evolution is to be thoroughgoing, and the priority of mind—the elementary tendency to resist the sinking into sterile order—is required if agapastic evolution is to be possible. Peirce, then, is committed to showing how the forms of hyperbolic evolution apply to all of creation, to the realms of nature, history, culture, and thought (6.58; 1.105–106). Triads must be constructed in all such realms; this was precisely the task of "The Principles of Philosophy" and "A Guess at the Riddle" (MS. 909), as well as of numerous uncompleted and unpublished papers. Of the triads given below, Peirce evidently had the greatest difficulty with those of physics, noting that that group would comprise "the germinal section" (1.354) of a work on the subject. In the physical realm, where determination functions with greatest influence, it would require the greatest effort to reveal the work of triadic generality. Indeed, one difficulty he confronted was that of explicating the concepts of physics in non-mechanistic categories when these concepts are, for the most part, heavily impregnated with mechanistic notions and assumptions. As usually stated, these notions require a denial of Thirdness, and perhaps for this reason Peirce had difficulty completing the sets of physical triads. The following is a list that would comprise, at least in part, a long list of categories based on the short list of Firstness, Secondness, and Thirdness. (Those given in brackets are in some cases interpolations, and in others are suggested directly from arguments and analyses Peirce presents in each relevant area.)

Physics
   Indeterminacy, Haecceity, [Process] (1.405)
   Chance, Law, Habit (1.409; 6.32)
   [*Rest, Velocity, Acceleration*] (1.337, 1.359)
   [*Inertia, Force, Causality*] (1.66–69)
   [*Neutrality, Charge, Attraction*] (1.459)
Biology
   Sensibility, Motion, Growth (1.393)
   Variation, Heredity, Selection (1.398; 6.32)

Physiology
   Cell Excitation, Excitation Transfer, Habitual
     Excitation (1.393)
   Irritation, Reflex, Repetition (5.373; 3.156–57)
Psychology
   Feeling, Willing, Knowing (1.375, 1.382)
   Feeling, Sensing, Conceiving (6.32)
   Feeling, Activity, Learning (1.377)
Reasoning
   Deduction, Induction, Hypothesis (1.354, 1.369)
   Names, Propositions, Inferences (1.354, 1.369)
   Sign, Signified, Cognition (1.372)
   Affirmative Propostion, Negative Proposition, Probable
     Proposition (1.369)
   Terminus, Connection, Branch (1.371)
   Icon, Index, Symbol (1.369)
   Absolute Term, Relative Term, Conjugative Term (1.354)

The triads from physics to psychics reveal a hierarchical order of evolution from an undetermined consciousness of pure feeling to the systematized and rationalized consciousness in the form of logical reasoning. But this very process reveals a new range of categories—*metaphysical* triads:

Philosophical Reasoning
   Mind, Matter, Evolution (6.32)
   Origin, End, Mediation (6.32)
   Pluralism, Dualism, Monism (6.32)
   Tychism, Anancism, Agapism (6.302)

And these are in addition to the very categories of Firstness, Secondness, and Thirdness and all of their conjugates. As reasoning becomes more abstract, as its diagrams become more sophisticated, it generates system-wide triads, not only of its object of reasoning but of the process whereby it interacts with its object; then still other triads become accessible:

Evolution of Reasoning
  Tychastic: chance association (6.307; 7.269)
  Anancastic: forced association
    1. *Cataclysmal (new discoveries)* (1.109; 6.312; 7.270)
    2. *Logical Association* (6.313)
  Agapastic: purposeful association (1.108; 6.315–17; 7.274)
    1. *Communal* (6.307)
    2. *Emotional* (6.307)
    3. *Intellectual* (6.307)

Using these categories, the progress of science can be measured as comprising an increase in the methods of reasoning. Scientific thought, while never fully departing from tychastic and anancastic influences, represents a triumph of agapastic evolution in that it investigates at once nature and the processes of knowing it. It systematizes the influences of tychastic evolution by means of probability and statistical theory, and it enhances the viability of communal agapism through the formation of scientific institutions and publications, thereby making research more economical and productive.

What is to distinguish agapastic activity from other forms of systematic and efficient communal endeavor such as is possible, for example, under fascism? Earlier Peirce may have replied that it is distinguished by selfless devotion to the community and an adherence to the social theory of logic. But fascism embraces these qualities as well. Where it is deficient, however, is in its lack of commitment to "the central doctrine of love" (6.450), and thus to true universality. In the religious notion of 'the Church' we approach such an ideal, but unfortunately most of contemporary institutionalized religion, Peirce thought, was dogmatic and factionalist, and did not have the agapastic potential of science (6.430). As he had argued in 1863 in his Cambridge High School Association lecture, Peirce again expressed the hope that religion might become inspired by the spirit of science and science become infused with traditional religious values and concerns:

> Man's highest developments are social; and religion, though it begins in a seminal individual inspiration

[emotional agapasm], only comes to full flower in a great church coextensive with a civilization. This is true of every religion, but supereminently so of the religion of love. Its ideal is that the whole world shall be united in the bond of a common love of God accomplished by each man's loving his neighbour. Without a church, the religion of love can have but a rudimentary existence; and a narrow, little exclusive church is almost worse than none. A great catholic church is wanted. (6.443)[5]

That catholic church is the community of truth-seekers. The bond of love that animates agapastic evolution synthesizes the under-determined effects of tychism and the overdetermined effects of anancasm: "The movement of love is circular, at one and the same impulse projecting creations into independency and drawing them into harmony" (6.288). In Lamarckian evolution, inheritance becomes possible through the sacrificial efforts of an organism to overcome disorder (6.299), both for itself and for its group, and in scientific evolution the education of individuals and groups results from similar efforts to check the influence of a dreamy Firstness and a brute Secondness. Love, as a mediation of real, separable individuals through a bond of affectionate concerns, is preeminently the activity of Thirdness in its more advanced stages.

Chapter
VI
Objective Logic

Having satisfied himself that the categories could be fruitfully if not finally applied to the various disciplines of knowledge, Peirce returned to the fountainhead of metaphysics—the analysis of the categories themselves. Until around 1895 he had taken the triads of earlier periods and had given them a metaphysical interpretation. As such, his treatment of them had been largely intuitive, discursive, and illustrative. We were simply told that Firstness, for example, was quality, feeling, etc., but we were not told specifically what the defining characteristics of the categories were. They could hardly remain 'tones' or 'tints' of conceptions if they were to serve so important a role in metaphysics.

One difficulty with the categories characterized as Firstness, Secondness, and Thirdness was that, not being described in terms of a logical system of notation, they afforded no means of generating other categories. We must not forget that the short list serves also as a foundation for a longer list of categories, and although the categories as stated could serve as a basis for classification, they did not clearly display the rationale behind the classification. Thus between 1896 and 1900, Peirce embarked upon a series of tasks designed to answer the sphinx's riddle clearly and to open fully the door of philosophy. He began work on his logical (existential) graphs, attempted to formalize more precisely the process of hyperbolic evolution in "The Logic of Continuity" (6.185–213), and produced one of his most brilliant metaphysical writings, "The Logic of Mathematics" (1.417–519), a work in which he attempted to link directly his mathematical and metaphysical categories so as to produce a "mathematical metaphysics" (6.213) and an "objective logic" in the form of a "logic of events" (6.214–35). A scant part of this new material he presented as lectures on "Reasoning and the Logic of Things" in February and March 1898 in Cambridge, Massachusetts. But these eager, erudite scholars who attended, perhaps having been forewarned of Peirce's penchant for architectonic speculation, requested something more palpable from him. In his first lecture, "Detached Ideas on Vitally Important Topics," Peirce told his audience:

> I was asked in December to prepare a course of lectures upon my views of philosophy. I accordingly set to work to draw up in eight lectures an outline of one branch of philosophy, namely, Objective Logic. But just as I was finishing one lecture word came that you would expect to be addressed on topics of vital importance, and that it would be as well to make the lectures detached. (1.622)

This was not the sort of distraction Peirce needed at this period. But he accepted the task and delivered the lectures as requested.

1. MATHEMATICAL METAPHYSICS

Around 1896 Peirce wrote a long essay entitled "The Logic of Mathematics; An Attempt to Develop My Categories From Within" (1.417–519). In it he attempted to do for metaphysics what Kempe's paper on mathematical forms had done for mathematics generally. By now he had become convinced that the insights of De Morgan, Cantor, and the other creative mathematicians "must spring from some truth so broad as to hold not only for the universe we know but for every world that poet could create" (1.417). Mathematics alone could not study this relationship, if only because its concepts derived from an exclusively mathematical point of view. Instead, Peirce called his inquiry "general semeiotic" because it examined the general conditions of all signs and the laws of the evolution of thought by means of signs (1.444). He describes his method in the following way:

> Our method must be to observe how logic requires us to think and especially to reason, and to attribute to the conception of the dyad those characters which it must have in order to answer the requirements of logic. (1.444)

Using this method Peirce became convinced that he had been mistaken in claiming that because Firstness could be prescinded from Secondness, but not vice versa, then Firstness was a category of being in its own right. In "The Logic of Mathematics" there is no section devoted to the monad in itself, which may suggest that he had come to see the monad as metaphysically less relevant than he previously had. The concept of the monad as previously understood is replaced by that of the *medad,* an entirely unrelated entity, and the monad is instead shown to have intrinsic links beyond itself. Among other things this would mean that *metaphysics actually begins with the dyad.*

The monad is composed of no parts, and yet is not conceivable without the notion of *part.* In order to see this, let us adopt, along with the usual logical conventions, the following notation:

$$0 = \text{absolute indetermination, or nullity (1.447)}$$
$$Mx = x \text{ is a monad}$$
$$Dx = x \text{ is a dyad}$$
$$yDx = x \text{ is dyadically related to } y$$
$$yRx = x \text{ is related to } y$$
$$Cx = x \text{ is thought or thinkable}$$
$$Fx = x \text{ is determined}$$
$$yFx = x \text{ is more determined than } y$$

Then we have $Mx \rightarrow \sim 0x;$ but $\sim 0x \rightarrow Fx$, and so $Mx \rightarrow Fx$. To be a monad is to be a *such,* and as such is to stand apart from nullity. At this point Peirce returns to the Appendix of Kant's Transcendental Dialectic for the principle:

$$Fx \rightarrow (\exists y)(xFy)$$

In terms of the x of Mx this may take either of two forms. In the first,

$$Mx \rightarrow (x = x)$$

$$(x = x) \cdot (x = 0) \rightarrow (\exists y)(x \neq y)$$

a dyad results simply from considering something not to be nullity, namely the dyad:

⟨monad, non-monad⟩

In the second form,

$$Mx \rightarrow Cx, \text{ and } Cx \rightarrow Fx$$

hence

$$Cx \rightarrow (\exists y)(xFy)$$

giving

⟨monad thought, monad⟩

The other two principles from Kant are as follows:

$$Fx \rightarrow (\exists y)(yFx)$$

$$yFx \rightarrow (\exists x)(yFz \cdot zFx)$$

In the first case a monad is more determined than a non-monad, but a non-monad is more determined than nullity. But then it follows that something must be *less* determined than absolute indetermination! This circumstance presents no problem to transcendental dialectic, for the following dyads are always possible in the form $\langle x,y \rangle$ such that yFx:

⟨non-monad, nullity⟩
⟨nullity thought, nullity non-thought⟩
⟨nullity-non-thought thought, nullity-non-thought non-thought⟩

and so on. In the second case, from a single dyadic relation two such relations may be formed, $\langle x,y \rangle \rightarrow \langle x,z \rangle \cdot \langle z,y \rangle$. Out of ⟨monad, nullity⟩ we get ⟨monad, non-monad⟩ and ⟨non-monad, nullity⟩. But what about ⟨monad, non-monad⟩? If we consider that couplet to belong to the set, S, then S' can be formed:

⟨monad-in-S, non-monad-in-S, monad-not-in-S, non-monad-not-in-S⟩

and so

$$\langle \text{monad-in-}S, \text{monad-not-in-}S \rangle$$

and

$$\langle \text{monad-not-in-}S, \text{non-monad-not-in-}S \rangle$$

can also be formed according to the third principle. Generally, for any determination of a set, S, there is a dichotomy of determinations 'x-in-S' and 'x-not-in-S'. This simply accords with the principle of excluded middle (1.450).

Peirce has now shown, first, that *there is no monad without a dyad,* each of these being considered in the most abstract manner possible, and second, that it is impossible to form a *single* class of dyads, for any determination of a dyad produces a dichotomy of classes of dyads. Thus there are *dyads of monads,* wherein dyadicity is manifest either in a 'relation of suchness' or in a 'relation of contemplation' (1.455–56). In terms of his earlier distinction, these are *utterly degenerate dyads* having the forms:

$$Mx \cdot My \cdot (x \neq y)$$

$$Mx \cdot My \cdot Cxy$$

where x and y must be thinkable together. Such dyads Peirce calls *essential dyads* because their dyadicity lies in the most superficial circumstances. This is not the case with a dyad comprised of two dyads which themselves contribute to their dyadicity. These are *dyads of dyads,* or *accidental dyads,* and consist of a 'relation of existence' or a 'relation of opposition'. Existence itself involves opposition and is vastly more than mere suchness for that reason, but opposition may involve more than existence. Accidental dyads of the first, self-existing sort are dyads of *inherence,* with the form:

$$Mx \cdot \exists x$$

while dyads of the second sort are other-directed dyads, dyads of *relation.* To complete the dichotomy of the dyads of inherence we would get $Mx \cdot \sim \exists x$, but this is simply another way of saying Mx, the elemental dyad of such and non-such; this branch of the dichotomy withers away. The dyads of relation, however, divide clearly and substantially into those of *identity* and those of *diversity:*

$$(\exists x) \cdot (\exists y) \cdot (x = y)$$

$$(\exists x) \cdot (\exists y) \cdot \sim Mx \cdot \sim My \cdot (x \neq y)$$

Dyads of identity differ by no quality but existence; they are two things in all respects similar except that one's existence is not the other's existence. As such each is a dyad of inherence, but is more than that, in that each is related to the other as a dyad of identity. Hence x and y need not be specified as inherently dyadic or monadic. In the case of dyads of diversity, however, where x differs from y *in some respect*, it is clear that neither x nor y can be monads. Dyads of diversity, then, can be further dichotomized according to the nature of the difference, either as *qualitative* diversity or *dynamical* diversity, giving:

$$(\exists x) \cdot (\exists y) \cdot (a \in x) \cdot \sim(a \in y)$$

$$(\exists x) \cdot (\exists y) \cdot (a \in x) \cdot (b \in y) \cdot bDa$$

It is at this point that dyadicity saliently emerges, $(Mx \cdot \exists x)$ is a self-existing monad, but establishes no positive dyadicity with any other thing. And its existence is existence *"abstractly and in itself considered"* (1.461). Considered in such a manner, it must be included within the list of pure forms of dyadicity, and yet if any thing or self exists, it exists in relation of opposition to something else. The case, then, in which we have two identical things, each existing, is a limiting case only, for if x influences y, and vice versa, then x has a quality y does not have, namely, the quality 'being influenced by y' and, again, vice versa. Existence and diversity emerge together and constitute the real relation of the dyadicity of dyads in the form bDa. At this point Peirce remarks:

> For what is a dyadic character? It is a character conferred upon one individual by another individual. It thus involves the idea of *action* and *force*, not in a narrow scientific sense, but in the sense in which we speak of the will as a force. (1.466)

In the narrow scientific sense $F = ma$, but to say this is to say nothing about force as *opposition*. In the sense of willing, however, is contained the notion of an opposition-to-be-overcome, and it is this sense that is implied in bDa.

When full reciprocity exists between the characters of two dynamical dyads, then they are *materially unordered*, while when a distinction can be made between the nature of the opposition each gives to the other they are *materially ordered*, giving respectively:

$$(\exists x) \cdot (\exists y) \cdot (a \ \epsilon \ x) \cdot (b \ \epsilon \ y) \cdot bDa \cdot (\exists c)[(c \ \epsilon \ x) \cdot (c \ \epsilon \ y)]$$

$$(\exists x) \cdot (\exists y) \cdot (a \ \epsilon \ x) \cdot (b \ \epsilon \ y) \cdot bDa \cdot (\exists c)[(c \ \epsilon \ x) \cdot \sim(c \ \epsilon \ y)]$$

Peirce gives as an example of a materially unordered dynamical dyad of diversity, '*A* is one mile from *B*' and of a materially ordered dynamical dyad, '*A* kills *B*'. In the latter case it is clear there belongs to one element of the dyad a character (a mortal wound) not belonging to the other. But what does each possess in the former case that constitutes a *material* character? 'Being one mile away from——' does not seem to possess a *materially* ordered character, unless distance *per se* confers material character. If we assume *A* and *B* to have mass, then the law of gravitation allows us to postulate reciprocally acting forces upon each. The problem with this, however, is that Peirce nowhere specifically equates existence with material existence. If mass is simply the resultant of attractive and repulsive forces (1.459), then the gravitational law would simply state that between any two centers of force an equilibrium of forces is established. Then the material character of *A* would be precisely the effect *B* has on *A*, and this would be the same *kind* of effect *A* had on *B*. Unfortunately, Peirce does not give us counsel on this question.

The intransitivity of materially-ordered characters raises the question of the relational order of the characters. We may ask: Can *either* of the dyads have the character, or must one alone have it? When amber and fur are rubbed together each contains a different electrical form (i.e., they are materially ordered), but neither is to be regarded as the condition for the material order. The amber could conceivably produce the given arrangement or just the opposite arrangement, and so the characters of the amber and fur are *formally unordered*. When, however, a distinction can be drawn between agent and patient, then the relation is *formally ordered*, thus giving:

$$(\exists x) \cdot (\exists y) \cdot (a \ \epsilon \ x) \cdot (b \ \epsilon \ y) \cdot bDa \cdot (\exists R^*)(yR^*x \lor xR^*y)$$

$$(\exists x) \cdot (\exists y) \cdot (a \ \epsilon \ x) \cdot (b \ \epsilon \ y) \cdot bDa \cdot (\exists R^*)(yR^*x \cdot \sim xR^*y)$$

Like *yDx*, which already contains the notion of *influence*, *yRx* combines that notion with that of *directionality*. *yR*x* is an asymmetrical causal relation. The attraction a magnet has for iron filings is an example of such a relation.

It only remains now to distinguish further among the dichotomous kinds of directional influence. Such an influence may be *actional* (partial) or *productive* (total), and now:

$$(\exists x) \cdot (\exists y) \cdot (a \ \epsilon \ x) \cdot (b \ \epsilon \ y) \cdot bDa \cdot Mb \cdot (\sim \exists x \ \rightarrow \ \sim \exists b)$$

$$(\exists x) \cdot (\exists y) \cdot (a \ \epsilon \ x) \cdot (b \ \epsilon \ y) \cdot bDa \cdot (\sim \exists x \ \rightarrow \ \sim \exists y)$$

When a character of one dyad is materially produced by the influence of the other dyad, the influence is actional. When all of the features of a dyad are produced by the other dyad, the influence is productive or *poietical* (1.469). In the latter case, without the poet there would be no poem *at all*.

Peirce has now traced the dimensions of dyadicity from inherence (the two-in-one) to separation, and back again. If we place the dyads of inherence following the dyads of production, we attain a hierarchy of increasing intimacy of relation, with the dyad of inherence representing at once the most intimate of relations and the transcendence of relation itself. Such a dyad is, to place such notions within the categories of categories, an illustration of the Concrete Unity, just as the relation of identity and diversity characterizes the the Abstract Unity (of Fig. 4). With the dyads of production something depends entirely upon something else, but the effect is still that two things exist. The agent remains alienated from the patient, while with the dyads of inherence this alienation is overcome. Having clarified the structures of dyadicity, Peirce is now prepared to unravel the tangled web of triadicity.

The dyad moves between the most abstract and the most intimate forms of dyadicity, approaching, at the very limits of existence, monadicity. Analogously, the triad traverses three degrees of relation from the monadically degenerate (three unrelated subjects) to the dyadically degenerate (two unrelated subjects) to the genuine triad (no unrelated subjects). Like an inherential dyad, the genuine triad is a monad of relations (1.472). What is required is a similar degree of intimacy between all three subjects. If *A* is the mother of *B* and *B* is the friend of *C*, then only the most oblique relation exists between *A* and *C* (in a physical sense). If *A*, *B*, and *C* are qualities of different suchness, then they form no triad at all internally, though they may form one in an act of contemplation or by means of some other form of adventitious closure. For this reason the only forms of genuine triadicity Peirce distinguishes are *laws:*

> I am satisfied that no triad which does not involve generality, that is, the assertion of which does not imply something concerning *every possible* object of some description can be a genuine triad. (1.476)

It is for this reason that he can find nothing of genuine philosophical interest in the possible structures of degenerate triads (1.481). They are not really triads and can best be considered as dyads or monads, though not medads. The act of contemplation differs in no philosophically interesting way in the monadically degenerate case of triads from that of monadically degenerate dyads.

As laws, genuine triads may be trichotomized into laws of monads, dyads, and triads. But this raises an interesting question. Have we not just previously considered the laws of monads and dyads *in general?* If so, as seems likely, then the very "Logic of Mathematics" belongs to the class of genuinely triadic phenomena in general. It appears, then, that of the three realms or 'worlds' subject to law—the worlds of quality, fact, and representation—the "Logic of Mathematics" belongs to the world of representation. Each category itself, then, is capable of taking on each of the three categorial dimensions, generating the following list, with the general category of relation on the left and its 'concrete' referent on the right:

Monad as Monad	Abstract Quality
Monad as Dyad	Existent Quality
Monad as Triad	General Quality
Dyad as Monad	Possible Relation
Dyad as Dyad	Existent Relation
Dyad as Triad	General Relation
Triad as Monad	Formal Mediation
Triad as Dyad	Existent Mediation
Triad as Triad	General Mediation

No wonder then that Peirce is able to speak of triads as monads, or dyads as monads. The three categories serve as *transcendentalia,* applying each to itself and to the others. But now a new list of categories emerges. Quality, fact, and representation, having the dimensions of monad, dyad, and triad, and of Firstness, Secondness, and Thirdness, emerge in each of three forms of *Abstract Unity, Concrete Plurality,* and *Concrete Unity.* Whatever is genuinely (transcendentally) monadic is *abstract, non-existent, non-particular, and yet a unity;* having no dimension of dyadicity, it enters into no relations. And, as the "Logic of Mathematics" reveals, it cannot be thought-of apart from dyadicity. The transcendental dyad is *concrete, determined, and related beyond itself.* It cannot be thought-of apart from the triad that links the many in a unified interaction (force). Finally, the transcendental triad is a *true unity* that binds many into one. A category, in the mind of the metaphysician, unifies many into one, but if it is a genuine category it does this only because what it categorizes comprises a genuine unity of the many itself. Hence corresponding to the category of representation there must be something represented by the category, in short, a concrete unity. If a genuine triad cannot resolve itself into a "formless aggregation" (1.477), it must only be because it contains an *internal* unity and not a unity contemplated.

The complete list of genuine triads should comprise General Qualities, General Relations, and the three forms of Mediation. Peirce, however, seems to overlook the first two and instead focuses only upon the latter three as laws of quality, fact, and relation. In all three forms of mediation there is generality and law, but there is also in each a different ontological grade of application. There is both law and the lawful object. In his classification of genuine mediation he indicates various degrees of lawfulness. (This classification is given in Fig. 8 below.) He distinguishes laws of quality from *general* laws of quality, the former being merely classificatory, and the latter genuinely nomological. Of a classificatory system of quality "we can have but a fragmentary knowledge" (1.484). Perhaps this is because we cannot conceive of mediation between qualities, that is, without introducing other qualities and in so doing making any previous classification obsolete. Such a classification would be of Existent Qualities and would be "fragmentary" simply because existent qualities are by nature plural and manifold. The general laws of quality apply, on the the other hand, to General Qualities (quality as a category) and are (1) that any quality perfectly represents itself, (2) that any two qualities are either comparable or determinable, and (3) that any two qualities are comparable according to the qualities of hue, intensity, and purity. The general laws of logic, as comprising a subdivision of the laws of fact or dyadicity, are (1) that every fact is definite, (2) that only two possible determinations (affirmative and negative) relate subject and predicate, and (3) that subject, predicate, and mediating thought can be related in a threefold inferential process.

Fig. 8

Genuine Triads
  Laws of Quality
  Laws of Fact
    Logical
    Metaphysical
      Necessary
        general laws of quality
        general laws of logic
        general laws of metaphysics
      Contingent
        logicalistic: laws of time
        non-logicalistic: laws of space
  Laws of Representation
  [General Semeiotic?]

The general laws of metaphysics are (1) that the root of all being is One, (2) that all existence lies in opposition, and (3) that "the end of being and the highest reality is the living impersonation of the idea that evolution generates. Whatever is real is the law of something less real" (1.487). In these laws of metaphysics we verge upon the realm of ontological realities, of which the laws are but cognitive reflections: the underlying Abstract Unity as the "root" of Being, the Concrete Plurality, when seen in light of the previous category, as a tension of opposites, and the Concrete Unity as the "living impersonation" of Abstract Unity.

As Peirce continued to work on his "Logic of Mathematics" it became increasingly clear to him where the course of his analysis was leading. A discovery and a classification of metaphysical categories in the form of abstractions of generalities (of quality, relation, and mediation), when seen themselves in light of the third law of metaphysics, imply the *reality* of concrete generalities as well. At this point the possibility that the order of logical analysis did not reflect the order of reality no doubt occurred to Peirce. There could surely be categories of Firstness, Secondness, and Thirdness. But what if the characters of Firstness imply those of Thirdness? Then Thirdness would be First. This is harmless enough until we consider whether quality is an ontological First, and almost everything Peirce had said about the complexity of experienced quality since the 'new list' paper would support the case that it was not. What is First is Abstract Generality, in the form of formal mediation, and this—as we shall see and as Peirce was also to realize—is what Hegel meant by the *Concept*. And so Peirce concludes:

> To get at the idea of a monad, and especially to make it an accurate and clear conception, it is necessary to begin with the idea of a triad and find the monad-idea involved in it. But this is only a scaffolding necessary during the process of constructing the conception. When the conception has been constructed, the scaffolding may be removed, and the monad-idea will be there in all its abstract perfection. (1.493)

The monad is simply the monad regarded as a representation, the representation of a monad as a metaphysical category. This is a far cry from being quality or pure feeling itself, and is closer to the idea of an abstract unity containing only self-mediation. But if the abstract perfection of the monad involves unity, an abstract unity, how can it be genuinely First?

In his work preparatory to the Cambridge Conferences of 1898 Peirce began to realize that the tychistic-evolutionary model of Firstness, Secondness, and Thirdness required some serious modification. It was also around this time, I surmise, that he revived his earliest theory of categories from beneath the heap of manuscripts he had preserved for nearly forty years. Recalling that early work, he wrote:

Suffice it to say that I seemed to myself to be blindly groping among a deranged system of conceptions; and after trying to solve the puzzle in a direct speculative, a physical, a historical, and a psychological manner, I finally concluded the only way was to attack it as Kant had done from the side of formal logic. (1.563)

But at that time he had failed to notice that the triads of *I*, *It*, and *Thou* and *simple, human,* and *perfect* provided an account only of relations, even where he used instances of the former in a role of logical subject, and that the long list, from Worlds to Manifests, could be arranged into a shorter list of general forms (as in Fig. 4 and in the nine-category list just given). Perhaps it was in rethinking these difficulties that he began to see the categories in Platonic terms once more, and in terms of Hegelian objective logic. For Hegel, the Concept evolves into the Absolute, or, in terms used herein, Abstract Unity becomes Concrete Unity. Now Peirce also begins speaking of two Worlds, an inner and outer, where "the idea in its purity is an eternal being in the Inner World" (4.161). In addition, he begins linking the abstract and the concrete through an Aristotelian conception of potentiality, where abstractions not only become possible, but are destined to become concretized. One argument for such "potential aggregates" is found in "The Logic of Continuity," one of the eight Cambridge lectures. There he proves that a potential multitude cannot be a collection of monads (6.187–88). A potential collection is indeterminate, yet determinable, for by taking on greater determination it becomes realizable. If the collection were simply comprised of monads, determination would have to take place by a realization of potential qualities. However, if determination is a process whereby something potential becomes distinct, and further, if any potential determination is at least determinate relative to some other potential collection (according to the three principles of determination from Kant), then any potential quality must be distinct. Yet the number of individuals is potentially more numerous than any given multitude, and if each individual is determined solely by quality, so must be the number of qualities. But then, Peirce concludes, "these qualities would form a collection too multitudinous for them to remain distinct" (6.188). Hence determination of a potential multitudinous collection cannot be by quality, and the members of the collection cannot be monads. As long as we assume monads, the only general character of a collection will be the numbers of monads. But, strictly speaking, monads are not the sorts of things that can be counted, for to do so is to put them into relation with each other, to give them a place in an order, and so is to destroy their monadicity. If the only dimension of potentiality is 'increase in number', then as the number of monads increases there must also be a distinct quality for each monad. These become progressively indistinct as the multitude grows, until the only quality possessed by a monad is that it *is* a monad, but somehow *not* a monad of anything. At this point the very notion of potentiality seems to dissolve as well.

Had he begun simply with dyadicity, or even with a monad relative to medadicity, he would have arrived at the same result. In order for the notion of potentiality to take on real meaning, we must begin with a collection subject to triadicity or generality. We begin with "relational generality" (6.190) and conceive of the determination of potentiality as the *concretization* of such generality. Real potentiality, then, is only possible if Thirdness is First! The implications of this change of perspective are vast. Now it no longer could be the case that the metaphysical categories must rest upon the logical categories. Logic derives on one level from the laws of metaphysics. However, it is only by first investigating the forms of logic that this could ever become known. But now Peirce is in a position to ponder once more, as he had forty years earlier, the question of the Platonic universe, and with it the logic of the universe, the logic of things, and the logic of events: "That the logic of the universe is more rudimentary than our subjective logic is a hypothesis which may be worth examination in some stage of culture, but it is too violently at war with all the lessons which this age has learned . . . " (6.189). The logic of the universe is based upon a continuum of "high generality" (6.191) that comprises the logic of concrete events in the form of thought-events (psychics) or force-events (physics). But there can be no such higher *generality* unless there is a commanding form (in the form of abstract unity) to *generate* it. And now Peirce's embryonic Platonism emerges clearly for the first time after lying dormant for forty years:

From this point of view we must suppose that the existing universe, with all its arbitrary secondness, is an off-shoot from, or an arbitrary determination of, a world of ideas, a Platonic world; not that our superior logic has enabled us to reach up to a world of forms to which the real universe, with its feebler logic, was inadequate. (6.192; see also 6.208)

It is our own logic that is feeble and the logic of the universe that is superior. This is not incompatible with the evolutionary view, for the abstract form can become concrete to one degree or another, and so:

The Evolutionary process is, therefore, not a mere evolution of the *existing universe,* but rather a process by which the very Platonic forms themselves have become or are becoming developed. (6.194)

Development, in this case, may be taken to mean that the forms themselves undergo development, but it is more likely, if the interpretation here given is correct, that the forms take part in development by entering into a "theatre of reaction" (6.195). Confusion may result from Peirce's continued use of the phrase "evolution of forms" (6.196, 6.200) in contrast with the notion of 'forms of evolution', but his actual descriptions of the process contain less ambiguity. For example:

Yet we must not assume that qualities arose separate and came into relation afterward. It was just the reverse. The general indefinite potentiality became limited and heterogeneous. Those who express the idea to themselves by saying that the Divine Creator determined so and so may be incautiously clothing the idea in a *garb* that is open to criticism, but it is, after all, substantially the only philosophical answer to the problem. (6.199)

The effect of this view is to diminish the status of tychism in the overall theory of development. Chance continues to operate, but simply as the temporary and localized absence of order:

> I chiefly insist upon continuity, or Thirdness, and, in order to secure to thirdness its really commanding function, I find it indispensable fully [to] recognize that it is a third, and that Firstness, or chance, and Secondness, or Brute reaction, are other elements, without the independence of which Thirdness would not have anything upon which to operate. (6.202)

And in other notes prepared for the Cambridge Conferences (MS. 943) Peirce concludes: "The second does not spring out of the first directly; but firstness looked at from a second point of view gives birth to a thirdness and the secondness comes out of the thirdness. This is the true logic of events." This is a somewhat puzzling remark even beyond its rejection of the firstness of Firstness. The "second" both "gives birth" to Thirdness and "comes out of" Thirdness. How can this be imagined except by thinking of the concretization of abstraction, turning the *I* into *It*, by a process governed by abstraction itself?

What, we may wonder, becomes of the long-standing criticism of Hegel? Hegel may have overlooked Secondness, as Peirce often remarked, but now Secondness is merely a perspectival nexus of relational generality. Not surprisingly, from 1897 or so onward Peirce steadily increased his praise for Hegel, so that by 1905 he would conclude that he had done not much better than Hegel when it came to the theory of categories (L–463)[1]. The difference between them finally turned on the question of whether or not Hegel's dialectic had to be given a rigorously mechanistic interpretation, whether "the whole universe and every feature of it, however minute, is rational, and was constrained to be as it is by the logic of events" (6.218). Peirce denied that the universe was so minutely determined, but did not deny that "the whole universe and every feature of it must be regarded as rational, that is as brought about by the logic of events" (6.218).

Another indication of the new priority of metaphysical categories over those of logic and psychology is found in Peirce's remarks on *quale*-consciousness contained in his discussion of the logic of events. *Quale*-consciousness contains unity and yet is irreducibly concrete and without parts. What then could be the origin of such a unity? Here Peirce rejects his previous efforts to derive unity either logically or psychophysically from, respectively, sign-action or neuron-action. Instead, unity cannot *originate* from plurality, he concludes (6.227), but must be grounded in some underlying metaphysical form (6.229).

2. THE LONG LIST REVISITED

As Peirce came to see the categories of Firstness, Secondness, and Thirdness in a perspectival and transcendental fashion it must have occurred to him that a method for generating the elusive long list of categories might finally be found. A long list cannot be generated without a method of generation, but the basic categories might reveal such a method if they could combine in some natural and systematic fashion. Since Firstness can characterize both a relation and some sort of subject, and since analogous possibilities accompany the other two categories, it becomes possible to take any subject and *firstize, secondize*, and *thirdize* it. This project emerges from several of Peirce's writings during 1902 and 1903, specifically in the unfinished "Minute Logic," in his eight lectures on pragmatism delivered at Harvard, and in the eight Lowell Lectures of 1903, including notes to the lectures printed as *A Syllabus of Certain Topics of Logic.*

Perhaps to indicate his changing attitude toward the categories, Peirce relabeled them *cenopythagorean categories,* and compared them closely with Hegel's dialectical 'moments' (2.84, 2.87; 1.351; 7.528). The reference to Pythagoras suggests number-like categories, and this in turn suggests the notions of an *operator* and a *recursive process.* Using the operation of 'firstization' on any given categorial subject, one can generate a different category altogether. And so Peirce became convinced once more that "all such metaphysical conceptions are but determinations of the categories; and consequently form a regular system" (2.117). However, unlike Hegel's "long wanderings" in the *Encyclopaedia,* Peirce's own system would display more clearly its own method (5.38, 5.43). As we have already mentioned, Peirce was changing his mind about Hegel. The major reason may have been due to his reading the *Phenomenology of Spirit*, which he considered superior to any other work of Hegel (5.37; 8.112), and which he called "a work . . . perhaps the most profound ever written" (MS. 478, p. 27). His own phenomenology, then, would undertake the construction of the long list by freeing the short-list categories from their logical origins. Then they would stand out in transcendental clarity, phenomenologically self-sufficient. Phenomenology would "unravel the tangled skein [of] all that in any sense appears and wind it into distinct forms" (1.280; 2.197; 5.122).

The turn to phenomenology, or perhaps the return to it after many years, forced Peirce to rethink his anti-intuitionism. For to the extent that phenomenological reflection holds up the inferential process, and fixes directly upon a noema, it seems to necessitate an introspection *of* signs, but not *in* signs. All that 'appears' is considered data in this view, and so it can no longer be true that 'there are no data'. In the "Minute Logic" Peirce returns to the intuitionism of Abbé Gratry's *La Logique*, which he had read forty years previously, by advocating a "natural light of reason" (2.23–25) as the basis upon which logical principles are discovered. And in the pragmatism lectures he observed: "Every philosopher who denies the doctrine of Immediate Perception—including idealists of every stripe—by that denial cuts off all possibility of ever cognizing a *relation*" (5.56). This modification of views is, however, less revolutionary than at first appears. Peirce would still deny that cognition could ever supply its own warrant, or that the feeling of immediacy could be apodictic. He continued to reject the German speculative and subjective method in favor of the English analytic method, and only concluded in favor of a reasoning instinct on the grounds of his theory that through experimental test we gain evidence of the telic dimension of cognition relative to truth. Now if this quidedness in inference is possible, with learning and effort (both inferential processes) it may also be possible to guide our attention to the qualities of consciousness itself (1.522). As he might have put it, we cannot *begin* with intuition and common sense, but after speculation we can *arrive* at their justification, now in the form of what was soon to be named *critical common-sensism*.

Yet if Peirce is to continue to maintain that no concentration can create unity where there is none originally, it follows that the unity of a noema could not result simply from our ability to discern what is in consciousness. Its unity must lie on some ground independent of phenomenological reflection. In the cases of inferential instinct and phenomenological instinct Peirce can claim abductively that their ground and possibility lie in the very constitution of the universe:

> If the universe conforms, with any approach to accuracy, to certain highly pervasive laws, and if man's mind has been developed under the influence of those laws, it is to be expected that he should have a *natural light*, or *light of nature*, or *instinctive insight*, or genius, tending to make him guess those laws aright, or nearly aright. (5.604)

Ultimately it is only the predictive power of experimental knowledge that gives us an intimation of the telic guidedness of cognition, but with that inkling we may hypothesize other possibilities of cognition, including the possibility that it contain the ability to grasp elemental features of experience. Peirce's phenomenology, then, does not claim to stand on its own ground as does Husserl's, a claim which in the latter case Peirce felt to be unfounded (4.7). It is part of a complex set of hypotheses devised to explain the workings of ordinary cognition.

From a phenomenological point of view the operator of 'firstization' instructs that a subject or phenomenon be looked at 'in itself'; the operator of 'secondization' instructs that the subject or phenomenon be compared with either internal or external characters or with its own environment; and the operator of 'thirdization' instructs that a subject or phenomenon be regarded as a totality of influences within a postulated unity. Then the result of any operation may itself, after hypostatic abstraction, be operated upon, provided there are sufficient characters in the subject to allow further categorization. In the "Minute Logic," where Peirce calls the three basic categories *Originality*, *Obsistence*, and *Transuasion*, he considers each of the categories as aspects of themselves. There is original Originality, original Obsistence, and original Transuasion; these are simply the most abstract definitions of the categories possible. In their "Obsistential aspect," on the other hand, they become quality, relation as relation, and mediation as mediation (not mediating as unity). Peirce does not continue with a transuasional description of the categories, but instead chooses to delineate some of the various aspects of the obsistential aspect of transuasion, particularly the 'originalian' aspect, the *sign*. This aspect may itself be operated upon, producing an originalian sign, or an *icon;* an obsistential sign, or an *index;* and a transuasional sign, or a *symbol*, making the latter a transuasional aspect of an originalian aspect of an obsistential aspect of Transuasion!

In preparing his Lowell Lectures of 1903 Peirce further clarified this recursive process:

> Here we make a new distinction. You see the principle of our procedure. We begin by asking what is the mode of being of the subject of inquiry, that is, what is its absolute and most universal Firstness? The answer comes, that it is either the Firstness of Firstness, the Firstness of Secondness, or the Firstness of Thirdness.

At this point we must keep in mind that the Firstness of Secondness is simply Secondness in its most abstract ("most universal") form, the 'essence' of Secondness, so to speak. He continues:

> We then ask what is the universal Secondness, and what the universal Thirdness of the subject in hand.
>
> Next we say that Firstness of Firstness, that Firstness of Secondness and that Firstness of Thirdness, that have been described, have been the Firstness of the Firstness in each case. But what is the Secondness that is involved in it and what is the Thirdness?
>
> So the Secondnesses as they have been first given are the Firstnesses of those Secondnesses. We ask what Secondness they involve and what Thirdness. And so we have endless questions, of which I have only given you small scraps. (1.543)

And so we also have the method of generating the long list of categories. If we recall the method of the "Logic of Mathematics" and also interpret categorial degeneracy as the application of the categories to themselves, three rules of recursive development emerge: (1) if something is a First it can only be a First in any respect; (2) if something is a Second, it may be either a first Second (FS) or a second Second (SS); and (3) if something is a Third, it may be either a first Third (FT), second Third (ST), or third Third (TT). Then if a second Second is a Second, it may either be a first Second-Second (FSS) or a second Second-Second (SSS). Letting X indicate "the subject of inquiry" and "the subject in hand" we get a branching system of regenerating categories:

Fig. 9

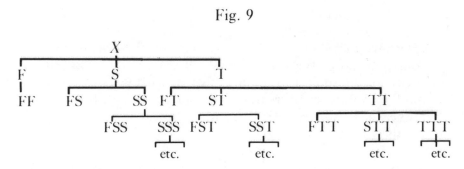

It becomes clear that for the recursive process to produce actual metaphysical categories, X must not itself be a category, but rather something possessing a "mode of being," and it is at this point that phenomenology turns into ontology. Something must be given or presented for categorial elaboration to take place. The categories themselves cannot supply this factor. From this point of view it becomes clear why Peirce's late philosophy required a *phaneron*. We see, for example, that certain categories are not allowed (SF, TF, TS, TF), and so if X is taken as a categorial First or Second, Fig. 9 would take an abbreviated form. It is only with Thirdness that the recursive process achieves its fullest potential, and, to the extent that any monad or dyad may be dialectically evolved into a triad according to the method of the "Logic of Mathematics," we are not surprised to see Peirce admitting that "Thirdness is the one and sole category. This is substantially the idea of Hegel; and unquestionably it contains a truth" (5.90). It also becomes clear that for X to be subject to the three operations, it must be capable of taking on differing degrees of reality and involvement, and if so, this suggests the existence of a hierarchy of ontological modes of being of which the categories

F, S, T, FF, FS, FT, etc., are but phenomenological manifestations. If we let X indicate the 'germ' of bare reality, a mere undifferentiated 'something', then we get (1.531–33):

FX   possible quality
SX   existent quality
TX   mediated quality

Then if we operate further on the barest dyads and triads we get (1.535–37):

FSX   referential quality
SSX   reactive quality
FTX   positive qualitative possibility
STX   existent thing
TTX   law

Here FTX is "something capable of being completely embodied" (1.536) as the quality of a complex Third like the play *King Lear* (1.531), while STX is no longer a mere qualitative existence, but the existence of an entity. The latter three categories of the list being thirds, something organized (mediated) must already be posited in order to be operated upon; this must apply to law as well. Law is not a generalization in this case, but a reality no less real than an existent thing. But law itself is the least concretized form of real generality. Further concretization occurs (1.537) as follows:

FTTX   thinkability
STTX   information
TTTX   cognition

In the first we have simply the *presence* of mind, in the second the concrete *use* of mind, and in the third the mediative use or *reflection* of mind, the latter being the proper use of mind in the form of sign-activity. And then TTTX becomes once more differentiated into representamen, object, interpretant, and these yet again into the various divisions of signs.

When the basic categories are thought of not as operators but as class names, they become the names of the modes of being. Peirce

initially doubted that the modes of being could be considered ontological isomorphisms of the phenomenological categories (2.116),
but eventually he settled on the connection as the best way to
proceed:

> My view is that there are three modes of being. I hold that
> we can directly observe them in elements of whatever is at
> any time before the mind in any way. They are the being of
> positive qualitative possibility, the being of critical fact,
> and the being of law that will govern facts in the future.
> (1.23)

The latter is embryonic being, being *in futuro,* which is rejected by
all nominalists. These modes correspond to possible, actual, and
necessary beings, except that Peirce's emphasis on "embodiment"
or "ensoulment" (1.218) contains the further notion that something
is becoming more ramified and more concretely unified. The
categories of Abstract Unity, Concrete Plurality, and Concrete
Unity attempt to capture this progress by combining the categories
of possibility, actuality, and necessity with those of unity, plurality,
and totality. Though Peirce made no such connection it may be
taken as understood in certain of his remarks. He speaks of a partially
degenerate Thirdness, ST, as an "Irrational Plurality" (5.70), as if
there were something unified, though not legitimately or essentially
(as is a Concrete Plurality); and he compares a thoroughly degenerate
Thirdness, FT, to pure self-consciousness as "a mere feeling that
has a dark instinct of being a germ of thought" (5.71). This is but a
unity, yet a unity of nothing particular, the "unity of monotony,"
in the words of his father;[2] in short, Abstract Unity. Completing the
triad, we turn to Thirdness as a genuine, full-bodied unity, a unity of
something concrete. As such it is both simple and complex (5.88):
as complex it is concrete, and as simple it is a unity (a Concrete
Unity). The quality of concrete unity, of unity in variety, is precisely what he would come to call *esthetic goodness:*

> In the light of the doctrine of categories I should say that an
> object, to be esthetically good, must have a multitude of
> parts so related to one another as to impart a positive simple
> immediate quality to their totality; and whatever does

this is, in so far, esthetically good, no matter what the
particular quality of the total may be. (5.132)

The recursively generated system of categories, then, was throughout subject to a fundamental principle: namely, *that abstract unity
become concrete unity*. This is the full meaning of synechism. For
any given X, what operations would be performed would depend
upon whether or not the movement (of modes of being) produced
satisfied that principle. The beauty of the recursive process, however,
was that if all licit possibilities were allowed, Thirdness would grow
at a progressively faster rate than either of the other categories.

Peirce never explicitly produced the long list of categories as
schematized here, though he had taken a major step in clarifying that
"regular system of relationships" he had worked on many years
earlier. My guess is that he had in mind the operating principles
embodied in Fig. 9, but that his mind was racing ahead to the fullest
implications of the unfolding of Thirdness in all areas. On this
account he may have been hesitant to begin a clear architectonic
formulation of the long list until it was clear where it was heading.
Of what we have, only the "Logic of Mathematics" approaches such
a formulation, and then only on its theoretical side. In the *Syllabus*
for the Lowell Lectures he included essays on the "Nomenclature
and Division of Dyadic Relations" (3.571–608) and the "Nomenclature and Divisions of Triadic Relations" (2.233–72), and here we
have another portion of the puzzle; however, the distinctions made
in these works derive from the metaphysical categories, and do not
generate the categories, as in the "Logic of Mathematics."

3. LIVING CATEGORIES

By now the whole framework of Peirce's thinking was beginning
to shift. Instead of trying to explain the emergence of Thirdness
out of Firstness and Secondness, he assumed Thirdness as a metaphysical postulate. But anything that could move of its own nature
toward concrete unity would be subject to final causation and so
would manifest the character of *life*. Objective logic, which studies
the 'life of the Concept' according to Hegel, studies for Peirce the
'life of signs' (2.111) and the "life-history" of symbols (2.112,

2.115). Certain ideas—and we notice Peirce now calling the categories *Ideas* (5.66)—have a "generative life" of their own (1.219–20). This notion connects nicely with the early arguments about signs and their *sui generis* activity, and with the arguments relating physical activity and signs. Now pragmatism becomes "a sort of instinctive attraction for living facts" (5.64), governed, we must presume, by a pragmatic clarification of the meaning of living ideas. Pragmatism, then, is not a method of the clarification of ideas, but a method whereby Ideas control the activity of inquirers. In this vein Peirce informed his perhaps bewildered audience in his 1903 Lectures of Pragmatism that pragmatism, if it is not to volatilize away in a vapor of subjectivity (5.33), must assume an *"active general principle"* operating in nature (5.99–100) and that this further implied the truth and acceptance of Scholastic Realism. Similar remarks about the dynamic and living dimension of thought were made in the Lowell Lectures (1.348; 5.594).

Is it a bald category-mistake to attribute 'life' to a concept? The answer to this question depends to a large extent upon one's metaphysical perspective. On more than one occasion Peirce may have looked up the definition of *life* in his copy of William Fleming's *The Vocabulary of Philosophy* and read:

> The theory of *evolution*. Schultz and others of the German writers of the same school, regard life as a regular evolution, created by opposing powers in the universe of existence, from the lowest forms of the vital functions to the highest spheres of thought and activity. To these speculators nature is not a fixed reality but a *relation*.[3]

In a sense Peirce had generalized upon this definition, extending the power of relation beyond biological organisms. Whenever something systematically manifests the ability to modify its surroundings, it possesses life (1.220; 6.158). A living category, then, is simply the schematization of this process. A sign is a living category because it can direct the flow of energies in an oganized direction; it is by its very nature an actively relating category. Any of the forms of relational generality would be capable of generating relations in this manner.

Two notions more than any others signal Peirce's changed

perspective: his increasing talk of final causes (and the resulting reclassification of the sciences in light of an increased emphasis on final, or nomological causation), and his Hegelian use of the term 'Reason'. After 1900 or so he modified his classification of the sciences by making logic a normative science governed by the results of ethics and ultimately esthetics (2.82; 5.35–36). No logical enterprise takes place outside of a context of goal-directed activity, and it is only in light of the study of goals and norms that the conduct of logic can be properly conceived. This view, however, did not commit him to a belief in a single global and conscious purpose behind all phenomena. He distinguished between *de facto* teleology and conscious, purposive teleology, much as did Aristotle. In the former case a process is telic to the extent that it can attain the same goal under varying conditions (1.204, 1.211). For this to be possible, it must be governed by a general schema, and so Peirce characterizes final causation generally as "logical causation" (1.250).

More interesting is Peirce's tendency at this time to attribute the general conduct of the universe to Reason. Again, this is not a providential Reason, but simply the operation of the categories of the short list. If there is a short list, then some schematizing organization is system-wide in the universe, but this is a scheming without cunning. He required that his Reason include the anti-rational tendency to create pluralities in nature (Secondness), and so insisted that Reason not govern all facets of existence (5.92). Yet though quality and existence are not deducible as the products of reason in their particularity, as W. T. Krug argued against Hegel's dialectic,[4] it does not follow that they are not, as classes of phenomena, subject to the generality of Thirdness and Reason. Quality and existence can play a rational role in the evolution of the universe, and in that sense can be rationally *aufgehoben*. Peirce's criticism of Hegel can be reduced to the observation that without real agency and efficient causation, a rational direction of change could not result. Efficient causation, as he observed (1.220), is required for the operation of final causation. Reason, then, is simply the lawful dimension of nature:

> But if there were no actual fact whatsoever which was meant by saying that the piece of carborundum was hard, there would be not the slightest meaning in the word hard as applied to it. The very being of the General, of Reason,

consists in its governing individual events. So, then, the essence of Reason is such that its being never can have been completely perfected. It always must be in a state of incipiency, of growth . . . . This development of Reason consists, you will observe, in embodiment, that is, in manifestation. The creation of the universe, which did not take place during a certain busy week, in the year 4004 B.C., but is going on today and never will be done, is this very development of Reason. (1.615)

This is a Reason without the hope of achieving the Absolute, for if reflection remains subject to the basic categories, new manifestations of previous fruits of Reason always remain possible. Such is the course of Peirce's objective logic.

Chapter
VII
The Foundation of Pragmaticism

1. The Pragmatic Maxim

If, in fact, an objective logic is at work in the universe, and if that logic constitutes an inherent reasonableness, then clearly any theory that entailed the denial of such a logic would have to be false. Yet the theory of objective logic is itself inferred to be true from a series of arguments relating metaphysical notions with psychological and experiential notions; it is not given to us from on high. In a sense those arguments are nothing other than Peirce's entire output in philosophy, insofar as his many tasks invariably involved either an application of the categories to some segment of reality or the formal articulation of the categories with an aim to achieving a better application.

In the last years of the nineteenth century and in the first half decade of this century Peirce watched his ideas on pragmatism grow into a movement of considerable vitality and variety. But he also witnessed the emergence of a theory or group of theories that entailed the denial of objective logic. In a general fashion, objective logic is refuted whenever it can be shown that a segment of reality is entirely unrelated with the rest of reality, for part of what it means for a logic to be objective is that its forms apply in all circumstances, though in differing degrees or manners. Beyond this, in Peirce's objective logic as in Hegel's, the priority of Thirdness stands out prominently, and so any theory that withholds the influence of Thirdness from a segment of reality also entails the denial of objective logic. In the spontaneous presence of pure feeling no Thirdness can be found, but in the life of cognition such qualitative presence takes on a greater meaning within the overall context of sign-activity.

Peirce dismissed the view popularly attributed to and advanced by most of the pragmatists that whatever was satisfactory was true: "As to this doctrine, if it is meant that True and Satisfactory are synonyms, it strikes me that it is not so much a doctrine of philosophy as it is a new contribution to English lexicography" (5.555). Such a doctrine was simply hedonism and nothing more (5.559). On 9 June 1904 he penned off a letter to John Dewey in which he remarked that the latter's *Studies in Logical Theory* (1903) exhibited a "spirit of intellectual licentiousness, that does not see that anything is so very false" (8.241). Responding to Dewey's psychologistic logic, Peirce noted:

> Thereupon, I remark that the "thought" of which you speak cannot be the "thought" of normative logic. For it is one of the characteristics of all normative science that it does not concern itself in the least with what actually takes place in the universe, barring always its assumption that what is before the mind always has those characteristics that are found there and which Phänomenologie is assumed to have made out. (8.239)

Peirce held himself partly responsible for this turn of events, noting of the "damnable error" (MS. 289) of the 1878 formulation that it easily suggested to the reader a nominalistic theory of meaning (8.208). But he was not entirely sure to what degree he was at fault in creating this impression. Exoneration could be found in the fact that the original formulation was presented in a popular monthly that seemed to have required popular exposition (5.453; 6.485), and yet damnation would also follow from the psychologistic emphasis on fixing belief and from the imprecise and inaccurate use of terms. There is considerable carelessness in Peirce's characterization of the question, "Is the untested diamond hard?"

as a "foolish question . . . except in the realm of logic" (5.403). Neither logic nor pragmatism was done justice by such a reply. In fact, the diamond *is* hard (1.27, n.1) while not being tested because the *meaning* of hardness is not what is at issue, but only the question of whether *this* diamond possesses that property; and insofar as the reality of the diamond as a diamond is also not at issue, it has to be considered really hard while not being tested. In 1905 Peirce concluded: "Is it not a monstrous perversion of the word and concept *real* to say that the accident of the non-arrival of the corundum prevented the hardness of the diamond from having the *reality* which it otherwise, with little doubt, would have had?" (5.457). Realities are not created by experimental operations, and neither are meanings. Results are, however; and results in turn become the occasion for further operations. Pragmatism, even in the early formulation, was not a theory of meaning, but of *usage*. Nothing prevents us from saying that diamonds remain soft until just prior to being scratched and then suddenly grow hard. This "would involve a modification of our present usage of speech with regard to the words hard and soft, but not of their meanings" (5.403).

We should also keep in mind that the pragmatic rule was suggested as a method of achieving a *third* grade of clarity of apprehension. The first two, intuitive clarity and logical distinctness, more properly covered the realm of meanings, and so Peirce was seeking to add yet another grade of clarity, not to undermine the previous two. His concern is with "the symphony of our intellectual life" (5.397), not with particular cadences. And here the pragmatic grade had a great deal to do with the coordination of thought, purpose, and action in a long-range, and distinctly intellectual, undertaking. As originally stated, the maxim is:

> Consider what effects, which might conceivably have practical bearings, we conceive the object of our conception to have. Then, our conception of these effects is the whole of our conception of object. (5.402)

Such a formulation was hardly inadvert. We notice at once that two sets of *conceptions* are being linked—those that pertain to certain effects and those that pertain to an object. No attempt is being made to link experienced sensible effects with conceptions.

To say that "our idea of anything *is* our idea of its sensible effects" (5.401) is not to say that an idea is a sign of sensible effects, but rather is a sign of *other signs*. For whatever reasons, Peirce chose not to introduce the semiotic apparatus into the "Illustrations" and the rendering, for that reason, could easily be seen as psychologistic.

How clear all of this was to him at the time is difficult to say. If his own attitude toward the 1878 paper was ambivalent, we must assume that he was not entirely sure how his interest in pragmatism had anything important to do with his other philosophical interests. He tells us in 1908 that he had passed through a period of doubt about pragmatism that lasted twenty years or so (MS. 300, pp. 15–16). This means that he may have begun to see new possibilities of interpretation at some time during the years 1898–1900, that is, if we assume the twenty-year period to commence with the publication of the "Illustrations." Possibly the doubt may have formed several years earlier or several years later, in the latter case during the Johns Hopkins period. What dispelled the doubt? Here a number of factors contribute to an answer—the formulation of a logic mathematics, the embracing of an Aristotelian view of real possibility and of a Hegelian view of Reason, and the formulation of the existential graphs. Together these helped to convince Peirce that he had available conceptual tools to keep pragmatism free from nominalism.

As a result, pragmatism, or now "pragmaticism," becomes increasingly formulated in abstract, intellectualist terms. There is nothing of 'brute' experience in it, or of radical empiricism; these had to do with other grades of clarity of apprehension. Pragmaticism is an advanced grade, one that makes possible a further articulation of apprehension beyond the previous two. Peirce himself was not sure whether the grades of clarity were stages wherein a later one could transcend an earlier one, or whether they were simply different kinds of clarity, each indispensable in its own right. Intuitive clarity seems to be an instance of Firstness and of logical 'character', analytic distinctness, an instance of Secondness and logical relation, and pragmatic clarity, an instance of Thirdness and logical representation by means of an interpretant. If so, then it is not surprising that Peirce may have had the same difficulties establishing ontological priority in the case of clarity of apprehension that he did in establishing a priority of the categories in general.

In its new formulation pragmaticism becomes "the master-key to all doors of philosophy, provided it be true" (MS. 328; also MS. 320). Unmistakably, then, if we recall on what occasions Peirce referred to the lock on the door of philosophy, particularly with reference to the conditions of inference in general, we can surmise that in its complete formulation, pragmaticism was to play a central role in objective logic. In 1905, as part of *The Monist* series on pragmaticism, he reworded the maxim in semiotic language: "The entire intellectual purport of any symbol consists in the total of all general modes of rational conduct which, conditionally upon all the possible different circumstances and desires, would ensue upon the acceptance of the symbol" (5.438). This is a theory of the *rational* purport of symbols, one that "eliminates their sential element" (5.428). But this is just the beginning. A host of assumptions lie beneath the maxim. In the first paper of the series one such assumption emerges almost at once:

> Since obviously nothing that might not result from experiment can have any direct bearing upon conduct, if one can define accurately all the conceivable experimental phenomena which the affirmation or denial of a concept could imply, one would have therein a complete definition of the concept, and *there is absolutely nothing more in it.* (5.412)

From this we learn that the experimentalist point of view has no limits in matters concerning human experience and that it may be possible for human beings to comprehend a conception in such a manner as to be able to comprehend all experimental implications of the meaning of the conception. This involves a question of accurate definition; it is also an extremely stringent condition. For in assessing it we are assuming a great deal about the nature of reality and mind and of the relationship between them. Among other things we are assuming that for a concept to contain generality, it must be thought of as being applicable *in principle* to something that *might* happen. What becomes of the generality of a conception when it is no longer possible (i.e., is impossible) that this conception ever be applicable to some future experience? What becomes of the generality of the conception of hardness in a world of immaterial souls, or of the generality of a probability assignment of a pair of dice now thrown into acid? What, in short, can guarantee in such circumstances a rebuttal to the nominalist's insistence that hardness and probability are conceptions pinned only to actual and past events? As long as conceptions are regarded as definitions of such a fixed reality, without regard to the interplay of reality and experience, the nominalist can hold his ground.

Against this the pragmaticist can reply that no such impossibility is possible, for one of the general modes of rational conduct that would ensue from the acceptance of the notion of hardness is the act of *making* something hard. Beginning with a very soft universe, it can be possible to make something harder and harder, provided of course that this remains a possibility in such a universe. But to say that it is a possibility is to say that hardness is a generality in that universe. This making-process is nothing but experimental science itself. Hardness can always be applicable to some experience, and if the dice are destroyed new ones can be made. It is not, then, that something *might* happen; rather, "whatever means something, means that something will happen" (8.194; 5.526). Experimentation itself is a kind of feedback process. To make an object hard, it must be continually tested, and to make a die it must be continually measured. This requires self-control, and so,

> the pragmaticist does not make the *summum bonum* to consist in action, but makes it to consist in that process of evolution whereby the existent comes more and more to embody those generals which were just now said to be *destined*, which is what we strive to express in calling them *reasonable*. In its higher stages, evolution takes place more and more largely through self-control, and this gives the pragmaticist a sort of justification for making the rational purport to be general. (5.433)

It is "rational experimental logic" (5.430) that gives "a sort of justification" to pragmaticism. But Peirce would not say that this means that generality must rely entirely upon the actions of humans. If this were so, meaning would be entirely contextual and nominalism would emerge once more. It is true that as long as we look only at the authority of human beings, anthropomorphism is a plausible conclusion (5.536); yet if it is possible to analyze other self-controlling mechanisms in nature, as is required by synechism, then a general character of self-control guarantees a non-anthropomorphic generality in nature. To embrace this position is to embrace objective logic itself.

To a significant degree one can dispel the hold of anthropomorphism even when considering humans alone if one can 'naturalize' the cognitive process, showing its continuity with natural phenomena. And this is the task Peirce had been involved in for nearly a half century. In this view, thinking itself is a kind of activity (5.429, 5.534; 8.191) having isomorphic features with all forms of activity in nature, and so if humans interact experimentally with nature, they do not do so exclusively from the standpoint of subjectivity.

2. The Proof of Pragmaticism

In linking the intellectual purport of a symbol with objective generality, a great deal of metaphysics is required. While Peirce continued to challenge the "rubbish" of certain forms of metaphysics (5.423; 8.191), pragmaticism itself became linked to a proper form of metaphysics (5.412, 5.423, 5.503) and in fact involved a "new metaphysical light" (MS.319). To justify the third grade of clarity of apprehension in a pragmatic form would require a "multitude of novel distinctions" (MS. 300, p. 17), such distinctions being necessary to dispel the nominalist attack on the purport of intellectual conceptions. Peirce called such a justification of pragmaticism a "proof" and promised to deliver this proof in the third article of *The Monist* series on pragmaticism. That article appeared, but from its title, "Prolegomena to an Apology for Pragmaticism," it is apparent that the proof in any clearly discernible form was missing. What is more, he never would clear for the reader that "thorny path" leading to the proof (5.10), so that we are left to reconstruct it, even if only in outline, as best we can ourselves.

What is the nature of the proof? Peirce spoke of it as "a scientific and logical proof" (MS. 296), but this gives us little clue as to its construction. He was aware that philosophic 'proofs' were not simply like logical or mathematical proofs, but rather required a great deal of subsidiary articulation. Yet it would be inaccurate to say that simply defending an articulated philosophy, such as materialism, or idealism, would constitute proof of whatever propositions were entailed by that philosophy. Something remained, to his way of thinking, that had to be proved, that is, some particular fact or relation; in this case, the claim that pragmaticism and pragmaticism alone makes possible a third grade of clarity.

Among the clues concerning the general form of the proof two stand out prominently. One is found in a passage on pragmaticism written in 1905, at a time when Peirce was undoubtedly trying to put the proof in clear and succinct language: "Pragmaticism was not a theory which special circumstances had led its authors to entertain. It had been designed and constructed, to use the expression of Kant, architectonically." This means among other things that the material of the period described in Part Two of the present work, the period in which pragmatism came to birth, followed naturally as an elaboration of the topics of Part One. Peirce knew that in 1878, but few if any others did. He continues:

> Just as a civil engineer, before erecting a bridge, a ship, or a house, will think of the different properties of all materials, and will use no iron, stone, or cement, that has not been subjected to tests; and will put them together in ways minutely considered, so, in constructing the doctrine of pragmaticism the properties of all decomposable concepts [the categories] were examined and the ways in which they could be compounded. Then the purpose of the proposed doctrine having been analyzed, it was constructed out of the appropriate concepts so as to fulfill that purpose. In this way, the truth of it was proved. There are subsidiary confirmations of its truth; but it is believed that there is no other independent way of strictly proving it . . . . (5.5)

The other clue is found in "The Bed-Rock Beneath Pragmaticism," written after 1905, wherein Peirce observes that the argument for pragmaticism "shall be treated as a hypothesis to be experimentally tested by developing the most striking of the consequences which this hypothesis necessitates, and then, on comparing them with the facts, by finding an inductive confirmation of its validity (MS. 300, p. 22). Both remarks suggest the idea of the proof as having a deductive form, an abductive origin, and an inductive confirmation.[1]

More specifically, we know that the proof would involve in some way (1) "a purified philosophy" (5.423), probably in the form of the phenomenological theory of categories; (2) the main body of our instinctive beliefs, or critical common-sensism (5.423, 5.499, 5.522; 8.207); (3) Scholastic Realism (5.453, 5.503; 8.208); (4) the truth of synechism (5.415); and (5) the existential graphs (4.535). We are also told that in its full formulation pragmaticism would be similar to Hegelian absolute idealism (5.436). Combining these features in a specific proof is no small feat, and yet Peirce believed that it was required. Even if only subsidiary confirmation was required, it still remained to be clearly outlined in what ways pragmaticism was justified by its architectonic construction.

Finally, Peirce tells us in 1908 that the proof first stood out clearly in his mind six or more years prior. This would put it roughly between 1896 and 1902. In 1899 Josiah Royce published the first series of his Gifford Lectures entitled *The World and the Individual,* and Peirce picked up the work for review in *The Nation* (1900). In the lectures Royce presented a theory of "the essentially teleological inner structure of consious ideas."[2] Ideas, he argued, are volitional as well as intellectual and their very formation the result of purpose and expectation:

> Yet *if we could* reach that limit of determination which is all the while our goal, if our universal judgments were confirmed by an adequate experience, not of *some* object (still indeterminate), but of *the individual* object, or of *all the individual objects,* so that no other empirical expression of our ideas remained possible, then, indeed, we should stand in the immediate presence of the Real.[3]

According to Royce, the full embodiment of an idea is simply the full realization of a purpose. Prior to that realization the idea is 'vague' and 'imperfect'.[4] From this Royce goes on to conclude that the coordination of all ideas is ultimately required for the fulfillment of any single idea; and this means that intellection must strive for an entire *life* of realized purpose: "the Being of the real object of which you now think means a life that expresses the fulfilment of just your present plan . . . ."[5] In reading this passage Peirce wondered how Royce could coordinate ideas in this manner. In his review he wrote:

> Royce evidently thinks that a purpose cannot be fully definite, until all the circumstances of the entire life are taken into account; so that, however meagre the internal meaning of an idea may be, as long as it remains general and "abstract," yet when that internal meaning is fully accomplished by its becoming in every respect determined, the external meaning will cover the whole life of the individual. Certainly, it is conceivable that such might be the result; but to prove that such would be the result, a far more exact examination of the question would be requisite than the author attempts. (8.122)

But how can a part *fully represent* the whole, even if only implicitly? Royce illustrates this possibility with the example of a perfectly miniaturized topographical map resting on the very terrain it maps.[6] The map will contain all features of the terrain, including a miniaturized map of itself. Peirce notes that this example requires a convergence to the formality of a single point, the latter being represented on all maps and not itself a representation of anything else but itself. He, on the other hand, requires not a representation and its object, but a series of representations and objects, each object being a representation of a still more determinate object, until the representation and the idea are both as nearly determinate as possible:

> A map is a section of a projection of which the surface mapped is another section. This projection itself is a sheaf of lines which diverge from one point. Instead of saying that a Self is a map, a more adequate metaphor would call it a projection of the reality, of which projection any one idea of the Self is a section. (8.125)

If, following Royce, we think of the journey from indetermination to determination as a process of moving from vague generality to concretely realized rational activity, we are in a position to link the vanishing point of representability as a kind of self-consciousness (8.122) with the fully externalized rationality of scientific activity. On the one hand we have the subjectivity of the phaneron, on the other, the objectivity of the icon. How are these two realms to be linked? The phaneron may be regarded as pure interiority and the icon as pure exteriority. The phaneron is "the collective total of all that is in any way or in any sense present to the mind, quite regardless of whether it corresponds to any real thing or not" (1.284). Peirce also speaks of it as a "presentment" (1.313), a "pure priman" (1.318; MS. 908, p. 9), and so as to introduce no extraneous notions, a "swa" (MS. 899). In all of his analyses the following conclusion is reached: while no decomposable conceptions can be found *within* the phaneron, there still remain decomposable conceptions of the *external* relations of it. This is simply the conclusion of the "Logic of Mathematics." A phaneron has "valency" (1.288–92), and in a draft of "The Basis of Pragmaticism" he indicates how this can be shown:

> If there is a Phaneron (which would be an assertion) or even if we can ask whether there be or no, there must be an idea of *combination* (i.e. having *combination* for its object thought of). Now the general idea of a combination must be an indecomposable idea. For otherwise it would be compounded, and the idea of combination would enter into it as an analytic part of it. It is, however, quite absurd to suppose an idea to be part of itself, and *not the whole*. Therefore, if there is a Phaneron, the idea of combination is an indecomposable element of it. (MS. 908, p. 8)

Something not present to consciousness cannot be a phaneron; but if something *is* present to consciousness it is assertion, and assertion is relative. Here we are reminded of the germinal idea behind the 'new list' of categories. There it was found that the modes of combination, in that case, of predication, had a stable logical structure. Now it is once more discovered that the combination of all phanerons is at least triadic in nature, and, from a theoretical point of view, only triadic in nature.

In "The Cenopythagorean Categories" (MS. 899) Peirce

approached this question from a slightly different point of view.
There the phaneron is designated as a "swa" so that no connotation
be carried into the analysis. Among the distinctions made, four are
of particular importance. An *individual sign* (*word* or *assertion*) is
one that allows the interpreter no choice as to what is intended by
it. Referring to someone by his proper name while pointing to that
person nearby is to use individual signs. A *general sign* (*word* or
assertion), on the other hand, is one in which there is ambiguity or
vagueness for the interpreter. An *individual thing* is one that either
determines nothing but itself or determines itself as well whenever
it determines anything else, while a *general thing* is one that can of
its nature determine something else without itself being determined.
An individual sign is *relatively* individual; it is not uniquely
individual, for as a sign it must share a relation with the signified.
This sharing may be more externalized, in the case of the icon, and
more internalized (in some interpretant), in the case of the index. Is
there then a wholly individual thing? To this Peirce replies: "A thing
that can neither determine anything else nor be determined by
anything else is not in this world at all (nor is it the world, since
it would have no parts); so that a better definition of absolute
nothing could not be given." This leaves the case in which an
individual thing continues to determine itself as it determines
anything else. The "swa" cannot be such an individual thing
because it is always only what it is. Hence it must be general. The
phaneron, then, is both general and externally related. As such it is
"vague" (MS. 908, p. 4) in the sense just given. What would an
icon be? Peirce tells us that "the only way of directly communicating
an idea is by means of an icon" (2.278). If communication is utterly
direct, then an icon would be an individual sign. And its opposite
would be a general non-sign, or, in other words, the phaneron. At
this point the link between them begins to emerge.

In another draft of "The Basis of Pragmaticism" (MS. 283) Peirce
supplies still more of the conceptual apparatus required for the proof:

> A *state of things* is an abstract constituent part of reality, of
> such a nature that a proposition is needed to represent it.
> There is but one *individual*, or completely determinate,
> state of things, namely, the all of reality. A *fact* is so
> highly a prescissively abstract state of things, that it can

be wholly represented in a simple proposition, and the
term "simple," here, has no absolute meaning, but is merely
a comparative expression. (5.549)

A phaneron, as a 'manifest', could not be an individual, but the
world as 'world' (to use the earlier distinctions) is an individual
thing because it is made of parts and determines only itself. A 'state
of things' is simply a combination of individuality and generality,
and a 'fact' is an aspect of a state of things. Both lie between completely
determinate individuality and complete generality. In the early
system these were the 'forms of fact' lying between complete
determination and complete indetermination. This is also true in
the current formulation:

> A *mathematical form* of a state of things is such a represen-
> tation of that state of things as represents only the sameness
> and diversities involved in that state of things, without
> definitely qualifying the subject of the samenesses and
> diversities. It represents not necessarily all of these; but if
> it does represent all, it is the *complete* mathematical form.
> Every mathematical form of a state of things is the complete
> mathematical form of *some* state of things. (5.550)

The last statement guarantees a connection between a complete
mathematical form and some state of things. But does this mean
that for any given state of things there is also a complete mathematical
form? If a state of things is an abstract constituent of reality, and a
mathematical form is an abstract representation of a state of things,
it is plausible that the first abstraction may be responsive to capture
by the second. If there is any similarity and diversity within a state
of things, some mathematical form should be able to represent it.
The problem is ascertaining a process whereby this can be assured.

The above distinctions are formal. Their application to the issue
of pragmaticism requires a material condition as well. Having shown
that a continuity of external forms can be conceived between the
extremes of the wholly inner and wholly outer being, it remains
to be shown that these external forms are in fact representations and
that externalization is a *process* that can be carried out. It is
necessary to search for the conditions for *semiosis* as the dynamical

interplay of signs Peirce found most significant in Royce's argument (8.122, n. 19). But can such dynamism be deduced from essentially non-dynamical (formal) conditions? The whole upshot of synechism is that Thirdness and living concepts are *sui generis* factors in the universe. The tendency for semiosis to take place is no less primordial, for what sort of argument, *not* entailing semiosis, could be formulated in such a way as to supply a ground for it? This is a circularity no philosopher can avoid. But from his earliest days in philosophy, when the question of philosophic foundations was clearly before him, Peirce chose to pursue indirect paths to his goal. The same had to be done now.

One condition of semiosis is that it be possible for one thing to have two perspectives, for how else could it be regarded both in itself and as represented, and how could a distinction between sign and signified be made in such a way as to maintain semiotic *unity?* This condition itself requires as a postulate a synthetic unity of apprehension, a unity in duality. Kant found such a unity in the *a priori* condition of intuition and understanding. For Peirce it was found in the concept of continuity, specifically when applied to the idea of the self. The self does not have an ideal phaneron-like reality, but, like the real phaneron of assertion, has an external form. This means that to be a self is to self-reflect, and to self-reflect is to discover perspective. This is Peirce's *dialogical* view of cognition, a position enunciated in the first of *The Monist* papers, "What Pragmatism Is." There he writes: "A person is not absolutely an individual. His thoughts are what he is 'saying to himself', that is, is saying to that other self that is just coming into life in the flow of time" (5.421). About five years later (1910) he expressed this point as follows:

> In reasoning, one is obliged to *think to oneself.* In order to recognize what is needful for doing this it is necessary to recognize, first of all, what "oneself" is. One is not twice in precisely the same mental state. One is *virtually* (i.e. for pertinent purposes, the same as if one were) a somewhat different person, to whom one's present thought has to be communicated. (7.103)

This establishes the condition for the possibility of a link between phaneron-like experiences, but does it establish a *semiotic* link, and the fact that that link is further linked in a directional fashion, the culmination of which is the icon? To this Peirce must reply that we cannot think of a link between experiences without thinking of that link as semiotically produced. For in any link there must be a linking condition. Even two 'individual things' can be linked if they are thought of as together. Then that becomes the property each of them shares. In this case they share an internal property, a certain idea or interpretant. And at once they cease being *individual* things. If two things are very alike they share external properties, and so contain a generality of their own. But in both cases a form of generality is required.

To the nominalist question—"How do we know that there are not only utterly individual things?"—Peirce would reply, because if there are signs, and if assertion involves signs, then there are no utterly individual things; and even if there were only seeming signs, they would still be signs! If the nominalist chooses to accuse the realist of living in a world of illusion, it cannot be because he has grounds in any way for finding falsity in the realist's claims. His doubt is only a paper doubt.

At this point, however, the proof still remains far off. The maxim of pragmaticism must be based upon "a theory as to the nature of the significations of general terms" (MS.296, p. A14). But to talk of generality is to talk of the future, and to talk of the future is to bring in the notion of reality. Just as there is no isolated person, so there is no isolated fact. Not realizing or emphasizing this was a major error in the 1878 formulation (5.457). Naturally, anything whatsoever can be thought of or represented as an isolated phaneron-like thing. But it is a mistake really to consider a diamond as an isolated entity. If we are thinking of it 'as a diamond,' then whatever fact we claim to discern in its state is a fact about diamonds generally. If it is regarded as a 'bare particular', in the manner of possible-world logicians, then there is nothing of a fact-like nature about it. A fact is already eminently abstract and cannot characterize bare particulars.

Peirce claims further that "all thoughts are interconnected" (4.553, n.2). This is a replay of the earlier view that 'the field of thought is extensive'. What, we might wonder, could guarantee this? We might imagine a Platonic heaven of all thoughts and investigate each individually to see if it is 'connected' with any other, and that other with another, etc. Such a picture would naturally suggest that no connection exists; for if all the thoughts are individually in heaven, no thought the investigator could have would not be in heaven as well, and no means of connection could be cognized. Any connecting relation would simply be a thought of a connecting relation in that heaven. Only a stratification of thoughts, with a possibility of thought *of* thoughts, enables us to avoid this problem. And this is just what the dialogical view of thinking makes possible. The guarantee that all thoughts are interconnected is a nexus of several claims:

> All thought involves some generality.
> Generality requries a future time.
> A future time requires a reality-to-be.
> Reality is a unity.
> ∴ All thought is a unity.

Now reality by definition is all that there is. And so if it contains a unity it cannot be an apprehended unity, for that would imply something real lying beyond reality. If there is a God, he does not lie beyond reality, but is part of what is real. The unity of reality must be internal, and yet differentiated, and this unity can only be captured in the notion of a *consequence*. Reality is a complexus of consequences, with no part of reality not a consequence to any other. As a result, thought must be connected in a consequential relation as well.

The proof begins to emerge out of the justification of the following condition:

> If the ultimate interpretation of a thought relates to anything but a determination of conditional conduct, it cannot be an intellectual quality and so is not in the strictest sense a concept. (MS. 908, p. 4)

Since reality is a complexus of consequences, then if some thought is a thought of reality it must refer to a set of consequences *to be*. It may also refer to consequences that were, but it must not restrict its scope to these alone. Thoughts of the past are present thoughts whose meaning is tied to futural generality. Feelings and sensations may be recalled, though not literally, and these, if thoughts, contain generality as well. But isn't it possible, we might wonder, that there be a thought of the past with literally no connection with the future? We may think of Napoleon winking his eye at Josephine one night in complete darkness. This seems to be a part of reality that could have no conceived connection with future-directed thought. But this Peirce denies. Against such a situation and the objector who advances it he replies:

> You speak of a wink as if it were a small event. How many trillions of corpuscles are involved in the action, through how many million times their diameters they move, and during how many billions of their revolutions in their orbits the action endures, I will not undertake to calculate. But certainly you cannot yourself think that so vast an operation will have had no physical effects, or that they will cease for ages yet to come. (8.195)

There is no reason in principle why the thought of Napoleon's wink in darkness cannot be made the object of a future act. It is not a matter of verifying the wink or of trying to give a futural account of that very act as rigidly designated; it is simply that some perspicacious thinker can refer to the wink by means of some future action. We normally do not do this, and for good reason: we cannot technically set up an experiment to experience the continuing effects of that wink. Instead, our thoughts are vague with respect to such a nexus of conditions, and most experimentation has to do with tenseless winks only. But is it false to say that the heat generated by the wink has still some localized effect? All features of the past do not dissipate into complete generality, but continue to establish determinations of reality. Some determinations endure in the same form longer than others; others are less enduring and so require different conditional acts.

Another formulation of the above condition to be established is found in an unpublished letter (1907) to the editor of *The Nation*. In it Peirce describes the "most pregnant principle" and the "kernal of pragmaticism" in these terms: "The *whole* meaning of an intellectual predicate is that certain kinds of events would happen, once in so often, in the course of experience, under certain kinds of existential conditions (5.468). We must take care to note the conceptual nature of the condition. It does not set out that certain events actually must take place, but only that certain *kinds* of events *would* happen under certain *kinds* of existential conditions. In the other formulation he spoke of the *ultimate interpretation* as relating exclusively to *conditional conduct*. Such a condition, could it ever be established, would seem to undermine entirely all theoretical concepts of any sort, for conduct seems to be a matter of brute Secondness and could not possibly supply the ultimate interpretation of something theoretical. We must assume that Peirce is not attempting to reduce Thirdness to Secondness, but that he is trying to distinguish several dimensions of the former. It is here that the central notion of vagueness, important in Royce's scheme also, enters the picture.

If reality consisted only of phaneron-like individual things, semiosis could not take place. But semiosis does take place, and so there are general things, things that determine other things (semiotically) while themselves not being determined. If they are to be determined, they are to be determined as a result of something else. If there is a bed-rock beneath pragmaticism, this fact is as good a candidate for it as any. Generality, however, is a form of vagueness (5.506), and in semiosis a sign is vague just to the very extent to which it is a sign. An "absolutely and completely" determinate sign is an impossibility (5.506). In that case it cannot serve as a sign. Does this mean that a physical object cannot be a rigid designator of something else? What would be indeterminate about a circumstance in which a particular pencil is stipulated as a sign of a particular shoe? In this restricted sense Peirce's requirement of a sign does not apply specifically, though it does generally. A determinate thing, granting for a moment its experiential possibility, can be designated only as a result of a process of sign-making and this, as Wittgenstein would say, requires a *form of life*. For Peirce it requires a mathematical form, namely an ostensive designating arrow from the sign maker to the pencil-to-be-sign. In the case of concepts as signs, generality is found throughout. To Mario Calderoni, an Italian pragmatist, he observed: "A concept determinate in all respects is as fictitious as a concept definite in all respects" (8.208).

If signs are vague, then so are those things that participate in sign activity. Communication is vague (5.506); so are feelings when reflected upon (1.310); so also our elementary categories and abstract concepts (5.501; MS. 908, p. 11) and our instinctive, common-sense beliefs (6.499; 5.505, 5.507ff, 5.516), including our concept of God (5.508ff; 6.466, 6.494). Something is vague if the principle of contradiction does not apply to it (5.488, 5.505). This means that if I know to what the sign refers specifically, I am in a position to say whether its use is contradictory or not. In the case of the pencil referring to the shoe the speaker 'speaks against himself' if he uses the pencil-sign to refer to a hat, that is, unless he first changes the sign-meaning. If he does this there is no vagueness. Peirce preferred to characterize vagueness in terms of the act of interpreting a sign. A sign-use that allows for *no* interpretation as to what is signified is completely determinate. In the pencil–shoe example the sign connection is still vague because an interpretation that the pencil is being used as a sign of the shoe is required, and this interpretation is based on an interpretation of the ostensive act of sign-making. We live in a universe of interpretation, a universe "perfused with signs" (5.448, n.1) and without interpretation there would be no vagueness or indetermination—and for that matter no semiosis. Both semiosis and interpretation are acts of sign-making, and this once more is an act of drawing a consequence upon an action: the consequence of the act of using S is to refer to P.

We are now in a position to answer the question of why an ultimate interpretation is only and always a determination of conditional conduct in light of certain kinds of existential conditions. We have established that the phaneron and the icon are relatable by degrees, and that the act of relating must be postulated in dialogical thinking, but, we may now wonder, why must there be a preferred *direction* of interpretation? According to Peirce this direction is found in the very nature of a consequential relation:

> Now the concept of a consequent is a logical concept. It is derived from the concept of the conclusion of an argument. But an argument is a sign of the truth of its conclusion; its conclusion is the rational interpretation of the sign. (5.448, n.1)

Two important distinctions are found here. Without an argument there can be no conclusion. Yet what it is in an argument that generates its conclusion is its *form*. The conclusion is true when the form is the correct form, and the act of making or 'drawing' the conclusion is simply the recognition of the form. But the sign of a whole argument is an iconic sign, and so all forms of interpretaion must involve iconic signs as well. Recognizing a direction in the icon is the second important feature, a feature supported by the fact that contained in the various uses of the verb "to draw" is the notion of directionality.

But why must iconic directionality eventually culminate in conditional conduct? Interpretation dispels vagueness when the sign used is interpreted in the manner prescribed. But how can we be assured that we have found the prescribed manner? If signs had a wholly private and idiosyncratic origin, this fact could never be established. If, on the other hand, they are thought of as being spontaneously made in that vague area where phaneron-consciousness becomes capable of sign-comprehension, then their spontaneity suggests the fact that they have a universal nature independent of this or that consciousness. The fact that the theory of signs and the theory of categories combines here so nicely seems to provide even more evidence of this fact. This allows interpretation to converge, and, given the fact that the growth of icons marks directionality, to converge on iconicity. It would seem, then, that the whole intellectual purport of a concept is to move toward a pure mathematical icon. Yet if this were the case, how could that ultimate icon serve to interpret a given sign-relation of which it is a form? The interpretation would have to be directly *intuited*, for no further interpretation is allowed. The word 'intuition' may not be altogether inappropriate for what Peirce wishes to convey here. If we interpret 'intuition' in the sense of an immediate act of cognitive apprehension, then the ultimate icon is an asserted sign, and this requires an even more ultimate interpretation. But if we interpret it as an immediate experience, in some specialized sense, then it is not far off to say that the ultimate interpretation is an 'intuition'. This is what Peirce is driving at, I think, when he claims that the relation between sign and object is not ultimately intellectual or internalizable:

But what does this correspondence or reference of the sign, to its object, consist in? The pragmaticist answers this question as follows. Suppose, he says, that the angel

Gabriel were to descend and communicate to me the answer to this riddle from the breast of omniscience. Is this supposable; or does it involve an essential absurdity to suppose the answer to be brought to human intelligence? In the latter case, "truth," in this sense, is a useless word, which can never express a human thought. (5.553)

If human intelligence is tied up with sign-making, it can never ground itself in intellectual apprehension alone, using signs *generally* to ground sign-relations. If there is a "right method of transforming signs" (5.553), it cannot be by an intellectualistic, formalistic kind of activity. Of the three kinds of interpretants—the *emotional* (first Thirdness), the *dynamical* (secondness Thirdness), and the *logical* interpretant (third Thirdness)—the latter would be an ultimate icon except for the fact that a logical interpretant must itself, when regarded as a sign, have a logical interpretant. Neither of the first two can be the ultimate icon because in the first case there is hardly any iconic dimension, and in the second, if there is, it is wholly particular. Generality is found in the third, but in that case there can be no ultimacy. And so the ground of sign-interpretation must be found elsewhere.

What is required is an intellectual *procedure* and not an intellectual *concept*, a procedure that incorporates generality and an apodictic ultimacy. Two things are required: an external icon and a guarantee that the procedure be carried out. These conditions are clearly satisfied in the case of machines. The blueprint of a machine design is always an icon, and the rigidity of the mechanism is the guarantee that a specific activity will be carried out when energy is supplied. *But it is in this sense also that the ultimate interpretation of the meaning of an intellectual concept must be a matter of procedural conduct.* In the 'conduct' we have the externalizing factor, and in the 'procedure' the nomic factor.

The above argument constitutes an involved conditional proposition comprised of a conjunction of propositions about signs, thinking, and phenomenological relations, but does it approach the status of a proof? *If* all of those claims are true, then there is a sense in which pragmaticism is proved. But are they true? It is not very persuasive to say that the purport of a low grade intellectual concept such as 'hardness' must be found exclusively in some conditional conduct. For that conduct must rely on an iconic apprehension of the act of testing for hardness, and this is a controlled act subject to other logical interpretants (the concepts of 'scratch', 'move', 'see', etc.). What we must find is an ultimate logical interpretant of something that requires no other logical interpretants, and further that makes it *logically* impossible that there be other logical interpretants of *that* ultimate logical interpretant.

Only one object could satisfy this condition: the symbolization of thinking or intellection *in general*. If a non-logical interpretation —for it must be non-logical in order to be an interpretant of (logical) thinking—can be found which is also ultimate in the externalized conditional sense, then not only the possibility but the necessity of pragmaticism can be established. Formal logic is an icon of thinking in general, though whether it is to the extent necessary here, is another question. What is required is a form of logic that is both *purely iconic and based simply upon procedural rules*. If any intuitive elements are required for the system to function, then logical interpretants are also required, and the system cannot have a procedure as its ultimate logical interpretant. Peirce was convinced that "the enigma of the nature of the logical interpretant" can be solved by observing how concepts are clarified in the highly formal systems of mathematics. It is not in intuition, but in the use of diagrams and operations that such concepts ultimately find their meaning. The general rule for such operations is as follows:

> Proceed according to such and such a general rule. Then, if such and such a concept is applicable to such and such an object, the operation will have such and such a general result; and conversely. (5.483)

In his more optimistic moments Peirce thought that he had found an adequate symbolization of thinking in general that was sufficiently procedural and non-intutionist in his system of *existential graphs*.[7] The development of the graphs more or less coincides with his quest for the proof of pragmaticism. They constituted an iconic system of thinking in the form of "a moving picture of the *essence of thought*" (MS. 298) and were "the chief premise" (MS. 905) of the argument for pragmaticism in relation to the categories. In 1910 he described the graphs as "the simplest possible system that is capable of expressing with exactitude every possible assertion" (MS. 654, p. 5). In terms of the previous distinctions, a graph is an individual sign because it leaves no room for interpretation, but it has become *so* determined as to be indeterminable in itself. Thus technically speaking, a graph cannot be placed on paper, but only a graph-instance can. For any mark placed on paper requires interpretation. And so when Peirce claims that the graphs make thinking "literally visible" (4.6) this statement cannot itself be taken literally. They are ultimate icons, the simplest possible, of thinking; but the graph itself is a conceptual form, a Platonic idea (MS. 296, p. A9). It is not a human concept, however, but a system of symbolizing the *arrangement* of concepts (to recall the 1878 formulation of pragmaticism). As such it is the form of a "concept-form," and the latter "cannot be in the field of consciousness any more than the graph can be on the Phemic Sheet" (MS. 296, p. A119). The ephemeral nature of the graph-instance also lies in its two-dimensional form:

> But in one respect at any rate Existential Graphs is essentially different from language. Namely, instead of being merely protracted in time, its expressions are diagrams upon a surface, and indeed must be regarded only as a projection upon that surface of a sign extended in three dimensions. Three dimensions are necessary and sufficient for the expression of all assertions. (MS. 654, pp. 6–7)

Besides satisfying the condition of total iconicity, the use of the graphs involves only procedural rules. Nothing of a logical intuition is required. The rules or 'permissions' only allow certain additions or erasures on the 'sheet of assertion'. This method is assisted by the fact that in the system of graphs all relations are relations of consequence (7.107). So the operations are entirely operations of specific manipulations controlled by the rules. There is no step in which one graph-instance is substituted for another on the basis of an intuited identity or equivalence. The graphs, then, can be construed as a purified form of scientific experimentation in general, and because they are graphs of the essence of thought, they can be used to justify the claim that all intellectual conceptions ultimately refer to a future experimental result. Regarded on their iconic side, they constitute the most abstract sign possible to symbolize externally the most abstract object possible (the idea of thinking). Regarded on their procedural side, they constitute the most concrete representation of the most concrete object representable (dynamic interaction). They not only appear to establish the truth of the pragmatic maxim *philosophically* in the form of a deduction, but also *pragmatically* and *inductively* by affording an efficient logical system whereby conceptions may be analyzed into their indecomposable elements. As an ultimate interpretant, the graphs do not require an endless investigation into logical interpretants of logical interpretants, for their ultimate interpretant is embodied in their being used; as such they are an extremely efficient way of symbolizing concepts. In the "Prolegomena to an Apology for Pragmaticism" (1906) Peirce explained this relation between low-cost investigation, induction, certainty, and the graphs:

> Not only is it true that by experimentation upon some diagram an experimental proof can be obtained of every necessary conclusion from any given Copulate of Premises, but, what is more, no "necessary" conclusion is any more apodictic than inductive reasoning becomes from the moment when experimentation can be multiplied *ad libitum* at no extra cost than a summons before the imagination. (4.531)

When the chemical valences were discovered, experimental possibilities proliferated greatly. This was an exercise in diagrammatic thinking. The only difference between the graphist and the chemist is that the latter must produce an actual result in the laboratory, while the former seeks only the distillation of conceptual generality (5.8). Yet they both use the same approach, and just as the chemist studies nature to control it, so also the graphs, being a central feature in the growth of concrete reasonableness, help establish in this fashion the truth of the philosophy of synechism.

Was Peirce satisfied with the role of the graphs in the philosophy of pragmaticism? At times he had reservations about their completeness or role in the proof (MS. 296, p. A15; MS. 300, p. 22; 4.11). Yet he took them to constitute at least a strong analogical clue to the truth of pragmaticism:

You apprehend in what way the system of Existential Graphs is to furnish a test of the truth or falsity of Pragmaticism. Namely, a sufficient study of the graphs should show what nature is truly common to all significations of concepts: whereupon a comparison will show whether that nature be or be not the very ilk that Pragmaticism (by the definition of it) avers that it is. (4.534, n.1)

Peirce realized that a graph-instance, as "the passive object of a geometrical *intuitus*" (4.534 n.1) may not be seen for what it is in light of the spectrum of logical and real objects between the phaneron and the icon. But this means that for its proper interpretaion, pragmaticism, being a philosophy primarily of method, requires a larger philosophical interpretation, and its true bed-rock remains ultimately the entire framework of objective logic and objective idealism.

3. The Humble Argument

During the period Peirce was engrossed in the proof, he devoted little time to other philosophical projects. Yet some of his other work reveals a continuing involvement with questions of the general philosophy of the universe. In fact, there is a sense in which it can be said that he continued to work on two sorts of argument, the detailed and thorny argument just presented, and a simple, even "humble" argument to justify such a philosophy. The proof of pragmaticism took semiosis for granted and did not raise the question of how it can be possible in the universe. This latter question involves the whole of objective idealism—the evolutionary theory of mind, Scholastic Realism, the categories, etc.—for its justification. In its simplified form this argument became known as "the neglected argument for the reality of God," and was published in *The Hibbert Journal* in 1908. The argument itself is based on an abduction that takes the following form:

There is a reason, an interpretation, a logic, in the course of scientific advance, and this indisputably proves to him who has perceptions of rational or significant relations, that man's mind must have been attuned to the truth of things in order to discover what he has discovered. (6.476)

Now the hypothesis of God's reality has traditionally come closest to expressing the ground of this logic. *If*, then, the theory of categories is correct in all of its wide implications, the God-hypothesis cannot be neglected. In this Peirce does not seem to be advocating traditional theism, only allowing a deep-structure-like viability of theism in light of objective logic. But this is not quite accurate. The God-hypothesis is "the natural precipitate of meditation upon the origin of the Three Universes" (6.487), and something like it is found in all scientific explanation. But the fact that it also appeals to the heart, involving "a deep sense of the adorability of the Idea" (6.487), does not mean that we experience a conflict of reason and feeling. The categories show the intertwining of the two in experience, and while belief in God seems a matter of instinct alone, it is an instinct elevated in the light of reason. Objective logic requires that it must be something like an "analogue of the mind" (6.502), a *logos* or active and universal Reason that first suggests such a hypothesis in the spontaneous play of "musement," so that both science and theology draw from the same wellspring:

> Over the chasm that yawns between the ultimate goal of science and such ideas of Man's environment as, coming over him during his primal wanderings in the forest, while yet his very notion of error was of the vaguest, he managed to communicate to some fellow, we are building a cantilever bridge of induction, held together by scientific struts and ties. Yet every plank of its advance is first laid by Retroduction alone, that is to say, by the spontaneous conjectures of instinctive reason; and neither Deduction nor Induction contribute a single new concept to the structure. (6.475)

During much of 1911 Peirce worked on a "logical critique of religious faith," evidently with the hope of being able to use his metaphysical notions to put religion in a respectable light. He was thereby keeping alive in his last years his lifelong endeavor to reconcile religion and science. But we have from this effort only a series of false starts (MSS. 846–56). Other more provocative ideas began to take shape also in this last decade or so of his life, and though the record is very fragmentary, it seems that he was attempting to develop a modal logic of possible worlds whereby whatever could be thought was true in some possible world. Rather than thinking of truth and reality as that toward which thought tends and that in which it rests, given sufficient time, he pondered the possibility of a reality as an entire universe of logical possibilities, perhaps because in his existential graphs he had now developed a notation with which to express this universe.[8] It only needed to be argued that "the domain of ideas (I purposely employ a vague term) and the domain of signs seem to coincide" (MS. 292, p. 41); thus just as all signs are linked, so would be all ideas as objective *logoi,* and "every idea or every element of idea not too subtle for us must be expected to be embodied somehow in the material universe" (MS. S–104). Along with the actualized, though formal universe, there is the "World of Hypothetical States of Things" (MS. 328) and both of these worlds are part of an even greater "universe of occasions" (MS. 806). In this light the system of signs is seen as an isomorphic reflection of the system of Platonic Ideas. After over half a century of continuous search for the answer to the riddle of the universe, Peirce's ideas were returning to their birthplace in the first brilliant flashes of insight of the early metaphysics, but now with decades of detailed elaboration included. He never departed from, nor achieved, his goal of producing a theory capable of justifying "a living practical belief, logically justified in crossing the Rubicon with all the freightage of eternity" (6.485). But no man has given it a better try, either. And although Peirce may have failed to produce a fully satisfying answer to the "riddle of the sphinx," his efforts in that direction have left us a legacy of a truly interdisciplinary metaphysics upon which to build.

Appendix
1

Fig. 1

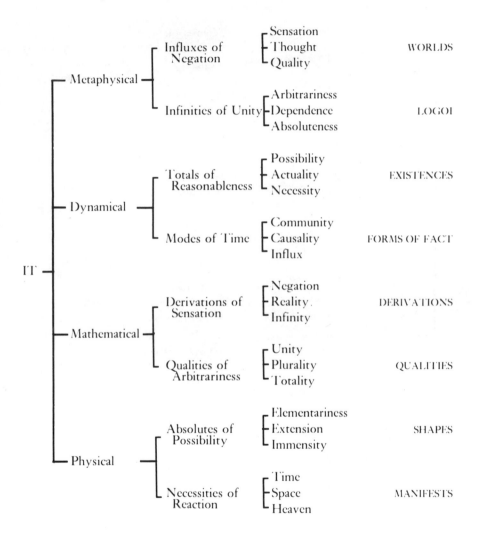

235

Fig. 2

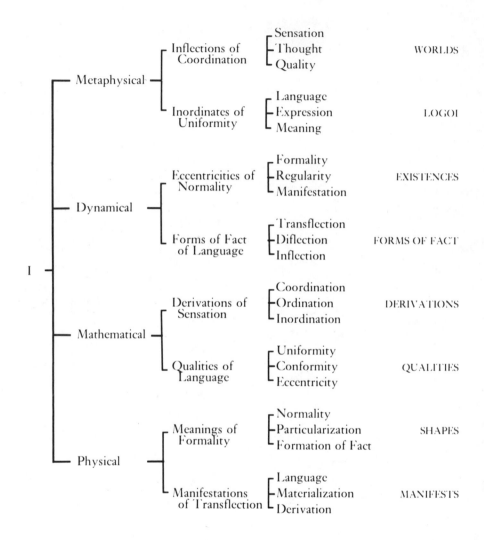

		Sensation	
Inflections of Coordination		Thought	WORLDS
		Quality	

| | | Language | |
Metaphysical | Inordinates of Uniformity | | Expression | LOGOI |
| | | Meaning | |

		Formality	
Eccentricities of Normality		Regularity	EXISTENCES
		Manifestation	

Dynamical

		Transflection	
Forms of Fact of Language		Diflection	FORMS OF FACT
		Inflection	

I

		Coordination	
Derivations of Sensation		Ordination	DERIVATIONS
		Inordination	

Mathematical

		Uniformity	
Qualities of Language		Conformity	QUALITIES
		Eccentricity	

		Normality	
Meanings of Formality		Particularization	SHAPES
		Formation of Fact	

Physical

		Language	
Manifestations of Transflection		Materialization	MANIFESTS
		Derivation	

Fig. 3

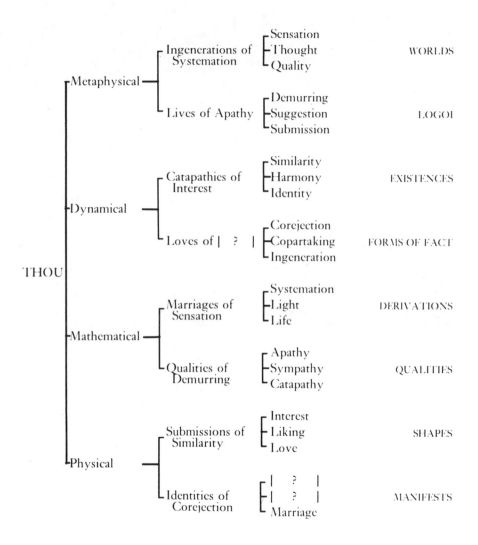

Fig. 4

IT

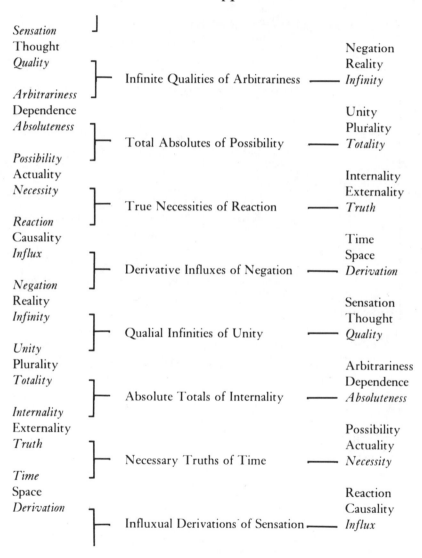

Fig. 5

I

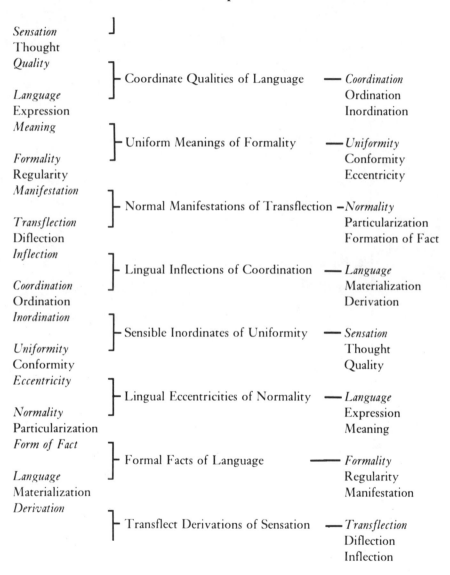

Sensation
Thought
Quality

Language ── Coordinate Qualities of Language ── *Coordination*
Expression   Ordination
Meaning   Inordination

Formality ── Uniform Meanings of Formality ── *Uniformity*
Regularity   Conformity
Manifestation   Eccentricity

Transflection ── Normal Manifestations of Transflection ── *Normality*
Diflection   Particularization
Inflection   Formation of Fact

Coordination ── Lingual Inflections of Coordination ── *Language*
Ordination   Materialization
Inordination   Derivation

Uniformity ── Sensible Inordinates of Uniformity ── *Sensation*
Conformity   Thought
Eccentricity   Quality

Normality ── Lingual Eccentricities of Normality ── *Language*
Particularization   Expression
Form of Fact   Meaning

Language ── Formal Facts of Language ── *Formality*
Materialization   Regularity
Derivation   Manifestation

── Transflect Derivations of Sensation ── *Transflection*
                                                    Diflection
                                                    Inflection

Fig. 6

THOU

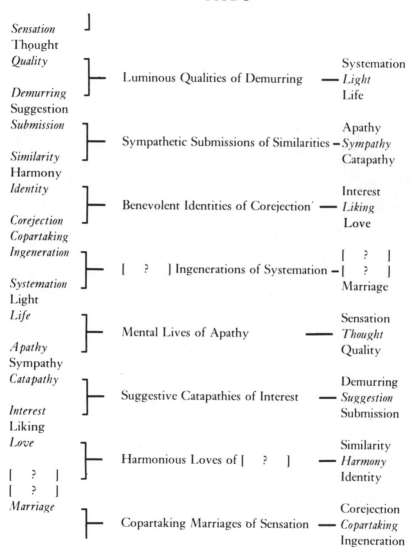

Sensation
Thought
Quality

Demurring — Luminous Qualities of Demurring — Systemation
Suggestion
— *Light*
Life

Submission — Sympathetic Submissions of Similarities — Apathy
— *Sympathy*
Similarity — Catapathy
Harmony

Identity — Benevolent Identities of Corejection — Interest
— *Liking*
Corejection — Love
Copartaking

Ingeneration — [?] Ingenerations of Systemation — [?]
— [?]
Systemation — Marriage
Light

Life — Mental Lives of Apathy — Sensation
— *Thought*
Apathy — Quality
Sympathy

Catapathy — Suggestive Catapathies of Interest — Demurring
— *Suggestion*
Interest — Submission
Liking

Love — Harmonious Loves of [?] — Similarity
— *Harmony*
[?] — Identity
[?]

Marriage — Copartaking Marriages of Sensation — Corejection
— *Copartaking*
Ingeneration

Appendix 2

List of Manuscripts Consulted

UNPUBLISHED

MS. 273: 60
MS. 283: 216
MS. 289: 206
MS. 292: 231
MS. 296: 211, 219, 226–228, 298
MS. 300: 208, 211, 213, 228
MS. 310: 12
MS. 319: 211
MS. 320: 209
MS. 328: 209, 231
MS. 340: 84
MS. 349: 72
MS. 357: 93
MS. 358: 94, 100
MS. 359: 94, 103
MS. 368: 132
MS. 372: 131
MS. 377: 131
MS. 441: 14
MS. 478: 195
MS. 587: 129
MS. 654: 227

MS. 720: 85, 88
MS. 726: 84
MS. 732: 89–92
MS. 741: 56
MS. 769: 85
MS. 802: 84, 86
MS. 806: 231
MS. 846: 231
MS. 858: 69
MS. 875: 153
MS. 891: 13, 30, 31, 39, 40, 80
MS. 899: 215
MS. 905: 226
MS. 908: 215, 216, 220
MS. 909: 174
MS. 916: 56, 61, 68
MS. 917: 47
MS. 919: 49, 52–54, 72
MS. 920: 29–32, 34–43, 45, 88
MS. 921: 14–16, 18–20, 22–29, 37, 68,

71, 72, 79, 89, 93
MS. 922: 43–45, 49, 50, 51, 86–88
MS. 923: 68, 74
MS. 923s: 70, 71
MS. 935: 133
MS. 943: 193
MS. 988: 46
MS. 1103: 32, 33
MS. 1104: 143
MS. 1105: 56–60
MS. 1310: 172
MS. 1311: 172
MS. 1555: 11
MS. 1569: 133
MS. 1606: 11
MS. 1608: 11
MS. 1633: 13
MS. 1638: 83
S–104: 231
L–107: 143
L–463: 193

PUBLISHED

1.27: 207
1.35: 156
1.83: 160
1.175: 165
1.211: 203
1.219: 202
1.280: 195
1.284: 215
1.300: 159
1.301: 160
1.313: 215
1.351: 195

1.353: 159
1.356: 159
1.405: 167
1.412: 166
1.417: 179
1.444: 180
1.447: 180
1.450: 182
1.461: 183
1.466: 183
1.481: 186
1.484: 187

1.487: 188
1.493: 189
1.522: 195
1.531: 199
1.543: 197
1.563: 190
2.33: 6
2.34: 6
2.84: 194
2.111: 201
2.117: 194
2.118: 40

Notes

INTRODUCTION

1. Murray Murphey, *The Development of Peirce's Philosophy* (Cambridge: Harvard University Press, 1961).
2. Israel Scheffler, *Four Pragmatists: A Critical Introduction to Peirce, James, and Dewey* (London: Routledge and Kegan Paul, 1974), p. 21.
3. *The Collected Papers of Charles Sanders Peirce*, Vols. 1–6, ed. Charles Hartshorne and Paul Weiss (Cambridge: Harvard University Press, 1931–1935); Vols. 7–8, ed. Arthur Burks (Cambridge: Harvard University Press, 1958). References to *The Collected Papers* will be given in the text by volume and paragraph number; for example, 6.25 indicates Vol. 6, par. 25.
4. R. M. Martin, "An Open Letter on Logic and God," in Paul Weiss, *First Considerations* (Carbondale: Southern Illinois University Press, 1977), pp. 255–56.

CHAPTER I   METAPHYSICAL ESSAYS

1. References to the unpublished papers and letters of Peirce are given according to the numbers indicated in the *Annotated Catalogue of the Papers of Charles S. Peirce*, ed. Richard S. Robin (Amherst: University of Massachusetts Press, 1967); "MS." and "L" indicate manuscript and letter respectively, followed by a specific number designation.
2. Friedrich Schiller, *On the Aesthetic Education of Man, in a Series of Letters*, trans. Elizabeth M. Wilkerson and L. A. Willoughby (Oxford: Clarendon Press, 1967), p. 4.
3. This list, found in MS. 921s, is presented in the order given by Peirce, though with his abbreviations expanded and with dates included. Those given by an asterisk (*) are either missing or not identified under the heading given. Other papers found in MS. 921 are not directly identifiable in terms of the list headings, but are very likely earlier or later drafts of papers included in

the list.

4. The list continues with four other highly abbreviated entries not identifiable with any known manuscripts.

5. Immanuel Kant, *Critique of Pure Reason*, trans. Norman Kemp Smith (New York: St. Martin's Press, 1965), A58, B82; "A" and "B" page references hereafter will be included in the text.

6. Immanuel Kant, "The Mistaken Subtlety of the Four Syllogistic Figures," Sec. II; Richard Whately, *Elements of Logic* (New York: William Jackson, 1834), p. 51.

7. Immanuel Kant, *Logic*, Introduction, Sec. VII.

8. Sir William Hamilton, *Lectures on Metaphysics and Logic* (Stuttgart-Bad Cannstatt: Friedrich Frommann, 1969), 4, 246.

9. This and the following descriptions of the stages are from the "Explanation of the Categories" found in MS. 921.

10. Murphey, p. 35.

11. *Kant's Introduction to Logic*, trans. T. K. Abbott (New York: Philosophical Library, 1963), p. 30.

12. Hamilton, 3, 103.

13. Henry Longueville Mansel, *The Limits of Religious Thought* (Boston: Gould and Lincoln, 1859), p. 23.

14. Mansel, p. 84.

15. Mansel, p. 91.

16. Mansel, p. 93. Similar views on consciousness are found in another book in Peirce's library: *Guesses at Truth* by Two Brothers [Julius Charles Hare and Augustus William Hare] (Boston: Ticknor and Fields, 1861). For example: "Can the spark of consciousness be elicited except by collision?" (p. 140). Also of interest is the remark: "After all, they are strange and mighty words, these two little pronouns, *I* and *Thou*, the mightiest perhaps in the whole compass of language" (p. 139). Peirce may have been in possession of an earlier edition of this work.

17. Mansel, pp. 95–96.

18. Mansel, pp. 108–9.

19. Mansel, p. 128.

20. Mansel, p. 85.

21. While a student at Harvard Peirce wrote two forensics on this subject, one an analysis of genius (19 March 1859) and the other on the question of whether wisdom is best learned from books or from observation (28 April 1859). See MS. 1633c.

22. "The Logical and Psychological Treatment of Metaphysics" (11 August 1861), from MS. 921.

23. Peirce was undoubtedly familiar with similar arguments in Mansel's *Limits*, p. 85, and in Jouffroy's *Introduction to Ethics* (Boston and Cambridge: James

Munroe, 1858), 1, 236. Both Mansel and Jouffroy turn to fideism in their reply to the skeptic.

24. This letter is probably lost. According to Max Fisch it was most likely sent to Harriet Melusina Fay, the woman Peirce would soon marry.

CHAPTER II   THEORY OF CATEGORIES

1. Jean Paul Sartre, *Being and Nothingness,* trans. Hazel E. Barnes, (New York: Philosophical Library, 1956), p. 251.
2. Sartre, p. 236.
3. Peirce tries to show this with respect to space in "The Axioms of Intuition: After Kant" (MS. 1003).
4. August Laurent, *Chemical Method, Notation, Classification, and Nomenclature,* trans. William Odling (London: Harrison and Sons, 1855), p. 320. Here we should also not overlook the possible influence of Hamilton's scheme of classification in his *Lectures on Metaphysics and Logic.*
5. Emanuel Swedenborg, *The True Christian Religion* par. 695; see also pars. 8, 12, 362, 364. W. P. Krolikowski's "The Peircean Vir" considers aspects of the Swedenborg/James, Sr. influence on Peirce, in *Studies in the Philosophy of Charles Sanders Peirce,* ed. Edward C. Moore and Richard S. Robin (Amherst: University of Massachusetts Press, 1964), pp. 257-70. The term *influx* is also found in W. Fleming, *The Vocabulary of Philosophy* (London and Glasgow: Richard Griffin, 1857), where it simply refers to the theory of how physical objects operate upon the senses (p. 257). Peirce owned a copy of this work.
6. On 4 April 1864 Peirce drafted a letter (L–82a) to Pliny Earle Chase, author of *Intellectual Symbolism: A Basis for Science:* "I have myself been studying Kant's categories for several years, and have called them the categories of the It—an obvious name for them but suggesting the existence of other categories." With the categories of the *I* and *Thou* now before us, it becomes clear what Peirce had in mind here.

CHAPTER III   THE NEW LIST OF CATEGORIES

1. *Cambridge Chronicle,* 21 November 1863; MS. 1638.
2. Murphey, p. 91.
3. *Journal of Speculative Philosophy,* 1 (1868), 255.
4. *The Logic of Hegel,* trans. William Wallace (London: Oxford University Press, 1931), pp. 161, 163.
5. G. W. F. Hegel, *Science of Logic,* trans. A. V. Miller (London: George Allen and Unwin, 1969), pp. 67, 69, 77, 82.

CHAPTER IV   TELEOLOGICAL THOUGHT

1. "Professor Porter's 'Human Intellect'," *The Nation,* 8 (18 March 1869), 211–13. Peirce's contributions to *The Nation* have been compiled and annotated by Kenneth L. Ketner and James E. Cook, *Graduate Studies, Texas Tech University,* No. 10 (December 1975). See Ketner and Cook, p. 28.
2. *The Nation,* 9 (25 November 1869), 461–62.
3. Ketner and Cook, p. 36.
4. *North American Review,* 110 (April 1870), pp. 463–64.
5. See also Chauncey Wright's defense of Peirce's review in *The Nation,* 13 (30 November 1871), 355–56, and Peirce's reply, both reprinted in Ketner and Cook, pp. 43–45.
6. See William James's letter to his brother Henry, in Ralph Barton Perry, *The Thought and Character of William James* (Boston: Little, Brown, and Co., 1935), 1, 332.
7. Benjamin Peirce, *Ideality in the Physical Sciences* (Boston: Little, Brown, and Co., 1881), pp. 51–52.
8. Ketner and Cook, p. 72.
9. Ketner and Cook, p. 63.
10. This is argued by Murphey, p. 298.
11. To my knowledge one of the few attempts to apply a Boolean algebra of continuity to metaphysical problems can be found in an obscure work by J. B. B. Burke, *The Emergence of Life* (London: Oxford University Press, 1931).

CHAPTER V   TYCHISM AND SYNECHISM

1. *The American Journal of Psychology,* 1 (November 1887), 168. On the following page Peirce writes: "We no more want an original machine, than a house-builder would want an original journey man, or an American board of college trustees would hire an original professor [!]."
2. *The Nation,* 59 (8 November 1894), 344.
3. *The Nation,* 59 (19 July 1894), 53.
4. See Vincent G. Potter and Paul B. Shields, "Peirce's Definitions of Continuity," *Transactions of the Charles S. Peirce Society,* 13 (Winter 1977), 20–34.
5. See also Peirce's remarks on the 'pythagorean brotherhood' in *The Open Court,* 6 (8 September 1892), 3375–77; MS. 888.

CHAPTER VI   OBJECTIVE LOGIC

1. A detailed account of Peirce's assessment of Hegel is given by Max H. Fisch, "Hegel and Peirce," in *Hegel and the History of Philosophy*, ed. Joseph J. O'Malley, Keith W. Algozin, and Frederick G. Weiss (The Hague: Martinus Nijhoff, 1974), pp. 171–93.
2. *Ideality in the Physical Sciences*, p. 52.
3. *The Vocabulary of Philosophy*, p. 291.
4. For an account of W. T. Krug's criticism of idealism see Joseph L. Esposito, *Schelling's Idealism and Philosophy of Nature* (Lewisburg: Bucknell University Press, 1977), pp. 162–64.

CHAPTER VII   THE FOUNDATION OF PRAGMATICISM

1. On the nature of the proof of pragmaticism as a deduction, see John J. Fitzgerald, *Peirce's Theory of Signs as Foundation for Pragmaticism* (The Hague: Mouton, 1966), Ch. 8; also Richard Smyth, "The Pragmatic Maxim in 1878," *Transactions of the Charles S. Peirce Society*, 13 (Spring 1977), 109.
2. Josiah Royce, *The World and the Individual* (New York: The Macmillan Co., 1904), p. 310.
3. Royce, pp. 298–99.
4. Royce, pp. 334, 337.
5. Royce, p. 359.
6. Royce, pp. 502–507.
7. For an account of the existential graphs see Don D. Roberts, *The Existential Graphs of Charles S. Peirce* (The Hague: Mouton, 1973).
8. Roberts, p. 81.

Index